T0305287

Valuing Complex Natural Resource Systems

THE FONDAZIONE ENI ENRICO MATTEI (FEEM) SERIES ON ECONOMICS, THE
ENVIRONMENT AND SUSTAINABLE DEVELOPMENT

Series Editor: Carlo Carraro, *University of Venice, Venice and
Research Director, Fondazione Eni Enrico Mattei (FEEM),
Milan, Italy*

Editorial Board

The Fondazione Eni Enrico Mattei (FEEM) was established in 1989 as a non-profit, non-partisan research institution. It carries out high-profile research in the fields of economic development, energy and the environment, thanks to an international network of researchers who contribute to disseminate knowledge through seminars, congresses and publications. The main objective of the Fondazione is to foster interactions among academic, industrial and public policy spheres in an effort to find solutions to environmental problems. Over the years it has thus become a major European institution for research on sustainable development and the privileged interlocutor of a number of leading national and international policy institutions.

The Fondazione Eni Enrico Mattei (FEEM) Series on Economics and the Environment publishes leading-edge research findings providing an authoritative and up-to-date source of information in all aspects of sustainable development. FEEM research outputs are the results of a sound and acknowledged co-operation between its internal staff and a worldwide network of outstanding researchers and practitioners. A Scientific Advisory Board of distinguished academics ensures the quality of the publications.

This series serves as an outlet for the main results of FEEM's research programmes in the areas of economics, energy and the environment.

Titles in the series include:

Green Accounting in Europe
A Comparative Study, Volume 2
Edited by Anil Markandya and Marialuisa Tamborra

Sustainable Management of Water Resources
An Integrated Approach
Edited by Carlo Giupponi, Anthony J. Jakeman, Derek Karssenberg and Matt P. Hare

Valuing Complex Natural Resource Systems
The Case of the Lagoon of Venice
Edited by Anna Alberini, Paolo Rosato and Margherita Turvani

Valuing Complex Natural Resource Systems

The Case of the Lagoon of Venice

Edited by

Anna Alberini

Department of Agricultural and Resource Economics, University of Maryland, USA and Fondazione Eni Enrico Mattei, Italy

Paolo Rosato

Department of Civil Engineering, University of Trieste and Fondazione Eni Enrico Mattei, Italy

Margherita Turvani

Department of Planning, University IUAV and School for Advanced Studies in Venice Foundation, Italy

THE FONDAZIONE ENI ENRICO MATTEI (FEEM) SERIES ON ECONOMICS, THE ENVIRONMENT AND SUSTAINABLE DEVELOPMENT

Edward Elgar

Cheltenham, UK • Northampton, MA, USA

Published by
Edward Elgar Publishing Limited
Glensanda House
Montpellier Parade
Cheltenham
Glos GL50 1UA
UK

Edward Elgar Publishing, Inc.
136 West Street
Suite 202
Northampton
Massachusetts 01060
USA

A catalogue record for this book
is available from the British Library

ISBN-13: 978 1 84542 847 1
ISBN-10: 1 84542 847 1

Printed and bound in Great Britain by MPG Books Ltd, Bodmin, Cornwall

Contents

List of Contributors   vii
Foreword   viii
Introduction   x

PART I   NON-MARKET VALUATION METHODS

1. Valuing Environmental Resources Using Stated Preferences
    Anna Alberini and Alberto Longo   3

2. Recreational Demand, Travel Cost Method and Flow Fixed Costs
    Edi Defrancesco and Paolo Rosato   23

3. The Appraisal Approach to Valuing Environmental Resources
    Edi Defrancesco, Paolo Rosato and Luca Rossetto   40

PART II   APPLICATIONS OF NON-MARKET VALUATION
          METHODS IN THE LAGOON OF VENICE

4. Using Contingent Valuation to Value the Island of S. Erasmo in
    the Lagoon of Venice
    Anna Alberini, Paolo Rosato, Alberto Longo and
    Valentina Zanatta   61

5. Evaluation of Urban Improvement on the Islands of the Venice
    Lagoon: A Spatially-Distributed Hedonic–Hierarchical Approach
    Paolo Rosato, Carlo Giupponi, Margaretha Breil and
    Anita Fassio   75

6. Valuing the Implementation Costs of Ecosystem Friendly Clam
    Fishing Practices in the Venice Lagoon: Results from a Conjoint
    Choice Survey
    Paulo A.L.D. Nunes, Luca Rossetto and Arianne de Blaeij   99

v

7.   The Value of Recreational Sport Fishing in the Lagoon of Venice
      Valentina Zanatta, Anna Alberini, Paolo Rosato and Alberto Longo 115

PART III   ASSESSING REMEDIATION OPTIONS AND POLICIES
           FOR CONTAMINATED SITES IN THE VENICE AREA

8.   What is the Value of Brownfields? A Review of Possible
      Approaches
      Stefania Tonin   143

9.   Developer Preferences for Brownfield Policies
      Anna Alberini, Alberto Longo, Stefania Tonin, Francesco
      Trombetta and Margherita Turvani   162

10. Governing Environmental Restoration: Institutions and Industrial
      Site Clean-ups
      Francesco Trombetta and Margherita Turvani   196

Index   213

List of Contributors

Anna Alberini, Department of Agricultural and Resource Economics, University of Maryland, USA and Fondazione Eni Enrico Mattei, Italy.

Margaretha Breil, Fondazione Eni Enrico Mattei, Italy.

Arianne de Blaeij, Department of Spatial Economics, Free University, Amsterdam, The Netherlands.

Edi Defrancesco, Department of Land and Agro-Forestry Systems, University of Padua, Italy.

Anita Fassio, Fondazione Eni Enrico Mattei, Italy.

Carlo Giupponi, Department of Crop Science, University of Milan, Italy and Fondazione Eni Enrico Mattei, Italy.

Alberto Longo, Department of Economics and International Development, University of Bath, UK.

Paulo A.L.D. Nunes, Department of Economics, Ca' Foscari University, Venice, Italy, Fondazione Eni Enrico Mattei, Italy and Department of Spatial Economics, Free University, The Netherlands.

Paolo Rosato, Department of Civil Engineering, University of Trieste and Fondazione Eni Enrico Mattei, Italy.

Luca Rossetto, Department of Land and Agro-Forestry Systems, University of Padua, Italy.

Stefania Tonin, Department of Planning, University IUAV, Italy.

Francesco Trombetta, Eni and Department of Planning, University IUAV, Italy.

Margherita Turvani, Department of Planning, University IUAV and School for Advanced Studies in Venice Foundation, Italy.

Valentina Zanatta, DICAS, Polytechnic of Turin and Fondazione Eni Enrico Mattei, Italy.

Foreword

The studies contained in this book, although written by different authors, are part of a unified and integrated research project designed to develop new methodologies to value complex natural resource systems. These studies emphasize the interlocking of resource management, urban regeneration, and economic development issues and policies surrounding certain natural resource systems, of which the Venice Lagoon is a prominent example.

The whole volume focuses on non-market valuation (methods and applications) and its use for policy analysis purposes, and on urban regeneration policies that have potentially important consequences on the natural resource system at hand. Although the research work is highly interdisciplinary, the volume is firmly rooted in the economics paradigm and economic analysis. Part I of the book provides excellent overviews of non-market valuation methods, which may well be adopted as course materials in appropriate PhD and undergraduate courses. Parts II and III of the book apply non-market valuation methods to the analysis of different aspects of the Venice Lagoon and the surrounding territory, including the valuation of measures to protect its coasts from erosion, the valuation of urban improvements, of ecosystem friendly clam fishing practices, of recreational sportfishing, and of measures for the remediation of contaminated sites.

The Venice Lagoon is a classic case that includes many of the problems that can be found in other complex natural systems. Therefore the studies of this book can be very useful to other scholars, students and policymakers who will study or manage other similar complex systems.

This volume is also one of the outputs of the FEEM research program on valuing natural resources and non-market goods. We have been working for several years on the valuation of environmental externalities and of composite goods like biodiversity, and on valuing intangible goods like health or the esthetics of urban developments. This book contains some applications to the Venice Lagoon of the methodologies developed in our research program.

The research efforts documented in this volume were managed by FEEM during a three-year research project funded by the Consortium for Coordination of Research Activities concerning the Venice Lagoon System (CORILA) within its 2000–2004 Research Program, 'An economic evaluation of interventions for the safeguarding and environmental protection in the Venice Lagoon'. I wish to thank the editors and the contributors to this volume, and CORILA for its financial and logistical support to the research. In particular Dr. Pierpaolo Campostrini has offered invaluable support to this work.

Carlo Carraro
Director of Research, Fondazione Eni Enrico Mattei

Introduction

Anna Alberini, Paolo Rosato and
Margherita Turvani

The Lagoon of Venice is a unique wildlife habitat and recreational site, and has been a World Heritage site since 1987. Its fisheries have provided sustenance to generations of residents of the city of Venice and of the surrounding region.

To the founders of Venice, the Lagoon had a special strategic significance, and the Republic of Venice – the Serenissima – was well aware of the importance of preserving and managing this natural resource carefully. In an effort to protect the fish stocks, for example, laws were passed that prohibited harvesting fish smaller than a certain size. Rivers were diverted to reduce sedimentation and regulate the depth of the Lagoon waters. As a result, the Lagoon's shallow waters protected the Republic of Venice from its enemies for one thousand years, making the city inaccessible from the sea and the mainland.

The Lagoon of Venice is a complex system where ecological and socioeconomic dimensions have co-evolved over time: the delicate and complicated interrelationships between water quality and movement, coastline, flora, fauna, and human health and wealth constitute an interrelated whole where any modification or disruption tends to affect many and diverse components of the ecological system, settlements and groups of people.

Clearly, the Lagoon has experienced a variety of natural and anthropic stimuli over the centuries. In recent decades, these stimuli have included agricultural pesticides and fertilizers runoff, hazardous wastes leachate and contaminated sediments from the chemical complex at Marghera and the industrial developments of the areas bordering on the Lagoon. 'High water' events and erosion from the wave motion created by boat traffic and by the digging of the *bocche di porto* (harbour access) to allow the growth of the industrial and tourist harbours have resulted in a serious deterioration of the ecological balance of wetlands and marshes, of the morphology and landscape of the Lagoon and its islands, and have caused damage to historical buildings and property in the city of Venice. Exotic species were introduced that compete with native species for habitat, and aggressive harvesting techniques were adopted in commercial fishing that wiped out native stocks and caused significant environmental damage.

The restoration of the historical centre of Venice has been a key political issue at the local, national and international level in the past century, and in the last decades increasing attention has been paid to the Lagoon. Public policies are under consideration that would restore environmental quality, fish stocks and habitat, and defend the morphology and landscape through the strict control of fishing practices, the restoration of island coastlines and marshes, and the protection of the islands from high tides. These policies therefore include a mix of (i) public works, such as the construction of floodgates, beach nourishment programmes, and containment of the hazardous wastes at the Marghera industrial site; (ii) regulation, such as restrictions on fishing equipment, sites and boat speed and access; (iii) urban regeneration programmes, zoning and remediation of the contaminated sites, and (iv) reliance on economic incentives, such as subsidies and others. Some funding for (iv) is available through European Union programmes.

In addition to pursuing environmental quality goals, these policies seek to promote economic growth. Economists would recommend that in examining such policies, at least some consideration be given to their costs and benefits. This means that the losses and gains brought by the policies must be monetized, and compared with one another.

In a typical cost–benefit analysis, the costs are comprised of both direct and indirect cost of investments and regulations. They therefore include the resources that are used up for construction or for private parties to comply with the regulations, monitoring and enforcement costs on the part of the relevant authority, welfare losses for consumer and producers associated with changes in price and quantities of goods traded on regular markets (such as fish and shellfish harvested in the Lagoon), transitional costs (e.g., unemployment) and any other adverse effects the policy may have on product quality, factor productivity, innovation, discouraged investment, and changes in markets indirectly affected by the policy. Ideally, much of the information necessary to compute the costs of the policy comes directly from the affected markets.

The benefits of these policies include, among others, the monetized value of the effects on human health, increased biodiversity, protection of landscape, and improved recreational opportunities for recreational anglers, boaters, swimmers, and the parties affected by the new economic opportunities created by the policies in many sectors. These benefits are experienced by the residents of the Lagoon area and by the relevant categories of users. In addition, it is likely that improving environmental quality, and protecting wildlife and landscape in the Lagoon will improve the well-being of many people that do not currently visit the Lagoon nor plan to in the future. The latter category of benefits is generally termed 'non-use values'.

To estimate the monetary value of benefits, it is necessary to find out how much people are willing to pay for them. It is, however, generally difficult to place a monetary value on benefits to recreationists and non-users, because these benefits are not bought and sold in regular markets. To circumvent this problem, it is possible to deploy non-market valuation methods. The travel cost method and contingent valuation are examples of such approaches. The former uses actual visits to a resource, and the cost of travelling to and spending time at this resource, to estimate a demand function, from which it is possible to compute an individual's willingness to pay for access to the resource and for improving its (environmental) quality.

Contingent valuation is an example of a survey-based, stated-preference method, which relies on what people say that they would do under well-defined but hypothetical circumstances. We wish to emphasize that non-market valuation methods are appropriate for placing a value on marginal changes in the level or quality of an environmental resource, and should not be construed as being able to provide the value of the resource *per se*.

This volume begins with three chapters that survey three important non-market valuation methods. In Chapter 1, Alberini and Longo describe the conceptual underpinnings of contingent valuation, and discuss practical considerations that researchers must face when conducting one such study. In Chapter 2, Defrancesco and Rosato briefly present the travel cost method, focusing on the role played by annual fixed costs (boat maintenance, license and equipment) when the evaluations are used for long term policy setting. In Chapter 3, Defrancesco et al. present a review of the use of appraisal methods in estimating the economic value of environmental resources. These techniques can be applied to computing both costs and benefits of environmental policies or the damage to natural resources caused by polluting events. Defrancesco et al. are very careful in highlighting the advantages and disadvantages of these approaches, and the fact that they necessarily rely on information from the markets. Absent markets for the harvests from the natural resource, or for goods whose quality is affected by the natural resource (e.g., homes in polluted neighbourhoods), it is necessary to resort to techniques based on directly questioning people about the value they place on a change in the resource.

Chapters 4 and 5 provide applications of these methods. In Chapter 4, Alberini et al. describe a contingent valuation study where residents of the Veneto Region were asked to report information about their willingness to pay for improvements in the environmental quality and resource management at and around S. Erasmo, one of the largest – and lesser known – islands in the Lagoon of Venice. The sample of respondents contained both users of the island – people who visit S. Erasmo for recreational purposes – and non-users, and Alberini et al. identify the use and non-use components of value for these environmental improvements. In Chapter 5, Rosato et al. present a model for the evaluation of environmental and urban improvements on the islands of the Lagoon of Venice that predicts the changes in residential real estate values using a mixed hedonic–hierarchical value function integrated with a Geographical Information System database that provides spatial distributions of changes in value.

As mentioned, the Lagoon of Venice has important fishing grounds, and both commercial and recreational fishing activities have taken place in them for centuries. In Chapter 6, Nunes et al. apply a stated-preference technique known as conjoint choice experiments for the economic valuation of alternative clam management practices in the Lagoon. They assess the preferences of commercial fishermen for various policies and restrictions on high-impact fishing techniques.

Commercial fishermen sometimes compete with recreational anglers for fishing stocks, and any Lagoon fish and fishing management policies that regulate the former will necessarily have an impact on the latter. In Chapter 7, Zanatta et al. use the travel cost method to estimate the welfare change implications for sports anglers of an improvement in catch rates brought about by controlling illegal clam fishing in the Lagoon. They combine information about actual trips at the current price per trip faced by anglers with intended trips for different, hypothetical prices and catch rates.

The state of conservation of the Lagoon of Venice is necessarily affected by the industrial activities taking place on the waterfront, and by the heritage of industrial activity and waste disposal practice that took place in the past. Sustainable development policies must, therefore, address the issue of cleaning up these sites while encouraging the productive reuse of these areas.

Clearly, land developers and investors are key players, and any cleanup and redevelopment has the potential to affect the value of the (formerly contaminated) land. In turn, any potential appreciation influences the attractiveness of contaminated sites to developers. Since the attractiveness of a parcel of land should be captured into its price, how can we find out how contamination, and subsequent remediation, affects the value of land? In Chapter 8, Tonin offers a survey of approaches for valuing contamination and for establishing the effect of contamination, and remediation, on real estate property. She concludes that the evidence of the effect of contamination and cleanup on the value of real estate is mixed, and that techniques that rely on observing market transactions on contaminated property vis-à-vis pristine property cannot be applied at Marghera, where property sales are few and far between.

Because of the limited number of transactions for the industrial area in Marghera, and the need to assess the attractiveness of its parcels – before and after remediation – to an international and domestic market, in Chapter 9 Alberini et al. resort to a survey of developers, deploying stated-preference questions to determine which policies – liability relief, fast-track review of cleanup plants, or financial incentives – can be used and which will be the most effective in stimulating productive reuse of these properties. This chapter, therefore, focuses on tradeoffs between economic incentives such as subsidies and imposing or relaxing liability, an economic tool that forces polluters to internalize the damages of pollution, and regulation, and tries to assess which is more effective in attaining remediation and redevelopment of contaminated sites.

Were these economic incentives and regulatory frameworks applied to the Marghera industrial area context, would they actually work? In Chapter 10, Trombetta and Turvani describe the legal and institutional context for remediation of contaminated sites in the Marghera industrial area, and discuss the promise of new policies based on voluntary agreements, which may be able to speed up and steer redevelopment.

We hope that this book offers useful guidance to those persons who are involved in studying or examining policy options for complex natural resource systems. The Lagoon of Venice is certainly one of the best possible case studies.

Finally, let us thank all those who supported our research work. In particular, we are indebted to the Consortium for Research on Venice Lagoon (CORILA) that provided financial support to the project; Martina Marian who managed the three-year research project on which this book is based; Professor Carlo Carraro of the University of Venice and FEEM, who coordinated the four research units who worked on the project; Mila Dallavalle for the valuable help provided in editing the final version of this book; and Martina Gambaro for her careful work in preparing the manuscript.

PART I

Non-Market Valuation Methods

1. Valuing Environmental Resources Using Stated Preferences

Anna Alberini and Alberto Longo

1.1 THE METHOD OF CONTINGENT VALUATION

Contingent Valuation is a method of estimating the value that a person places on a good. The approach asks people to directly report their willingness to pay (WTP) to obtain a specified good, or willingness to accept (WTA) to give up a good, rather than inferring them from observed behaviors in regular market places.

Because it creates a hypothetical marketplace in which no actual transactions are made, contingent valuation has been successfully used for commodities that are not exchanged in regular markets (for example improvements in water or air quality, national parks, reductions in the risk of death, days of illness avoided or days spent hunting or fishing), or when it is difficult to observe market transactions under the desired conditions. Contingent Valuation (CV) remains the only technique capable of placing a value on commodities that have a large passive-use[1] component of value.

Much controversy surrounds the use of CV when most of the value of the good derives from passive use, as has been typical in litigation over the damages to natural resources and amenities caused by releases of pollutants. Critics of contingent valuation allege that the quality of stated preference data is inferior to observing revealed preferences, consider contingent valuation a 'deeply flawed method' for valuing non-use goods and point at the possible biases affecting contingent valuation data (Hausman, 1993).

Despite these criticisms, CV has formed the basis for a significant amount of policymaking in the US (see Cropper and Alberini, 1997, for examples), and is increasingly used in developed and developing countries (Alberini and Cooper, 2000).

The remainder of this chapter is organized as follows. In section 1.2 we provide formal definitions for the welfare measures (WTP or WTA) elicited through a contingent valuation survey. In section 1.3 we discuss use and non-use values. In section 1.4 we describe survey methods and in section 1.5 the typical structure of a CV questionnaire. In section 1.6 we discuss alternative elicitation methods, and in section 1.7 statistical models of WTP. Section 1.8 presents ways of testing the internal validity of the responses to the WTP questions. Section 1.9 introduces the conjoint (choice) approach, and statistical models of the responses to conjoint choice questions are presented in section 1.10. We discuss the design of a conjoint (choice) study in section 1.11. Section 1.12 provides some concluding remarks about conjoint (choice) studies and contingent valuation surveys.

1.2   WTP AND WTA

The goal of contingent valuation is to measure the compensating or equivalent variation for the good in question. Compensating variation is the appropriate measure when the person must purchase the good, such as an improvement in environmental quality. Equivalent variation is appropriate if the person faces a potential loss of the good, as he would if a proposed policy results in the deterioration of environmental quality. Both compensating and equivalent variation can be elicited by asking a person to report a willingness to pay amount. For instance, the person may be asked to report his WTP to obtain the good, or to avoid the loss of the good.

Formally, WTP is defined as the amount that must be taken away from the person's income while keeping his utility constant:

$$V(y - WTP, p, q_1; Z) = V(y, p, q_0; Z) \qquad (1.1)$$

where V denotes the indirect utility function, y is income, p is a vector of prices faced by the individual, and q_0 and q_1 are the alternative levels of the good or quality indexes (with $q_1 > q_0$, indicating that q_1 refers to improved environmental quality). Z is a vector of individual characteristics.

Willingness to accept for a good is defined as the amount of money that must be given to an individual experiencing a deterioration in environmental quality to keep his utility constant:

$$V(y + WTA, p, q_0; Z) = V(y, p, q_1; Z) \qquad (1.2)$$

As shown in equations (1.1) and (1.2), WTP or WTA should depend on (i) the initial and final level of the good in question (q_0 and q_1); (ii) respondent income; (iii) all prices faced by the respondent, including those of substitute goods or activities; and (iv) other respondent characteristics that may influence the rate at which the individual trades off income for environmental quality.

In theory, absent income effects and when WTP is a small fraction of income, WTP and WTA for a given commodity should be approximately equal. However, a number of CV studies have found that WTA is often much larger than WTP for the same commodity. Various explanations are possible for this finding. One explanation is that the difference between WTP and WTA depends on the elasticity of substitution between the commodity to be valued (a public good) and private substitutes. The lower such elasticity, and the fewer the available substitutes, the greater the difference between WTP and WTA (Hanemann, 1991). Another explanation – the theory of prospects – is that individuals value losses more heavily than gains.

It is also possible that individuals react to their perception of who has the property rights over the commodity in question. If the proposed policy contradicts their perception of the existing property rights, individuals might express their rejection of the scenario through high WTA values. This might happen if, for example, individuals believe that they are entitled to clean air, and are outraged at a proposed degradation in air quality. In practice, some or all of these alternative explanations may coexist. Carson (1991) suggests that WTP should be used whenever the individual might incur benefits from the proposed policy, and Mitchell and Carson (1989) offer ways to frame the payment question to elicit WTP.

1.3   USE AND NON-USE VALUES

When people take trips to recreational areas, visit cultural heritage sites, or use natural resources, they experience a gain in their utility. However, it is reasonable to believe that people place monetary values on natural resources, ecosystems, or cultural goods independently of using these resources. If so, they may be willing to pay to preserve these resources even if they do not currently use them nor plan to in the future.

In the economic literature, natural resource values that are independent of people's present use of the resource are called 'passive-use' or 'non-use' values. The total economic value of a resource can, therefore, be broken into two components: the 'use value' component, which expresses the monetary value of that resource associated with the present use of that resource, and the 'non-use value' component, which contains the remaining monetary values people attach to that resource, independently of the present use of that resource. If non-use values are large, ignoring them in natural resource policymaking could lead to serious errors and resource misallocation. In some cases, non-use values have been found to account for most of the value of a resource. Desvousges et al. (1996) survey CV studies that have examined the various components of WTP.

Non-use values can be broken down into four classes of values: 'option', 'quasi option', 'bequest', and 'existence' values (Perman et al., 1996). *Option value* refers to the value that arises from retaining an option to a good or service for which future demand is uncertain. The option value is an additional value to any utility that may arise if and when the good is actually consumed. If individuals are certain about their future preferences and the future availability of the resource, the option value is zero. But if individuals are not certain about either their future preferences or the future availability of the resource, they may be willing to pay a premium – the option value – to keep the option of future use open.

Quasi option value refers to the utility gains expected to be realized from not undertaking irreversible decisions, and so maintaining options for future use of some resources, given expectations of future technological advance and/or the growth of knowledge. *Bequest value* is the value placed on the resource by individuals who are not users and wish to preserve the resource for future generations to use and enjoy. Bequest value is based on the idea that people gain welfare from the possibility that other people can consume the resource at some point in the future.

Finally, individual preferences may exist for maintaining resources in their forms even where no actual or future use is expected to be made of the resource. These preferences are the basis for the *existence value*. Existence value derives from human preferences for the existence of resources as such, unrelated to any use to which such resources may be put.

1.4 SURVEY METHODS

As previously explained, the contingent valuation method relies on directly querying individuals about their WTP (WTA) for a specified improvement (degradation) in environmental quality in the course of an interview.

Various survey methods are possible. In-person interviews are generally held to produce the highest-quality WTP data, but are very expensive. Telephone surveys are much less expensive and can produce high-quality data, but do not lend themselves to lengthy descriptions of the scenario, nor to the use of photographs and visual aids.

Mail surveys are even less expensive than telephone surveys, but completion of the questionnaire by the respondent may be correlated with his WTP for the commodity being valued, implying a self-selected type of sample. However, Cameron et al. (1998) show how to correct for sample-selection bias using Census information at the zipcode level for the addressees to whom the questionnaires were mailed. Mail surveys also make it difficult to ask questions that depend on the answer to previous questions, as is the case with follow-up questions about WTP.

Finally, some studies have been conducted using convenience samples drawn from University staff, college students, and by intercepting passers-by at shopping malls. Such samples may be acceptable when the purpose of the study is to test methodological aspects (such as the effect of the wording of the questionnaire, or the effect of presenting respondents with commodities defined in different ways), but do not allow the researcher to extrapolate values to the general population. In addition, when the subjects participating in the study are college students, insufficient variation in their individual characteristics usually prevents the researcher from investigating the relationship between these characteristics (such as age, income, family status) and WTP.

1.5   STRUCTURE OF THE QUESTIONNAIRE

Most contingent valuation surveys open with general ('warm-up') questions aimed at making the respondent comfortable with participating in the survey and answering questions. This is usually followed with a description of the scenario depicting a plan for the provision of a public good, a change in environmental quality, or a change in the private commodity to be valued.

Respondents are then queried about their WTP for the proposed plan (or about their WTA to accept a degradation in environmental quality or the loss of access to a natural resource). It is important that respondents be explicitly told how payments would be made by people to finance the provision of the good or the policy delivering the improvement in environmental quality (i.e., the payment vehicle). Questions about socio-demographics are usually placed in the last portion of the survey questionnaire. These typically include the respondent's age, household income, marital status, number of dependents, educational attainment, and 'attitude' questions, such as whether the respondent considers himself or herself an environmentalist.

1.6   WTP ELICITATION QUESTIONS

In early applications of the method of contingent valuation, respondents were often asked open-ended questions about their WTP. An open-ended question might be worded as follows: 'What is the most you would be willing to pay for …?' and is intended to elicit a point estimate of the respondent's WTP. Appealing as this approach might be, it is nowadays less and less frequently used, due to the obvious respondent difficulty in answering the payment question, which results in many missing values for WTP.[2]

An alternative approach is to list a number of possible WTP values on a card, and to ask the respondent to pick the amount on the card that best represents his willingness to pay. The amount chosen by the respondent can be interpreted as the respondent's WTP. A more precise interpretation, formalized in Cameron and Huppert (1988), is that the chosen amount is a lower bound for the respondent's WTP, the upper bound being the next highest amount on the card. Although under this interpretation WTP is not directly observed, statistical models can be fit that allow one to obtain the parameters of the distribution of WTP, and to make a prediction about a respondent's expected WTP amount. The payment card approach remains a popular way of eliciting WTP.

The most widely used approach to eliciting information about the respondent's WTP is the so-called dichotomous-choice format. A dichotomous choice payment question asks the respondent if he would pay $X to obtain the good. A frequently used wording of the payment question is whether the respondent would vote in favor of the proposed plan or policy if approval of the plan would cost his household $X (in the form of extra taxes, higher prices of products, etc.). There are only two possible responses to a dichotomous choice payment question: 'yes', and 'no' (or 'vote for' and 'vote against'). The dollar amount $X is varied across respondents, and is usually termed the bid value.

The dichotomous choice approach mimics behavior in regular markets, where people usually purchase, or decline to purchase, a good at the posted prices. It also closely resembles people's experience with political markets and propositions on a ballot. The dichotomous choice approach has also been shown to be incentive-compatible: provided that respondents understand that provision of the good depends on the majority of votes, and the respondent's own vote in itself cannot influence such provision, truth-telling is in the respondent's best interest (Hoehn and Randall, 1987). In addition, the dichotomous choice approach is also credited with reducing the cognitive burden placed on the respondent.

It is important to note that the dichotomous choice approach does not observe WTP directly. At best, we can infer that the respondent's WTP amount was greater than the bid value (if the respondent is in favor of the program) or less than the bid amount (if the respondent votes against the plan), and form broad intervals around the respondent's WTP amount. Mean WTP is estimated by fitting special statistical models of the responses (see section 1.7).

To improve the precision of the WTP estimates, in recent years researchers have introduced follow-up questions to the dichotomous choice payment question (for example Hanemann et al., 1991). To illustrate, consider a respondent who states he is not willing to pay $10 for the proposed plan. The follow-up question might ask him if he would pay $5. If the respondent answers 'no' to both questions, it is assumed that his WTP amount falls between 0 and $5. If the respondent answers 'no' to the initial question, and 'yes' to the follow-up questions, it is assumed that his WTP amount falls between $5 and $10. The bid level offered in the follow-up question will be greater than that offered in the initial payment question if the answer to the initial payment question is 'yes'.

1.7   STATISTICAL ANALYSIS OF THE RESPONSES

The purpose of the payment question is to obtain information about the respondent's WTP amount. WTP responses must be statistically modeled to obtain an estimate of mean WTP, which is multiplied by N, the size of the population affected by the proposed policy, to produce total WTP. Total WTP can then be compared with the cost of implementing the policy to determine whether the proposed policy passes a benefit–cost test.

If the payment question is open-ended, the WTP figures reported by the respondents can simply be averaged to produce an estimate of mean WTP:

$$MWTP = \frac{1}{n}\sum_{i=1}^{n} y_i \qquad (1.3)$$

where n is the sample size and each y is a reported WTP amount.

Average WTP may be deceptively high if a few individuals report very high WTP amounts. Carson (1991) proposes using an α-trimmed sample mean, where α is set at a predetermined percentage. An α-trimmed average is essentially a weighted average that attaches a weight of zero to the largest and lowest $\alpha \cdot 100$ percent of the observations, effectively disregarding them.

The sample average is the best (that is, lowest-variance) estimator of the true population mean only if the distribution of WTP is a normal. However, it is reasonable to assume that in many CV studies the distribution of WTP is not a normal: A normal distribution allows negative values, which can be ruled out for many of the commodities under investigation in a CV survey.

If the distribution of the population is not a normal, the sample average remains a valid way to estimate the true population mean, but the maximum likelihood estimate of mean WTP is more statistically efficient. Estimating the mean by the method of maximum likelihood requires that a distribution be specified for WTP. For instance, one may wish to assume that distribution of WTP is a Weibull with parameters θ and σ, and cdf

$$F(y) = 1 - e^{-(y/\sigma)^{\theta}}.$$

The most efficient estimate of mean WTP in this case is obtained as:

$$\hat{\sigma} \cdot \Gamma\left(\frac{1}{\hat{\theta}} + 1\right)$$

where $\hat{\sigma}$ and $\hat{\theta}$ denote the maximum likelihood estimates of the parameters, and $\Gamma(\cdot)$ is the gamma function.

Dichotomous choice payment questions typically require a different type of statistical analysis, based on the assumption that if the individual states he is willing to pay the bid amount, his WTP must be greater than the bid. If the individual declines to pay the stated amount, then his WTP must be less than the bid. In both cases, the respondent's actual WTP amount is not observed directly by the researcher. Let WTP* be unobserved willingness to pay, which is assumed to follow a distribution $F(\theta)$, where θ is a vector of parameters, and form an indicator, I, that takes on a value of one for 'yes' responses and 0 for 'no' responses. The probability of observing a 'yes' (or $I = 1$) when the respondent has been offered a bid equal to B_i is:

$$\Pr(I_i = 1) = \Pr(WTP_i^* > B_i) = 1 - F(B_i;\theta) \qquad (1.4)$$

whereas the probability of observing a 'no' (or $I = 0$) is simply $F(B_i;\theta)$, that is the cdf of WTP evaluated at the bid value. The log likelihood function of the sample is:

$$\sum_{ii=1}^{n}\left\{I_i \cdot \log[1 - F(B_i;\theta)] + (1 - I_i) \cdot \log F(B_i;\theta)\right\}. \qquad (1.5)$$

If WTP is normally distributed, $F(\cdot)$ is the standard normal cumulative distribution function, and $F(B_i; \theta) = \Phi(B_i/\sigma - \mu/\sigma)$, where the symbol Φ denotes the standard normal cdf, μ is mean WTP and σ is the standard deviation of the distribution. If WTP follows the log normal distribution (and is hence defined only for non-negative values), $F(B_i; \theta) = \Phi(\log B_i/\sigma - \mu/\sigma)$ where μ and σ are the mean and standard deviation of the logarithmic transformation of WTP, and mean WTP is equal to $\exp(\mu + 0.5 \cdot \sigma^2)$. Other distributions are possible: for example, WTP is often assumed to be a logistic with cdf equal to $1/[1 + \exp(-z)]$, where $z = \mu/\sigma - B/\sigma$. After equation (1.6) is specialized to the desired WTP distribution, the parameters can be estimated directly by maximizing (1.5).

If WTP follows the normal or logistic distribution, the coefficients can be estimated using a probit or logit estimation routine. Specifically, one runs a probit (logit) regression of the dependent variable I (the yes/no indicator) on a constant and on an independent variable consisting of the bid level. The intercept, α, of the probit model obtained in this fashion is equal to μ/σ, whereas the slope coefficient, β, is equal to $-1/\sigma$. One recovers estimates of the original μ by dividing $\hat{\alpha}$ by $(-\hat{\beta})$, and of the original σ as $\hat{\sigma} = -1/\hat{\beta}$.

The probit or logit routine produces standard errors for $\hat{\alpha}$ and $\hat{\beta}$, but not for $\hat{\mu}$ and $\hat{\sigma}$.[3] To obtain the variances of the latter estimates, researchers have resorted to a variety of techniques. The most straightforward is that based on the 'delta method', illustrated for dichotomous choice contingent valuation data by Cameron (1991). To obtain the covariance matrix of $\hat{\mu}$ and $\hat{\sigma}$, one first needs the covariance matrix of $\hat{\alpha}$ and $\hat{\beta}$ produced by the probit routine, here denoted as **V**. The expression for **V** is:

$$
\mathbf{V} = \left\{ \sum_{i=1}^{n} w(z_i) \begin{bmatrix} 1 & B_i \\ B_i & B_i^2 \end{bmatrix} \right\}^{-1} \tag{1.6}
$$

where $z_i = \hat{\alpha} + \hat{\beta} \cdot B_i$, and $w(z_i) = \phi^2(z_i)/\{\Phi(z_i)[1 - \Phi(z_i)]\}$, with $\phi(\cdot)$ the standard normal probability density function (pdf). Next, it is necessary to compute the matrix **G**, with

$$
\mathbf{G} = \begin{bmatrix} -1/\hat{\beta} & 0 \\ \hat{\alpha}/\hat{\beta}^2 & 1/\hat{\beta}^2 \end{bmatrix}
$$

The final step requires calculating the matrix product $\mathbf{V_1} = \mathbf{G}' * \mathbf{V} * \mathbf{G}$, with $\mathbf{V_1}$ the covariance matrix of $\hat{\mu}$ and $\hat{\sigma}$.

A second approach relies on the asymptotic distribution of $\hat{\alpha}$ and $\hat{\beta}$, which is a bivariate normal with means α and β and covariance matrix approximated by **V**. A large number (m) of draws from the above bivariate normal distribution is taken, and for each draw (consisting of two values, one for $\hat{\alpha}$ and one for $\hat{\beta}$) $\hat{\mu}$ and $\hat{\sigma}$ are calculated. Finally, one averages all of the values of $\hat{\mu}$ and $\hat{\sigma}$ thus obtained, and computes the standard deviations of those values. The standard deviations thus calculated provide the standard errors for $\hat{\mu}$ and $\hat{\sigma}$. Confidence limits can be calculated using these standard errors, or by sorting $\hat{\mu}$ and $\hat{\sigma}$ in ascending order, and identifying the 2.5th percentile and the 97.5th percentile of each set (assuming that the desired confidence interval is 95 percent), although bias corrections to this interval may be appropriate (Cooper, 1994).

If elicitation is based on an initial dichotomous choice question, followed by one dichotomous choice follow-up question (the 'double-bounded' approach), a likelihood function based on interval data must be specified. To write out the likelihood function, first notice that four possible pairs of responses to the payment questions are possible: (a) yes, yes; (b) yes, no; (c) no, yes; and (d) no, no. Since the follow-up bid amount, B2, is greater than the first for those respondents who answered 'yes' to the initial payment question (lower for those respondents who answered 'no' to the initial payment question), the pairs identify intervals around the respondent's WTP amount.

Specifically, WTP is greater than B2 for 'yes, yes' respondents; it lies between B1 and B2 for 'yes, no' respondents, and between B2 and B1 for 'no, yes' respondents. Finally, WTP is less than B2 for 'no, no' respondents. This yields the log likelihood function:

$$\log L = \sum_{i=1}^{n} \log \left[F(WTP^{H}; \theta) - F(WTP^{L}; \theta) \right] \qquad (1.7)$$

where WTP^{H} and WTP^{L} are the lower and upper bound of the interval around WTP defined as explained above. (For respondents who give two yes responses, the upper bound of WTP is infinity, or the respondent's income; for respondents who give two 'no' responses, the lower bound is either zero (if the distribution of WTP admits only non-negative values) or negative infinity (if the distribution of WTP is a normal or a logistic).)

It should be borne in mind that if the distribution of willingness to pay is positively skewed, the estimate of mean WTP exceeds – sometimes greatly – the estimate of median WTP. Median WTP – the value at which 50 percent of the respondents would vote in support of the program, and hence the cost at which the majority of the population would be in support of it – is thus frequently reported by researchers as a robust lower-bound estimate of WTP.

Finally, it is important to remember that, as shown in equation (1.6) and in the formula for recovering the covariance matrix of the original parameters of the distribution of WTP, the standard error around mean or median WTP – and hence, the precision of the results from the survey and the power of tests of hypotheses about WTP – is crucially affected by the bid values assigned to the respondents as part of the payment question. Alberini (1995), Kanninen (1991) and Cooper (1993) examine the issue of the choice of bids in dichotomous-choice contingent valuation surveys.

1.8   INTERNAL VALIDITY OF THE WTP RESPONSES

After WTP responses have been collected through the survey, it is important to test for internal validity, that is to estimate models of willingness to pay that relate the respondents' WTP amounts to the individual characteristics of the respondents, and to the quantity and mode of provision of the commodity being valued (if the latter have been varied to the respondents). Formally, the underlying regression equation is:

$$WTP_i^* = \mathbf{x}_i \beta + \mathbf{z}_i \gamma + \varepsilon_i \tag{1.8}$$

where WTP^* represents the WTP amount,[4] $\mathbf{x}$ is a $1 \times k$ vector of indicators and continuous variables representing aspects of the commodity or of the provision mechanism that have been varied to respondents in the study, and $\mathbf{z}$ is an $1 \times m$ vector of individual characteristics of the respondents. β and γ are vectors of unknown coefficients, and ε is the econometric error term.

If respondents have been asked to value commodities of different size and quality, one would expect WTP to increase with the size and the quality of the commodity. In the contingent valuation literature, this expectation is termed the 'scope' effect. It can be empirically tested by checking that the coefficients on the variables capturing size and quality are statistically significant and of the appropriate sign. The size and quality of the commodity can be expressed in a number of ways, such as the number of species affected by a wildlife management or recovery program, the size of the geographical area affected by the program, etc.

If the mode of provision of the commodity or the payment vehicle is varied across respondents, dummy variables should be included in the right-hand side of the WTP equation to check whether WTP changes with these aspects of the scenario. Researchers have also investigated whether the amount of information provided to respondents about the commodity, and/or the way it was presented to them (Magat and Viscusi, 1992) has an impact on willingness to pay.

The vector $\mathbf{z}$ usually includes individual characteristics such as age, education, gender, income, measures of attitude towards the commodity being valued (for example in the case of environmental resources, whether the respondent considers himself or herself an environmentalist), past behaviors that could explain willingness to pay, and other conditions that could influence WTP (for example health).

1.9 CONJOINT METHODS

Contingent valuation, the non-market valuation technique we have presented thus far, can be interpreted as a special case of conjoint choice methods. Conjoint choice experiments are increasingly popular non-market valuation methods in environmental economics. Conjoint analysis and conjoint choice experiments are stated-preference techniques, in the sense that they infer preferences and values by asking individuals what they would do under hypothetical circumstances, rather than observing actual behaviors on marketplaces.

In a typical conjoint analysis survey, respondents are shown alternative variants of a good, which are described by a set of attributes. The alternatives differ from one another in the levels taken by two or more of the attributes.

Conjoint questions may be employed to ask the respondent rate, rank, or just choose between alternative representations of a specified good. The most popular variants of conjoint exercises are (i) contingent ranking, (ii) contingent rating, and (iii) conjoint choice. Statistical analyses of the responses obtained in any one of these ways can be used to obtain the marginal value of these attributes and the willingness to pay for any alternative of interest.

In a contingent ranking exercise, respondents are asked to rank a set of alternative representations of the good from the most preferred to the least preferred. One of the alternatives that is usually part of the choice exercise is the 'do nothing' alternative, or the status quo. One disadvantage of this technique lies in the cognitive burden associated with ranking choices with many different attributes and levels, or with the number of representations to be ranked, especially when the respondent is asked to choose among goods that he is not familiar with. Moreover, response reliability is likely to be affected by the number of options ranked and the degree of preference for each. One would expect reliability to decrease with more options, in the sense it might be relatively easy to identify the most preferred and the least preferred options, but it might be not so easy to rank the options in the middle (Louviere et al., 2000).

In a contingent rating exercise respondents are shown different representations of the good and are asked to rank each representation on a numeric or semantic scale. In this variant, there may not be a direct comparison between alternatives and there is no formal theoretical link between the expressed ratings and economic choices (Hanley et al., 2001).

One of the major drawbacks of this technique is the strong assumptions that must be made in order to transform ratings into utilities. These assumptions relate to the issue of how to evaluate ratings from different respondents and how to weight the cardinality of ratings. For example, the same representation of a good might receive the same rate by two different respondents, but this does not necessarily mean that the two answers are identical: a rate of '8' by a respondent might be completely different from the '8' given by another respondent. Therefore, contingent ratings are inconsistent with consumer theory and do not produce welfare-consistent value estimates (Hanley et al., 2001).

In a conjoint choice exercise, respondents are shown a set of alternative representations of a good and are asked to pick their most preferred. If the 'do nothing' or status quo option is included in the choice set, the experiments can be used to compute the value (WTP) of each alternative. This approach has the advantage of simulating real market situations, where consumers face two or more goods characterized by similar attributes, but different levels of these attributes, and are asked to choose whether to buy one of the goods or none of them. Another advantage is that the choice tasks do not require as much effort by the respondent as in rating or ranking alternatives.

The first applications of conjoint analysis were in the fields of marketing research and transportation. Since then, conjoint analysis and conjoint choice approaches have been applied in several other disciplines. In Table 1.1 we report an example of conjoint choice question used by Hanley et al. (2001) to value rock-climbing sites in Scotland.

Table 1.1   Conjoint choice question

Which route would you prefer to visit in the summer, given the two routes described below?

Characteristics of route	Route A	Route B
Length of climb	100 meters	200 meters
Approach time	3 hours	2 hours
Quality of climb	2 stars	0 stars
Crowding at route	Crowded	Not crowded
Scenic quality of route	Not at all scenic	Not at all scenic
Distance of route from home	160 miles	110 miles

Prefer Route A?   ☐
Prefer Route B?   ☐
Stay at home? (Choose neither?) ☐

Source: Hanley et al. (2001)

1.10   MODEL AND ECONOMETRIC ANALYSES OF THE CONJOINT RESPONSES

In this section, we discuss the underlying economic theory and the econometric models for conjoint choice experiments. The reader is referred to Beggs et al. (1982) for models for rating questions.

To motivate the statistical analysis of the responses to conjoint choice experiment questions, it is assumed that the choice between the alternatives is driven by the respondent's underlying utility. The respondent's indirect utility is broken down into two components. The first component is deterministic, and is a function of the attributes of alternatives, characteristics of the individuals, and a set of unknown parameters, while the other is an error term. Formally,

$$V_{ij} = \overline{V}(\mathbf{x}_{ij}, \boldsymbol{\beta}) + \varepsilon_{ij} \qquad (1.9)$$

where the subscript i denotes the respondent, the subscript j denotes the alternative, $\mathbf{x}$ is the vector of attributes and individual characteristics, and ε is an error term that captures individual – and alternative – specific factors that influence utility, but are not observable to the researcher. Equation (1.9) describes the random utility model (RUM).

In most applications, it is further assumed that $\overline{V}$, the deterministic component of utility, is a linear combination of the attributes of the alternatives and of the respondent's residual income, $(y - C)$, where y is income and C is the price of the commodity or the cost of the program to the respondent:

$$V_{ij} = \beta_0 + \mathbf{x}_{ij}\boldsymbol{\beta}_1 + (y_i - C_j)\beta_2 + \varepsilon_{ij} \qquad (1.10)$$

Clearly, the coefficient β_2 is the marginal utility of income.

When faced with a given choice set, it is assumed that the respondent chooses the alternative that results in the highest utility. Because the observed outcome of each choice task is the selection of one out of K alternatives, the appropriate econometric model is a discrete choice model that expresses the probability that alternative k is chosen. Formally,

$$\begin{aligned} \Pr(k \text{ is chosen}) &= \Pr(V_k > V_1, V_k > V_2, ..., V_k > V_K) \\ &= \Pr(V_k > V_j) \end{aligned} \quad \forall j \neq k \qquad (1.11)$$

where the subscript i is suppressed to avoid notational clutter. This means that

$$\begin{aligned} \Pr(k) = \Pr[\beta_0 + \mathbf{x}_k\boldsymbol{\beta}_1 + (y_i - C_k)\beta_2 + \varepsilon_k \\ > \beta_0 + \mathbf{x}_j\boldsymbol{\beta}_1 + (y_i - C_j)\beta_2 + \varepsilon_j] \end{aligned} \quad \forall j \neq k \qquad (1.12)$$

from which follows that

$$\Pr(k) = \Pr[(\varepsilon_j - \varepsilon_k) < (\mathbf{x}_k - \mathbf{x}_j)\boldsymbol{\beta}_1 - (C_k - C_j)\beta_2] \quad \forall j \neq k \qquad (1.13)$$

Equation (1.13) shows the probability of selecting an alternative no longer contains terms in (1.10) that are constant across alternatives, such as the intercept and income. It also shows that the probability of selecting k depends on the difference in the level of the attributes across alternatives, and that coefficient of the difference in cost or price across alternatives is equal to minus the marginal utility of income.

If the error terms ε are independent and identically distributed and follow a standard type I extreme value distribution,[5] the probability that respondent i

picks alternative k out of K alternatives is:

$$\Pr(k) = \frac{\exp(\mathbf{w}_{ik}\boldsymbol{\beta})}{\sum_{j=1}^{K} \exp(\mathbf{w}_{ij}\boldsymbol{\beta})} \qquad (1.14)$$

where:

$$\mathbf{w}_{ij} = \begin{bmatrix} \mathbf{x}_{ij} \\ C_{ij} \end{bmatrix}$$

is the vector of all attributes of alternative j, including cost; and

$$\boldsymbol{\beta} = \begin{bmatrix} \boldsymbol{\beta}_1 \\ -\beta_2 \end{bmatrix}.^{6}$$

Equation (1.14) is the contribution to the likelihood in a conditional logit model. The full log likelihood function of the conditional logit model is:

$$\log L = \sum_{i=1}^{n} \sum_{k=1}^{K} y_{ik} \cdot \log \Pr(i \text{ chooses } k), \qquad (1.15)$$

where y_{ik} is a binary indicator that takes on a value of 1 if the respondent selects alternative k, and 0 otherwise, and $\Pr(i$ chooses $k)$ is equal to $\Pr(k)$ in equations (1.12)–(1.14).

Once model (1.15) is estimated, the rate of tradeoff between any two attributes is the ratio of their respective $\hat{a}$ coefficients. The implicit marginal value of each attribute is computed as the negative of the coefficient on that attribute, divided by the coefficient on the price or cost variable.[7] Willingness to pay for a commodity is computed as

$$WTP_i = \frac{\mathbf{x}_i \hat{\boldsymbol{\beta}}}{\hat{\beta}_2},$$

where $\mathbf{x}$ is the vector of attributes describing the commodity assigned to individual i.

The conditional logit model described by equations (1.14)–(1.15) is easily amended to allow for heterogeneity among the respondents. Specifically, one can form interaction terms between individual characteristics, such as age, gender, education, etc., and all or some of the attributes, and enter these interactions in the indirect utility function.

Whether or not interaction terms are included, implicit in the conditional logit model is the assumption of Independence of Irrelevant Alternatives (IIA), which states that the ratio of the odds of choosing any two alternatives depends only of the attributes of the alternatives being compared, and is not affected by the attributes of other alternatives. IIA generally imposes restrictive substitution patterns among the alternatives, and researchers are thus advised to test for violations of this assumption.[8]

One way to avoid imposing IIA is to fit a multinomial probit model. In a multinomial probit model, the error terms in equation (1.10) are jointly normally distributed. While the error terms of different individuals continue to be independent of one another, the joint normal distribution allows for correlation between the error terms associated with different alternatives (within one individual).

Another model that avoids imposing IIA is the random-coefficient logit, which also has the advantage of allowing for heterogeneity of marginal utilities across respondents. In a random-coefficient model, the vector of coefficients β breaks down into two components: its expectation, $\bar{\beta}$, and a vector of error terms, u_i, that vary over respondents. The individual-specific error term u creates correlation between the indirect utilities associated with the different alternatives, ruling out IIA. Estimating this model requires that assumptions be made about which coefficients are random, and about the joint distribution of the individual-specific errors u_i.

Since in many applications of conjoint choice the same respondent is faced with multiple choice tasks, it is reasonable to worry whether the error terms associated with the different choice occasions are correlated within the same respondent. All of the models here considered – the conditional logit, the random-coefficient logit, and the multinomial probit – can be amended to allow for random effects, whereby all error terms for a respondent share a common component. This component is fixed within the respondent, but varies between respondents, and is supposed to capture idiosyncratic, unobservable factors that can influence utility.

1.11   DESIGNING A CONJOINT ANALYSIS STUDY

In developing a conjoint choice survey, the researcher must first select the attributes that define the good to be valued. The attributes should be selected on the basis of the goal of the valuation exercise, prior beliefs of the researcher, and evidence from focus groups.

Clearly, valuation requires that one of the attributes be the 'price' of the commodity or the cost to the respondent of the program delivering a change in the provision of a public good. It is also important to make sure that the provision mechanism, whether private or public, is acceptable to the respondent, and that the payment vehicle is realistic and compatible with the commodity to be valued.

The next step in the development of the conjoint choice experimental design is the choice of the levels of the attributes. Given the levels of all other attributes, Kanninen (2002) derives the d-optimal values of the cost attribute, as well as the percentage of the sample that should be assigned to these amounts. Regardless of optimal statistical design considerations, the levels of the attributes should be selected so as to be reasonable and realistic, lest the respondent rejects the scenario and/or the choice exercise.

When choosing both the attributes that describe the commodity to be valued and the levels of the attributes, one that should keep the sample size in mind.[9] Once the experimental design is created, the researcher needs to construct the choice sets. The choice sets may consist of two or more alternatives, depending on how simple one wishes to keep the choice tasks. The 'status quo' should be included in the choice set if one wishes to estimate WTP for a policy package or a scenario.

If the status quo is not present, it is not possible to estimate the welfare change from the status quo. However, there are some situations where the status quo cannot be considered as a feasible choice, and therefore should not be included in the choice set. When grouping alternatives together to form the choice sets, it is important to rule out alternatives that are obviously dominated by others. For example, if house A and B were compared, and the levels of all attributes were identical, but B were more expensive, A would be, clearly, a dominating choice.

1.12   DISCUSSION: IS CONJOINT ANALYSIS BETTER THAN CONTINGENT VALUATION?

Hanley et al. (2001) discuss whether conjoint analysis or choice experiments may prove better than contingent valuation, in the sense that the former would avoid biases that have been ascribed to contingent valuation. For example, regarding hypothetical bias – which is feared to result in overstated valuation, as the respondent does not actually make a payment – Hanley et al. point out that a systematic comparison of WTP elicited from contingent valuation and in revealed preference studies (Carson et al., 1996) shows that there is a remarkable degree of consistency between stated and revealed preferences.[10] Hanley et al. conclude that there is no particular reason to believe that surveys employing conjoint analysis would perform differently than contingent valuation as far as hypothetical bias is concerned.

Regarding sensitivity of WTP to scope, most conjoint analysis studies respondents are asked to engage in the choice (or alternatively, rating or ranking) multiple times, and the size of the commodity being valued is typically varied across alternatives and choice sets. This implies that subjects are given an internal scope test, allowing the researcher to check whether utility, and hence WTP, varies with the size of the good being valued. This is a desirable feature of conjoint analysis, but it should be borne in mind that internal scope tests are not judged to be as rigorous as external scope tests, where respondents are randomly assigned to different subsamples and are asked to valued commodities of different size.

Several analysts believe that conjoint analysis questions reduce strategic incentives, because individuals are busy trading off the attributes of the alternatives and are less prone to strategic thinking (Adamowicz et al., 1998). The same reasoning and the fact that conjoint choice questions may appear less 'stark' than the take-it-or-leave options of contingent valuation has led other researchers to believe that 'protest' behaviors are less likely to occur in conjoint analysis surveys. No evidence has yet been produced, however, in support of or disproving either of these claims.

Some valuation researchers (for example Carson, personal communication; Hanemann, personal communication) do not believe in conjoint analysis because they believe that much effort must be spent in stated preference studies to provide a scenario that is fully understood and accepted by the respondent. Changing this scenario from one choice question to the next, they point out, results in a loss of credibility of the scenario and may induce rejection of the choice task.

In sum, we believe that conjoint choice experiments are potentially useful to value environmental resources and public goods, but that much research is needed to fully understand their advantages and drawbacks.

NOTES

1. Passive-use values (also termed non-use values) relate to the utility that a person experiences from knowing that a natural resource or amenity exists and may be experienced by other people or future generations, even though he/she has never visited it nor plans to.
2. We also believe that the open-ended format encourages people to underreport their willingness to pay.
3. The statistical software SAS is an exception: Its probit routine prints out standard errors for the intercept and slope, as well as the variances and covariance of $\hat{\mu}$ and $\hat{\sigma}$.
4   This amount is unobserved if the payment questions are in the dichotomous-choice format.
5. The Type I extreme value distribution is defined over the real axis. The probability density function for x is:

$$f(x) = Be^{-B(x-A)}e^{-e^{-B(x-A)}}$$

where B is the scale parameter and A is the location parameter. A Standard type I extreme value distributions restricts A to be equal to 0 and B to be 1.

6. The intercept in equation (1.10) is not identified and is therefore normalized to zero.
7. Various approaches can be used to calculate the standard errors of the estimates of the marginal utilities, which are ratios of asymptotically jointly normally distributed variates. One approach is the delta method, which is based on a first-order Taylor series approximation. Another approach follows Krinski and Robb, and generates a large number of draws, M, from the asymptotic distribution of the estimated coefficients (which is a multivariate normal). Given a draw, the marginal utility of an attribute is then computed. The standard deviation of the M computed marginal utilities is taken to be the standard error around the point estimate of marginal utility.
8. Specifically, a change in the attributes of one alternative changes the probabilities of the other alternatives proportionately to satisfy the conditional logit's requirement that the ratio of these probabilities remain the same.
9. The maximum total sample size is given by the number of respondents receiving the questionnaire, times the number of conjoint choice questions asked in the questionnaire. Ideally, this maximum sample size should be large enough to accommodate all of the possible combinations of attributes and levels of the attributes, that is the full factorial design. To illustrate, consider a house described by three attributes: square footage, proximity to the city center, and price. If the square footage can take three different levels (1500, 2000, 2200), proximity to the city center can take two different levels (less than miles, more than three miles) and price can take 4 different levels ($200 000, $250 000, $300 000, and $350 000), the full factorial design consists of $3 \times 2 \times 4 = 24$ alternatives. The number of alternatives of the full factorial design increases with the number of attributes and the number of levels per attribute. When the full factorial design contains too many combinations for the planned sample size, one may resort to fractional designs. Fractional designs usually allow one to estimate the 'main effects' (that is they are suitable for situations when the attribute enter in a linear fashion in the utility function, as in equation (1.10)), and can sometimes be specified to allow one to estimate some, but not all, of the interactions between attributes. Orthogonal designs are an important subset of all fractional designs. One of their advantages is that they allow for efficient identification of main effects. However, in some cases it is not realistic to vary the levels of the attributes in an orthogonal manner. If so, the researcher is advised to use correlated designs.
10. In most cases where contingent valuation (or conjoint analysis) appears to have overstated WTP, voluntary donations were the payment vehicle. Voluntary donations have been shown to be incentive-incompatible, and to encourage free-riding behaviors on the part of respondents.

REFERENCES

Adamowicz, W.L., J. Louviere and J. Swait (1998), 'Introduction to Attribute-based Stated Choice Methods', Final report submitted by Avanis, Silver Spring, MD: Resource Valuation Center, Damage Assessment Center, National Oceanic and Atmospheric Administration.

Alberini, A. (1995) 'Optimal Designs for Discrete Choice Contingent Valuation Surveys: Single-bound, Double-bound and Bivariate Models', *Journal of Environmental Economics and Management*, **28**, 187–306.

Alberini, A. and J.A. Cooper (2000), 'Applications of the Contingent Valuation Method in Developing Countries: A Survey', FAO Economic and Social Development Paper 146, Food and Agricultural Organizations of the United Nations, Rome, Italy.

Beggs, S., S. Cardell and J. Hausman (1981), 'Assessing the Potential Demand for Electric Cars', *Journal of Econometrics*, **17**(1), 1–19.

Cameron, T.A. (1991), 'Interval Estimates of Non-Market Resource Values from

Referendum Contingent Valuation Surveys', *Land Economics*, **67**(4), 413–21.

Cameron, T.A. and D.D. Huppert (1988), 'OLS versus ML Estimation of Non-market Resource Values with Payment Card Interval Data', *Journal of Environmental Economics and Management*, **17**, 230–46.

Cameron, T.A., W.D. Shaw and S. Ragland (1998), 'Nonresponse Bias in Mail Survey Data: Salience v. Endogenous Survey Complexity', in J.A. Herriges and C.L. Kling (eds), *Valuing the Environment Using Recreation Demand Models*, Cheltenham, UK and Lyme, USA: Edward Elgar Publishing.

Carson, R.T. (1991), 'Constructed Markets', in Braden J. and C. Kolstad (eds), *Measuring the Demand for Environmental Commodities,* Amsterdam: North-Holland.

Carson, R.T., N.E. Flores, K.M. Martin and J.L. Wright (1996), 'Contingent Valuation and Revealed Preference Methodologies: Comparing the Estimates for Quasi-public Goods', *Land Economics*, **72**(1), 80–99.

Cooper, J.A. (1993), 'Optimal Bid Selection for Dichotomous Choice Contingent Valuation Surveys', *Journal of Environmental Economics and Management*, **24**(1), 25–40.

Cooper, J.A. (1994), 'A Comparison of Approaches to Calculating Confidence Intervals for Benefit Measures from Dichotomous Choice Contingent Valuation Surveys', *Land Economics*, **70**(1), 111–22.

Cropper, M. and A. Alberini (1997), 'Contingent Valuation', Entry in *The New Palgrave Dictionary of Economics and the Law.*

Desvousges, W.H., S.P. Hudson and M.C. Ruby (1996), 'Evaluating CV Performance: Separating the Light from the Heat', in Bjornstad J.D. and R.J. Kahn (eds), *The Contingent Valuation of Environmental Resources: Methodological Issues and Research Needs*, Cheltenham, UK and Brookfield, USA: Edward Elgar Publishing.

Hanemann, W.M. (1991), 'Willingness to Pay and Willingness to Accept: How Much Can They Differ?', *American Economic Review*, **81**(3), 635–47.

Hanemann, M.W., J. Loomis and Kanninen (1991), 'Statistical Efficiency of Double-Bounded Dichotomous Choice Contingent Valuation', *American Journal of Agricultural Economics*, **73**(4), 1255–63.

Hanley, N., S. Mourato and R.E. Wright (2001), 'Choice Modelling Approaches: A Superior Alternative for Environmental Valuation?', *Journal of Economic Surveys*, **15**(3), 435–62.

Hausman, J.A. (1993), *Contingent Valuation, A Critical Assessment*, Amsterdam: North-Holland.

Hoehn, J.P. and A. Randall (1987), 'A Satisfactory Benefit Cost Indicator from Contingent Valuation', *Journal of Environmental Economics and Management*, **14**, 226–47.

Kanninen, B.J. (1991), 'Optimal Experimental Design for Contingent Valuation Surveys', Ph.D. dissertation, University of California Berkeley.

Kanninen, B.J. (2002), 'Optimal Design for Multinomial Choice Experiments', *Journal of Marketing Research*, **39**(2), 214–27.

Louviere, J., D.A. Hensher and J.D. Swait (2000), *Stated Choice Methods*: *Analysis and Applications*, Cambridge, UK: Cambridge University Press.

Magat, W.A. and W.K. Viscusi (1992), *Informational Approaches to Regulation*, Cambridge: MIT Press.

Mitchell, R.C. and R.T. Carson (1989), *Using Surveys to Value Public Goods: The Contingent Valuation Method*, Washington, DC: Resources for the Future.

Perman, R., M. Yue and J. McGilvray (1996), *Natural Resource and Environmental Economics*, New York: Addison Wesley Longman.

2. Recreational Demand, Travel Cost Method and Flow Fixed Costs

Edi Defrancesco and Paolo Rosato

2.1 INTRODUCTION

The Travel Cost Method (TCM) is one of the most frequently used approaches to estimating the use values of recreational sites. The TCM was initially suggested by Hotelling (1949) and subsequently developed by Clawson (1959) in order to estimate the benefits from recreation at natural sites. The method is based on the premise that the recreational benefits at a specific site can be derived from the demand function that relates observed users' behaviour (i.e., the number of trips to the site) to the cost of a visit.

One of the most important issues in the TCM is the choice of the costs to be taken into account. The literature usually suggests considering direct variable costs and the opportunity cost of time spent travelling to and at the site. However, some authors (Walsh, 1986, p. 275) have underscored the importance of studying the effect of fixed costs (equipment, license fees, and so on) on the long-run price elasticity of demand.

The first aim of this chapter is to discuss the role played by a category of fixed costs that we term annual flow fixed costs, that is annual fixed expenses related to the recreational activity, on the consumer decision-making process under different time horizons. These considerations are important when, as is often the case, a recreational user incurs substantial fixed costs directly related to the recreational activity on an annual basis, regardless of the number of trips undertaken (for example, an annual site licence). Second, we develop a simple model to account for the effect of flow fixed costs on consumer surplus and behaviour in a full annual perspective.

The chapter is organized as follows. Section 2.2 briefly summarizes the economic theory underlying the TCM. Section 2.3 discusses the role played by flow fixed costs. Section 2.4 presents a model incorporating the effects of flow fixed costs in TCM evaluations and proposes an approach to estimate these effects based on the data usually collected through user surveys. Section 2.5 shows an empirical application and, finally, Section 2.6 summarizes the main findings and further research needs.[1]

2.2   THE TRAVEL COST METHOD AND THE EFFECT OF PRICE

The classical model derived from the economic theory of consumer behaviour postulates that a consumer's choice is based on all the sacrifices made to obtain the benefits generated by a good or service. If the price (p) is the only sacrifice made by the consumer, the demand function for a good with no substitutes is $x = f(p)$, given income and preferences.

However, the consumer often incurs other costs (c), in addition to the out-of-pocket price, such as travel expenses, and loss of time and stress from congestion. In this case, the demand function is expressed as $x = f(p, c)$. In other words, the price is an imperfect measure of the full cost incurred by the purchaser.

Under these conditions, the utility maximizing consumer's behaviour should be reformulated in order to take such costs into account. Given two goods or services (x_1, x_2), their prices (p_1, p_2), the access costs (c_1, c_2) and income (R), the utility maximizing choice of the consumer is:

$$\max U = u(x_1, x_2)$$
$$\text{subject to:} \ (p_1 + c_1)x_1 + (p_2 + c_2)x_2 = R \qquad (2.1)$$

Now, let x_1 denote the aggregate of priced goods and services, x_2 the number of annual visits to a recreational site, and assume for the sake of simplicity that the cost of access to the market goods is negligible ($c_1 = 0$) and that the recreational site is free ($p_2 = 0$). Under these assumptions, equation (2.1) can be written as:

$$\max U = u(x_1, x_2)$$
$$\text{subject to:} \quad p_1 x_1 + c_2 x_2 = R \qquad (2.2)$$

Under these conditions, the utility maximizing behaviour of the consumer depends on: a) his preferences [$u(x_1, x_2)$], b) his budget (R), c) the prices of the private goods and services (p_1) and d) the access cost to the recreational site (c_2). Figure 2.1 shows the optimal choice between private goods and recreational activity, given the budget constraint: This is the point where the marginal rate of substitution is equal to the slope of the budget line and/or where the marginal utilities weighted by the cost of the good are equal:

$$\frac{U_1'}{p_1} = \frac{U_2'}{c_2} .$$

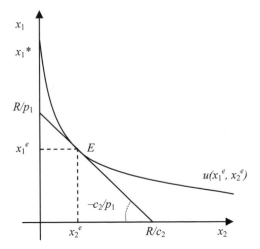

Figure 2.1   Utility maximization of a recreational services user

Much theoretical and empirical research focuses on 'interior' solutions of optimization problem (2.2), in which positive amounts of both goods are consumed ($x_1 > 0$ and $x_2 > 0$). When the income elasticities of the demand functions for x_1 and x_2 are different, as in the example shown in Figure 2.1, it is possible to obtain a corner solution. This corner solution is represented by the point (x_1^*,0) in Figure 2.1. The user could renounce the recreational activity, allocating his budget only on x_1, but he will not set x_1 to zero (the utility function curve intersects the y axis at x_1^*), because x_1 includes also necessary goods.

In other words, the individual considers access to and use of the recreational site if income is greater than a certain threshold, once other needs[2] have been satisfied. As income increases, the marginal rate of substitution grows, the consumer starts the recreation activity and the optimal solution moves from the corner solution to an 'interior' one.

The TCM is based on the assumption that changes in the costs of access to the recreational site (c_2) have the same effect as a change in price: the number of visits to a site decreases as the cost per visit increases. Under this assumption, the demand function for visits to the recreational site is $x_2 = f(c_2)$ and can be estimated using the number of annual visits as long as it is possible to observe different costs per visit.[3]

There are two basic approaches to the TCM: the Zonal approach (ZTCM) and the Individual approach (ITCM). The two approaches share the same theoretical premises, but differ from the operational point of view. The original ZTCM takes into account the visitation rate of users coming from different zones with increasing travel costs. By contrast, ITCM, developed by

Brown and Nawas (1973) and Gum and Martin (1974), estimates the consumer surplus by analysing the individual visitors' behaviour and the cost sustained for the recreational activity. These are used to estimate the relationship between the number of individual visits in a given time period, usually a year, the cost per visit and other relevant socio-economic variables. The ITCM approach can be considered a refinement or a generalization of ZTCM (Ward and Beal, 2000).

Figure 2.2 depicts the expected relationship between the number of visits and cost per visit, given other variables, showing that the number of visits decreases as the cost per visit increases. If we assume that all users have the same preferences and the same income,[4] the number of visits is a function of the cost per visit:

$$x_2 = g(c_2) \tag{2.3}$$

Therefore, if an individual incurs c_2^e per visit, he chooses to do x_2^e visits a year, while if the cost per visit increases to c_2^p the number of visits will decrease to x_2^p. The cost cp is the choke price, that is the cost per visit that results in zero visits. The annual user surplus is easily obtained by integrating the demand function from zero to the current number of annual visits, and subtracting the total expenditures on visits.

In this chapter, we wish to consider the effect of a change in the cost of recreation on the demand for trips. We begin our analysis with the simple case where the price per trip does not include fixed costs, focusing on an increase in the price per trip.

Figure 2.3 shows the effect of raising the price of a trip. Briefly, the additional cost (*ca*) changes the slope of the budget line and reduces the optimal number of visits (Figure 2.3a), bringing the individual to a new

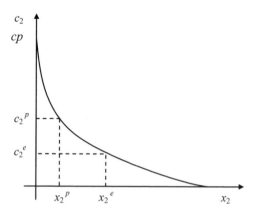

Figure 2.2   Individual's recreational demand function

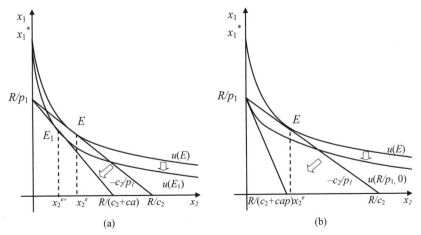

Figure 2.3   User behaviour if the price per trip increases

optimal point (E_1), which corresponds to a lower utility level. In Figure 2.3a, this new optimal point E_1 is an interior solution implying fewer visits to the recreational site and a slightly higher consumption of all other goods than in the original optimum E.

As shown in Figure 2.3b, a larger increase in the cost per trip may result in a corner solution with zero visits $(x_2 = 0)$, and the entire budget spent on x_1. The additional cost per visit at which visits are set to zero is cap, and the choke price is $(cap + c_2)$. When the cost per visit is equal to the choke price $(cap + c_2)$, the consumer's utility is $u(R/p_1, 0)$. The portion of individual demand function that refers to prices higher than current travel expenses, $[x_2 = z\,(ca),$ the inverse demand function being $ca = \delta(x_2)]$, is the curve I in Figure 2.4 where in the y axis we put ca, the additional cost per trip.

The aggregate demand function from zero to the total present visits (A) $[\,x_2 = h(ca)\,,$ and inverse demand function $ca = \varphi(x_2)]$ is obtained summing up the individual demands (I) at the different additional costs. This function intersects the y axis at the maximum additional cost incurred by the users. The recreational user's annual surplus is obtained taking the present value of the definite integral of the aggregate demand function (A) from zero to total number of annual visits. Assuming that the annual surplus is constant over time and an infinite time horizon, the present value of the surplus (S) is:

$$S = \frac{\displaystyle\int_0^{\Sigma_i x_{i2}^e} \varphi(x_2)\,dx_2}{r} \tag{2.4}$$

where r is an appropriate discount rate.

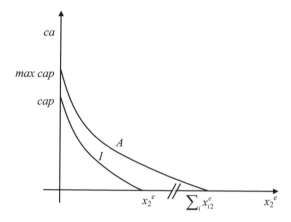

Figure 2.4   Individual's and aggregate recreational demand function

2.3   TYPES OF COST AND USER BEHAVIOUR

The basic model described in Section 2.2 shows that the aggregate recreational demand function is closely related to a 'travel generator function' (2.3) that includes the costs perceived as relevant by the users in their decision-making process in establishing the number of annual visits. At a minimum, the price of a trip should include direct variable costs, such as fuel, tolls, tickets, and so on. In addition, the opportunity cost of the time spent travelling to and at the site is usually included in the price per trip, and is usually measured as a fraction of the wage rate.[5] See Randall (1994) and Common et al. (1999), for a discussion of the difficulties associated with measuring the value of time and other components of cost that are subjective and not easily measured, or must be captured with proxy variables.

Another potentially important category of costs is incurred on an annual basis, regardless of the number of trips undertaken by the individual. This is because the recreational use of natural resources often involves annual fixed costs that are independent of the number of visits. For example, with recreational fishing in open waters or sea, it is necessary to pay for an annual fishing licence and to incur boat-related annual expenses (that is laying-up, maintenance and insurance) that are generally independent of the annual number of visits. Such costs are unrecoverable in the short period (sunk costs), but can be avoided over a longer period by renouncing the recreational activity.[6] The cost of laying-up and of a fishing licence, which becomes a sunk cost after it has been incurred, can be avoided the following year by renouncing the visits. We term this category of costs as flow fixed costs.

The literature on fixed costs and TCM is rather elusive. Some authors

(Hanley and Spash, 1993, p. 88) argue that the welfare measures will be different, depending on whether the fixed costs are included or not, and recommend excluding the fixed travel costs because 'Individuals, maximizing utility, are assumed to compare the marginal utility with the marginal costs of consumption'. Ward and Beal (2000, p. 44) argue that 'TCM uses the cash costs directly incurred by visitors to travel to given the demand equation to that site'. Likewise, Walsh (1986, p. 100) suggests considering only the direct costs only since '. . . the concept of fixed costs is not applicable to consumer decisions to take an additional trip to recreation site'. However, he points out (p. 256) that the presence of high fixed costs related to equipment specific to the recreational activity reduces the price elasticity of the demand in the short run compared to that in the long run.

The practice of ignoring flow fixed costs seems reasonable when a) the amount of flow fixed costs is low relative to variable costs, b) the fixed costs are incurred for multi-purpose equipment or costs (for example a car) and, even more important, c) the analysis is strictly a short-term one. But are these assumptions reasonable in the presence of substantial annual fixed expenses specific to the recreational activity, and when the benefit estimates are used for guidance in medium- or long-term public decisions, such as a license fee policy? In our view, in these cases the opportunity cost of annual flow fixed expenses should be taken into account, and the analysis of the choices of the individuals should refer to a full annual perspective.

In the remainder of this section, we examine the decision process of an individual who wishes to go boating or fishing in order to predict the number of visits when the access fees are raised. Assuming that the individual has to make his decision before the beginning of the recreational season, the decision-making process involves two sequential steps.

The first step answers the question 'Do I fish/go boating this year?' (full annual perspective). The decision to sustain the annual fixed costs related to the recreational activity[7] – or spend this amount of money on other goods – depends on the comparison between a subjective prediction of the number of visits he will do during the season and a minimum threshold. In general, this valuation is analogous to the decision of buying specific equipment for the recreational activity (fishing rod, hunting gun, and so on).

The second step answers the question 'Do I fish/boat today?' (infra annual perspective). After having incurred annual fixed expenses, the user decides on the number of visits to carry out on the basis of the variable cost per visit. The usual approach of estimating the recreational demand function based on the observed user behaviour and the direct variable travel cost, therefore, focuses only on the second step of the decision-making process.

To examine this two-step decision process, we study the utility maximization decision of an individual that incurs both a variable cost per visit and an annual fixed cost (c_0). In what follows, we assume that R is the available budget net of the annual fixed expenses c_0, p_1 the price of the other goods and services, and c_2 the direct variable cost per visit. As before, x_1 and x_2 signify aggregate consumption and the number of visits to the recreational site. In a full annual perspective, the optimal choice can be obtained by solving:

$$
\begin{aligned}
\max U &= u(x_1, x_2) \\
\textit{subject to}: \quad p_1 x_1 + c_2 x_2 &= R \qquad \textit{if } x_2 > 0 \\
p_1 x_1 &= R + c_0 \qquad \textit{if } x_2 = 0
\end{aligned}
\qquad (2.5)
$$

The optimal solution can be found by comparing the utility level

$$
\left[u\left(\frac{R + c_0}{p_1}, 0 \right) \right],
$$

which is attained by spending the entire budget $R + c_0$ on x_1, with the utility level $[u\,(x_1^{\,0}, x_2^{\,0})]$ attained by spending R on the optimal combination of x_1 and x_2 with $x_2 > 0$. Of these two possible pairs of consumption and number of visits, the individual will choose the one with the higher utility level. The optimal solution depends on all of the parameters of (2.5), including all prices, income, annual fixed cost and on the shape of the utility function.

The presence of annual fixed expenses does not change the slope of the budget line, but produces an effect similar to a change in income. If the demand for visits to the recreational site is elastic with respect to income, then changes in income will also change the marginal rate of substitution at the optimum. For example, a low income will favour a corner solution that allocates all income on x_1. As income increases, the MRS increases, favouring interior solutions.

To grasp interior versus corner solutions, it is useful to examine the equilibrium condition (indifference) between recreational site use x_2 and the exclusive consumption of x_1. This condition, which represents the marginal angler or recreational boater, is obtained by solving the following equation:

$$
u(x_1^m, x_2^m) = u\left(\frac{R + c_0}{p_1}, 0 \right)
\qquad (2.6)
$$

where x_1^m and x_2^m are the level of consumption and number of visits of the marginal user that accepts to incur annual direct fixed costs (C_0) for the recreational activity (Figure 2.5). Assuming a convex, monotonic and non-

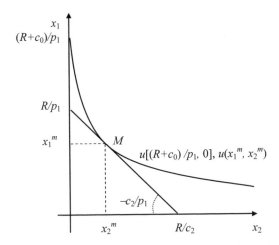

Figure 2.5   Utility maximization of a private and public recreational services user with annual direct fixed costs

homothetic utility function, an annual fixed expense implies the existence of a minimum number of annual visits per user x_2^m, where x_2^m is greater than zero. This can be seen in Figure 2.5, which shows that the indifference curve passing through point $M = (x_1^m, x_2^m)$, also passes through the point $[(R + c_0)/p_1, 0]$.

In a full annual perspective, starting from point M representing the marginal equilibrium described by equation (2.6), an increase of the cost of recreation will set the visits to zero. In other words, as costs increase, the number of trips jumps from x_2^m directly to zero. Otherwise, in an infra annual perspective, an increase in the price per visit will gradually reduce the number of visits from x_2^m to zero. As a consequence, in a full annual perspective, taking into account only the variable cost of a visit ignores the option, which is always available to the user, of forgoing the purchase of a license, which in turn implies that the user will not go to the site. This frees up income that can be spent on other goods. In sum, ignoring that the fixed costs can be avoided by forgoing the recreational activity predicts a less elastic response to a change in the price of a trip than the true response.

2.4   TCM AND FLOW FIXED COSTS

When the user's decision-making process is similar to that outlined above, the TCM must take into account the alternative of not incurring the annual fixed expenses, which implies a corner solution. The end result is that, on a full annual base, the estimated number of annual visits decreases with increasing prices per trip more than the reduction predicted on an infra annual basis (that is ignoring the fixed cost). This is due to the fact that, in a full annual perspective, further increases in additional unit costs ultimately reduce visits to a minimal value x_2^m greater than zero.

The minimal annual visits number can be obtained from equation (2.6) taking into account its corresponding 'choke' price (point M, Figure 2.6). In this particular case, the 'choke' price is not the price at which all visits cease on an infra annual perspective, but the price at which the user decides to avoid annual fixed costs.

This has two important implications. The first is that the choke price when annual license fees are considered (cap) is lower than the choke price (cap^*) in the situation when all costs are variable and the perspective is an infra annual one (see Figure 2.7). The second is that the individual demand function is discontinuous (see Figure 2.7): it is equal to zero when the price per trip is greater than cap, and when the price is equal to cap the demanded number of trips is x_2^m.

Now we have to estimate x_2^m and/or cap. The minimal number of visits (x_2^m), is not observable, because it is evaluated by the user in phase (a) of his decision-making process, but it can be obtained from the indifference conditions of (2.7) described in Figure 2.6. Under these conditions, utility derived from allocating his entire budget ($R + c_0$) for the consumption of x_1, is equal to the utility that he obtains in M. Since:

$$x_1^m = \frac{R - cap\, x_2^m}{p_1}$$

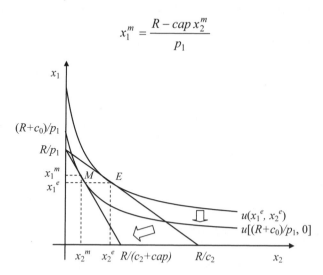

Figure 2.6   User behaviour at increasing additional fees with annual direct fixed costs

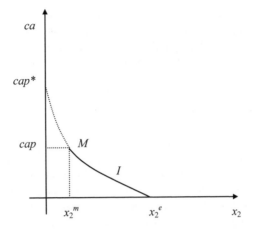

Figure 2.7   The individual's recreational demand function with annual fixed costs

equation (2.6) can be written as:

$$u\left(\frac{R+c_0}{p_1}\right) = u\left(\frac{R - cap\, x_2^m}{p_1}, x_2^m\right) \qquad (2.7)$$

Consider the marginal consumer, assume that $p_1 = 1$, and let

$$cap = \delta(x_2^m), \quad u(x_2^m) = \int_0^{x_2^m} \delta(x_2)dx_2, \quad \text{and} \quad u\left[c_0 + x_2^m \delta(x_2^m)\right] = c_0 + x_2^m \delta(x_2^m).$$

This yields:

$$c_0 + x_2^m \delta(x_2^m) = \int_0^{x_2^m} \delta(x_2)dx_2, \qquad (2.8)$$

which can be solved for x_2^m.

The total recreational benefit of the site experienced by all users is:

$$S = \sum_i \frac{\displaystyle\int_0^{x_{i2}^e} \delta_i(x_2)\, dx_2 + \frac{1}{r} \int_{x_{i2}^m}^{x_{i2}^e} \delta_i(x_2)dx_2}{1+r} \qquad (2.9)$$

In practice, estimating x_2^m due to annual fixed costs sustained presumes that users are able to estimate with precision their future visits. It is, however, possible to ignore x_2^m when the flow fixed costs do not influence the user decisions. This would happen, for example, when the flow fixed costs are negligible or they are typically incurred every few years.

2.5   APPLICATION

We illustrate the proposed approach using data from a recent survey of boaters in the Lagoon of Venice, and focusing on the prediction of the impact of an increase in fees on the number of annual trips and on welfare measures. The data were collected through a survey conducted in spring and summer 1999 for estimating the recreational benefits of the Lagoon. The survey questionnaire deployed both the contingent valuation and the ITCM approaches. A detailed description of the data is presented in Defrancesco and Rosato (2000).

This exercise is based on a relatively homogeneous subsample of 129 recreational users that incurred high annual fixed expenses, paying an annual fee to keep their boat in a marina. Given the limited sample size and the unrepresentative sample, these results should be considered as an illustration and the results from the calculations below should not be extended to the entire population of recreational users of the Lagoon.

The ITCM was based on the number of annual trips reported by the respondents. The variable costs include: a) the direct variable cost sustained by each user in order to reach the boarding point, off-site travel time valued at a fraction of the wage rate (€6 per hour), b) the cost of fuel for the boat, c) food and beverages, and d) in the case of anglers, the cost of bait. The annual fixed cost takes into account the cost incurred in order to keep the boat in a marina, boat insurance and maintenance costs, and, if applicable, the annual cost of a fishing license. Descriptive statistics of the data are reported in Table 2.1.

We estimate a recreational demand function (2.3) that predicts the

Table 2.1   Descriptive statistics

	Mean	Standard Deviation
Annual trips	26.8	5.8
Direct Variable Costs per Trip (€)	59.0	27.7
Annual Direct Fixed Expenses (€)	1071.0	592.9
Annual Income (.000€)	17.5	15.3

Notes: Defrancesco and Rosato (2000).

individual annual trips as a linear function of the logarithm of variable costs per visit and income. Regression results are displayed in Table 2.2. The OLS coefficients are individually significantly different from zero at the 1 percent level and have the expected signs. The R^2 of the regression is 0.53, indicating a good fit.

In order to compute the individual recreational surplus we truncate the demand function to one visit, since it is asymptotic to the y axis (Ward and Beal, 2000, p. 92), valuing the first trip on the basis of its marginal benefit obtained solving the demand function for the cost that would produce one trip. On an infra annual perspective, the net recreational surplus of a user is equal to the difference between the total annual surplus (the area under the demand function between one visit and the actual trips, plus the surplus related to the first trip) and the total variable cost incurred. The mean recreational surplus per visit is equal to €611.8, the standard deviation over the mean is equal to 48 percent and the median value is €567.3.[8]

By contrast, under a full annual perspective the behaviour of the Lagoon recreational user is influenced by annual fixed expenses sustained for recreation, given his income. Accordingly, $x_2{}^m$ must be found by solving numerically equation (2.8) for each user. In this case, (2.8) is equal to:

$$c_0 + x_2^m e^{\frac{x_2^m - (c + \beta \ln R)}{\alpha}} = \frac{1 - (c + \beta \ln R)}{\alpha} + \int_1^{x_2^m} \left(e^{\frac{x_2 - (c + \beta \ln R)}{\alpha}} \right) dx_2 - ca \cdot x_2^m \quad (2.9)$$

where R = user income, c_0 = annual fixed costs, and ca = variable cost per visit.

In this case, the annual recreational surplus of the user is equal to the difference between the definite integral of the demand function from $x_2{}^m$ to the actual number of annual trips, and the related total variable costs. In other words, if the agency managing the Lagoon estimates the net recreational users' surplus in order to better define a fee policy, it has to take into account the surplus under a full annual perspective, estimated using $x_2{}^m$. If the agency raises the entrance fees, many users may decide to renounce altogether trips to the Lagoon.

Table 2.2   The individual's recreational demand function coefficients

		Coefficient	Standard Error
Constant	(c)	42.56	2.25
Ln(Direct Variable Cost per Visit)	(α)	−6.94	0.62
Ln(Annual Income)	(β)	4.44	0.50

Our calculations indicate that for this application, the minimal number of visits per year, calculated solving (2.9) for each user, ranges between 2 and 12; the mean x_2^m is equal to 3.36 and standard deviation equals 1.22. The estimated coefficients of a regression model (see Table 2.3), expressing x_2^m as a function of log income, log variable cost and annual fixed costs (adj $R^2 = 0.85$), show that the minimal number of visits per user estimated solving 2.9 decreases as income increases and is positively related to the amount both of fixed and variable costs.

In addition, the number of visits carried out by all users decreases more rapidly on a full annual perspective, that is taking into account their behaviour facing annual fixed cost. Figure 2.8 shows that, extending the analysis to the medium run, an additional annual fee higher than €500 results in several users renouncing the recreational activity, as their number of annual visits would be less than the minimum justifying the annual fixed costs sustained.

Therefore, the dotted line showing annual trips taking into account the annual fixed cost lies below the curve depicting visits on an infra annual perspective, which are based only on variable costs. Obviously, the distance between the lines increases as additional fees increase. In this particular example the distance between the two demand functions is quite small. This is due to the semi-log specification of the individual demand function adopted in the simulation which implies very high surplus values gained by visitors for the initial trips of the year. Using different demand functions (for example a linear specification) the number of visits assuring a surplus that cover the annual fixed costs would significantly increase. On a full annual perspective, the net mean surplus per visit is equal to €377.8, the standard deviation over the mean equals 55 percent (median €352.1). The unit mean surplus is, therefore, 38 percent less than the welfare estimate obtained applying the traditional TCM (annual perspective). So, the exercise clearly highlights the effects of flow fixed costs on the total visits and the recreational value of the selected users' sample.

Table 2.3   Regression equation for the minimum annual number of visits

	Coefficient	Standard Error
Constant	4.89	0.28
Annual Fixed Costs	0.002	0.00
Ln(Variable Unit Cost)	0.182	0.08
Ln(Annual Income)	−1.62	0.07

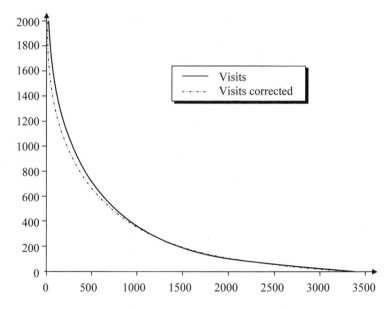

Figure 2.8   Total annual visits at increasing additional fees on an infra annual and on a full annual perspective

2.6   CONCLUDING REMARKS

The aim of this chapter is to propose a modified TCM approach, taking into account flow fixed costs. In our view, when recreational users incur substantial annual direct fixed expenses, their behaviour could be influenced by them, on a full annual perspective. As a result, the agency managing a natural site for outdoor recreation should use caution and apply a full annual perspective when valuing recreational users' behaviour in the presence of high fixed costs.

By ignoring flow fixed costs TCM, both surplus estimate and annual number of visits at different additional fees could be overestimated. So, in a medium-run perspective it is important to take into account the annual fixed expense that is directly connected to recreation. When flow fixed costs are substantial relative to the variable costs, the proposed approach works as follows:

a) estimate the recreational demand function based on observable users' behaviour (actual annual trips and related variable costs in an infra annual perspective);

b) estimate the minimum number of annual visits ($x_2{}^m$) that justifies the annual fixed expenses incurred by each user;

c) derive the adjusted demand function.

Using this approach the user behaviour can be described on a full annual perspective, taking into account a more precise estimate of the number of visits with different additional fees. Under an annual perspective, that is ignoring $x_2{}^m$, would lead one to overestimate both recreational surplus and the number of annual trips when annual fees are increased. Correctly estimating this surplus and number of visits is important for setting fee policies and for medium- to long-run decision-making for policy purposes. The traditional TCM approach would produce questionable results, when substantial annual direct fixed costs are incurred by recreationists.

Under certain circumstances, however, the annual fixed costs do not impact welfare appreciably. The effect of flow fixed costs is negligible even on a full annual perspective when, for example, their amount is modest or their timing is not frequent (for example they are sustained every 3–4 years).

However, further research is needed to achieve a better definition of the types of cost really valued by the users in their decision-making process, when relevant annual fixed costs are incurred. For this purpose it would be interesting to compare the minimum number of visits calculated using the demand function obtained with TCM and the one derived with direct interviews.

NOTES

1. The authors are grateful to Anna Alberini for the valuable comments to the earlier versions of the chapter. We remain responsible for the contents of the chapter.

2. The consumer utility function is non-homothetic.

3. The basic TCM model is completed by the weak complementarity assumption, which states that trips are a non-decreasing function of the quality of the site, and that the individual forgoes trips to the recreational site when the quality is the lowest possible. We omit the dependence of x_2 on quality Q in our notation to avoid clutter, and because the focus of this chapter is the effect of a change in price and in the license fees, keeping the quality of the site the same. See Freeman (1993) and Herriges et al. (2004).

4. The function can also be estimated for non-homogeneous sub-samples introducing among the independent variables income and socio-economic variables representing individual characteristics (Hanley and Spash, 1993, p. 84).

5. For a comprehensive discussion of these issues see, for example, Ward and Beal (2000, pp. 36–9).

6. Whether a cost should be classified as fixed depends crucially on the time period considered (Tirole, 1991, p. 532). For example, the cost of an annual licence is regarded as fixed if a period of less than 12 months is considered, but variable if the horizon is extended to one year or longer.

7. The fixed annual costs include the fishing licence, boat-related expenses, and so on.
8. This large mean is due to the algebraic form of the demand function and to the particular subsample analysed.

REFERENCES

Brown, W.G. and F. Nawas (1973), 'Impact of Aggregation on the Estimation of Outdoor Recreation Demand Functions', *American Journal of Agricultural Economics*, **55**, 246–9.

Clawson, M. (1959), 'Method for Measuring the Demand for, and Value of, Outdoor Recreation', *Resources for the Future*, 10, Washington, DC.

Common, M., T. Bull and N. Stoeckl (1999), 'The Travel Cost Method: an empirical investigation of Randall's Difficulty', *The Australian Journal of Agricultural and Resource Economics*, **43**(4), 457–77.

Defrancesco, E. and P. Rosato (2000), 'Recreation Management in Venice Lagoon', FEEM, *Nota di lavoro*, **65**.2000.

Freeman, A.M. III. (1993). *The Measurement of Environmental and Resource Values: Theory and Method*, Washington, DC: Resources for the Future.

Gum, R.L. and W.E. Martin (1974), 'Problems and Solutions in Estimating the Demand for and Value of Rural Outdoor Recreation', *American Journal of Agricultural Economics*, **56**, 558–66.

Hanley, N. and C.L. Spash (1993), *Cost Benefit Analysis and the Environment*, Aldershot, UK and Brookfield, USA: Edward Elgar.

Herriges, J.A., C. Kling and D.J. Phaneuf (2004), 'What's the Use? Welfare Estimates from Revealed Preference Models when Weak Complementarity Does Not Hold', *Journal of Environmental Economics and Management*, **47**(1), 53–68.

Hotelling, H. (1949), *Letter, In An Economic Study of the Monetary Evaluation of Recreation in the National Parks*, Washington, DC: National Park Service.

Randall, A. (1994), 'A Difficulty with the Travel Cost Method', *Land Economics*, **70**(1), 88–96.

Tirole, J. (1991), *Teoria dell'organizzazione industriale*, Milano: Hoepli.

Walsh, R.G. (1986), *Recreation Economic Decisions: Comparing Benefits and Costs*, Pennsylvania: Venture Publishing, Inc. State College.

Ward, F.A. and D. Beal (2000), *Valuing Nature with Travel Cost Method: A Manual*, Cheltenham, UK and Northampton, MA, USA: Edward Elgar.

3. The Appraisal Approach to Valuing Environmental Resources

Edi Defrancesco, Paolo Rosato and Luca Rossetto

3.1 INTRODUCTION

Environmental protection decisions are often based on comparisons of monetary values, such as cost–benefit analyses, which means that it is important to supply public decision makers with reliable valuations methods.

When placing a monetary value on an environmental resource, the first order of business is to define the environment and, consequently, the relationships between environment and economic system. In our judgment, the most helpful definition of the environment is the one adopted by the European Council and found in the 'Green Book' (EU Commission, 1993):

> the environment includes the abiotic and biotic natural resources such as the air, water, land, fauna and flora, the interaction between these factors and the goods that form the cultural heritage and characteristic aspects of the landscape.

The European Union's 'White Book' (EU Commission, 2000) has recently reinforced this definition and extended it to biodiversity effects in sensitive natural areas.

When attention is restricted to interactions between environment and human activity, a more suitable definition is given by the World Health Organisation (Molesti, 1988):

> the environment is a set of processes and physical, chemical, biological and social influences that directly or indirectly have a significant and clear effect on the health and welfare of the individual or the community.

The value of the environment may thus be analysed from three different but complementary standpoints (Howe, 1990): (i) the scientific standpoint, which stresses the role of physical and biological systems; (ii) the economic standpoint, which measures the economic value accruing to *homo economicus*; and (iii) the social standpoint, which assesses the changes in the social system taking into account the needs of society.

The economic approach is sometimes criticized by non-economists for trying to put a 'price tag' on an environmental resource. However, it should be emphasized that the valuation process does not *give* a resource market value, but rather measures the welfare accruing to the people (including present and future generations) enjoying an environmental resource using monetary units.

In this chapter, we adopt the economic standpoint for the valuation of environmental resources. The economics literature agrees on the notion of total economic value (TEV), which includes both use and non-use (or passive) values (option, existence, and bequest), and links them not only to individual preferences but also to public needs, including physical, chemical, biological functions and services (Krutilla, 1967). It should also be pointed out that any valuation method is applied to value a change in the quality or quantity of an environmental resource, and not to value the resource *per se* (e.g. CBA, environmental damage assessment, etc.).

Not all TEV components are always relevant in all valuation scenarios. In other words, the valuation of a damaged/improved resource should take into account use and non-use TEV components significantly appreciated by society.

In particular, the value that people place on an environmental resource, especially for non-use categories within the TEV, should depend on a) the irreversibility of any environmental resource change; b) the uncertainty for future generations on resource availability; and c) its uniqueness.

In the past, the notion of TEV, especially for environmental resources, was investigated by several Italian appraisal researchers who proposed the notion of 'social value'. In particular, Famularo (1943) first proposed the so-called social use value which is particularly useful in valuing non-market goods or services (public goods, externalities), while reflecting social needs and preferences.

Forte (1970) took up the concept of social use value as a method to overcome market failures and to assess the social benefits of goods with historical and cultural features. Under the notion of social use value, many appraisal researchers tried to overcome the limits of market-based approaches in valuing an environmental resource while considering public benefits accruing to all society.

In particular, Fusco Girard (1993) suggests that an environmental and/or cultural resource change should be valued considering not only the people currently involved, directly or indirectly, in a welfare change but also future generations. Extending the idea previously expressed by Forte, he proposes the notion of 'complex social value' which takes into account all benefits accruing to society: direct and indirect, present uses potential and future uses.

With this extension, the concept of value developed by appraisal researchers is consistent with the notion of total economic value of a resource (TEV), in the sense that it subsumes all reasons for placing a monetary value to an economic good (private and public components, present and future generations).

In this chapter we present a theoretical–methodological framework for valuing public and environmental goods that follows the appraisal approach, and discuss the premise and the limitation of this framework. The remainder of the chapter is organized as follows. Section 3.2 presents a theoretical background on appraisal methods based on the dual approach to consumer behaviour theory. Section 3.3 illustrates appraisal methods for valuing environmental resources. Section 3.4 highlights the possible limitations of appraisal approaches. Section 3.5 discusses practical implementation issues, and Section 3.6 provides concluding remarks.

3.2   THE DUAL APPROACH IN THE ENVIRONMENTAL RESOURCE VALUATION

In the previous section we presented definitions of the concept of 'environment' and 'value'. This framework, while useful for understanding the key concepts, provides little practical guidance. It is understood, however, that any valuation procedure should rely on a logical relationship between economic theory and appraisal practice.[1] In particular, the valuation of an environmental good should be necessarily based on the relationship between the resource and the behaviour and level of satisfaction of the economic agents involved.

In this context, it is useful to distinguish between situations where the change in the environment quality (environmental resource level) forces people to change their behaviour, and situations where this adjustment does not occur. In the former case, the environmental change may be assessed as an expenditure function variation; in other words, the people affected by the environmental change adopt a strategy for maximizing utility under the changed situation. In the latter case, people do not change their behaviour and the environmental change is directly turned into a utility variation. Presumably, if there is a change in behaviour, it should lead to a higher utility level than that one achieved without it. In practice, examples of environmental changes where the economic agents are totally non-reactive are very rare. Obviously, when an environmental quality change leads to a behavioural adjustment, the welfare change may be assessed through the corresponding adjustment costs (indirect estimate). By contrast, when these adjustments do not occur, the welfare change may be assessed only through the changes in individual utility function (direct estimate).

Therefore, when an environmental change produces adjustments in the behaviour of economic agents, the market equilibrium may be modified as the quantity exchanged and/or prices may change.[2] To properly value environmental change it is therefore important to make a comparison between the situation with the change and the one that would have occurred without it (Cochrane, 1993).[3]

Before we turn to appraisal methods for placing a monetary value on an environmental change, we present a brief theoretical introduction on consumer behaviour. Assuming a given income level and preferences, each individual chooses the set of economic goods (private and public) that ensures the highest utility.

Formally, the consumer behaviour may be analysed following two approaches. The first, known in economic literature as the primal problem, is based on the maximization of the utility function subject to the market prices and income constraint. The second, known as dual problem, looks for the allocation of goods and services ensuring a given utility level with the minimum expenditure. The primal approach is more intuitive but its application is often difficult because it requires specifying and estimating the utility function of the consumer. The dual approach, on the other hand, requires specifying the expenditure function, which can be easily observed and estimated from the market. Accordingly, the dual approach figures out the consumer utility changes through changes in the expenditure function (Nicholson, 1995).

The dual model can be expressed by the following:

$$\operatorname*{Min}_{x}\left[\sum_{j=1}^{n} p_j \cdot x_j \middle| u(X,Q) \geq \overline{U}; \overline{\mathbf{Q}}\right] \tag{3.1}$$

where $u(\cdot)$ is the utility function; $\mathbf{Q}$ is a vector of the public goods and services; $\mathbf{X}$ is a vector of market goods and services; p_i is a vector of prices of market goods and services; x_i is the vector of market goods and services; $\overline{\mathbf{Q}}$ is environmental quality level; and $\overline{U}$ is a given utility level.

The economic meaning of (3.1) can be explained as follows: the consumer chooses a set of market goods and services in order to minimise total expenditure subject to a given utility ($\overline{U}$) and environmental quality ($\overline{\mathbf{Q}}$).

The expenditure function satisfying (3.1) is the following:

$$E^* = E^*\left(\mathbf{P}, \overline{U}, \overline{\mathbf{Q}}\right) \tag{3.2}$$

Models (3.1) and (3.2) can be used to value changes in the quality and/or quantity of environmental goods (Q).

When a consumer can mitigate the effects of the environmental change, the welfare change can be measured by the change in the expenditure function. Suppose, for example, that environmental quality Q deteriorates from Q_s to Q_c ($Q_s > Q_c$), leading to a different allocation in income (for example because of defensive expenses) and a utility reduction ($U_s > U_c$). The change in the expenditure function is:

$$\Delta E = \left| E\left(\mathbf{P}_c, U_c, \mathbf{Q}_c\right) - E\left(\mathbf{P}_s, U_s, \mathbf{Q}_s\right)\right| \qquad (3.3)$$

where $\mathbf{P}_c$ is the vector of prices with the change, $\mathbf{P}_s$ is the vector of prices without the change, U_c is utility with the change, U_s is utility without the change, $\mathbf{Q}_c$ is the state of the environment with the change, and $\mathbf{Q}_s$ is the state of the environment without the change.

In this case, the monetary measure (V) of the utility lost with the environmental quality change is the compensation changing the expenditure function and restoring the original utility of the consumer. Formally, this is

$$V = \left| E\left(\mathbf{P}_c, U_s, \mathbf{Q}_c\right) - E\left(\mathbf{P}_s, U_s, \mathbf{Q}_s\right)\right| \qquad (3.4)$$

The expenditure function with the compensation is not necessarily equal to the previous one (without environmental change). Only if the original environmental conditions $\mathbf{Q}_s$ are fully restored the expenditure function is equal to the original one.

This approach assumes substitutability between market and environmental (non-market) goods and services since information on expenditure changes can be found in the market only: this condition is also necessary when appraisal methods are used.

Figure 3.1 illustrates the two different paths for valuing a deterioration in environmental quality:

- A behaviour adjustment can be observed and valuated (path 1). In this case, modifications in individual behaviour may be recognized as a change in the expenditure function, i.e., expenses avoided, defensive costs, substitution of benefits lost, and restoration cost. The valuation can be easily done by detecting these effects.
- When strategies for reducing negative effects are not observable or not feasible, the valuation can be performed only through direct methods (path 2). In other words, when no behaviour adjustment is observed, the utility change is restricted to the individual perception. In this case the effect should be assessed using techniques for direct elicitation of the value.

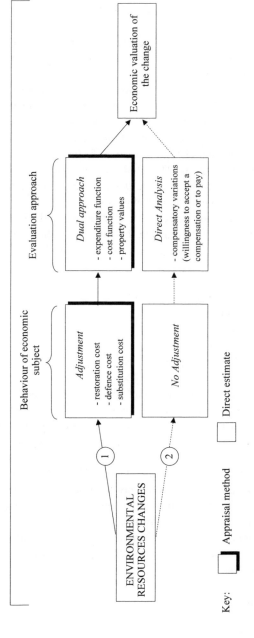

RESOURCE VALUATION PROCESS

Behaviour of economic subject

Evaluation approach

Adjustment
- restoration cost
- defence cost
- substitution cost

Dual approach
- expenditure function
- cost function
- property values

No Adjustment

Direct Analysis
- compensatory variations (willingness to accept a compensation or to pay)

Economic valuation of the change

ENVIRONMENTAL RESOURCES CHANGES

1

2

Key: ▮ Appraisal method   ☐ Direct estimate

Figure 3.1   Approaches in environmental resource valuation

3.3   THE APPRAISAL APPROACH TO THE VALUATION OF ENVIRONMENTAL GOODS

The valuation of an environmental resource may be obtained as the variation in income necessary to restore the original utility. Formally, the dual approach can figure out this income variation through changes in the cost or expenditure function, i.e., the valuation of an environmental resource is indirectly measured through private market goods (Simonotti, 1982). Similarly, appraisal methods can be extended to environmental resources valuation even if their application involves market goods. The key point in valuing an environmental change is to identify the most appropriate method measuring its effects properly. This choice is a critical point since the relation between goods and utility is more fleeting and elusive in the case of environmental goods than with market goods.

In appraisal theory, by selecting a specific method, the researcher first identifies the value considered as the 'best' proxy of the expenditure change. The appraisal literature identifies five main appraisal criteria for valuation purposes:

1. market value (capitalization);
2. production/reproduction cost;
3. substitution value;
4. transformation value;
5. hedonic (complementary) value.

Table 3.1 lists and briefly describes these five appraisal criteria. In other words the value of an environmental good can be assessed by choosing the appropriate appraisal criterion valuing private goods linked to the environmental resources. Only in special cases, however, do these measures fully assess the TEV. Most likely, they only capture *part* of the TEV, because they are usually restricted to use values only. This approximation is reasonable when non-use values are not significant, i.e., the environmental resource change is limited in time and extension or, more generally, when an environmental resource is fully restorable or reproducible. Eventually, it should be remembered that an environment resource valuation might require several appraisal methods working together, since it often involves different aspects and services.

The Market Value

The market value of a good can be considered as the value determined through a market transaction.[4] A good has a market value when there is a

Table 3.1 The appraisal criteria in environmental resource valuation

Appraisal criteria	Applications for environmental resource valuation purposes	Economic benchmark
1 Market value	Environmental goods or services actively exchanged in the market	Market price of similar goods
Capitalization value	Resources with limited or no market, providing an income over time	Income
2 Cost or production value	Restorable resources without market	Costs or prices of production factors
3 Substitution value	Replaceable resources without market	Prices or costs of substitutes
4 Transformation value	Environmental resources without market but transformable into market goods or services	Prices of goods transformed and transformation costs
5 Hedonic (complementary) value	Environmental resources or externalities affecting the value of private goods	Market value of the good with and without the externality (characteristic)

Source: Merlo (1991) amended by the authors.

seller and a purchaser who are willing to improve their utility through an exchange. The market value is definitively the most important valuation criterion and it has a key role in any appraisal valuation. The market value depends not only on the purchaser's appreciation of a good or service but also on the market structure. Indeed, the more active the market, the more precise is the estimate of the market value.

In valuing an environmental resource, there are usually only limited opportunities for applying the market value. In fact, the market value is only applied on environmental goods strictly linked to goods and services actively exchanged in the market. Yet, the market value is the benchmark criterion in the appraisal literature, i.e., all other criteria can be derived from it.[5]

Economists and appraisers agree that the market price is the most reliable and preferred way to capture the value of a good, even when the good is not one usually traded on markets or when it is one with uniqueness attributes making any comparison difficult (e.g. works of art, irreproducible environmental goods such as certain landscapes, etc.). In these cases, the economic benchmark should be either the income coming from the good or to economic goods purchased or sold linked, directly or indirectly, to the one being valued.

In the former case, the capitalization value method is used; in the latter, criteria such as the cost, substitution, transformation or complementary value (Merlo, 1990) can be used (see next sections).

The capitalization value of a good is the sum of the discounted future income generated by the good itself. So, the utility coming from a good (Medici, 1953) and measured by income provided is the ratio between market price and capitalization rate.[6] In the case of environmental goods this approach may be applied when:

1. the market for the environmental good does not exist or is poor, or market bargaining does not lead to significant values;
2. the good generates a stable income over time whose magnitude is proportionate to the utility generated by it.

The capitalization value of marketable services can be seen as a proxy for the value of the environmental resources. For example, the capitalization value of a public park can be calculated by discounting the revenue coming from selling products or permits for recreational use (Merlo, 1990). The fertility decline of a polluted agricultural area can be monetized as the discounted value of the production losses associated with it.

The Cost Value

The cost value of a good is defined as the market value of the resources required for producing it.[7]

This method is applied when an environmental resource has to be restored. This restoration may consist of a) reproducing exactly the original good, or b) restoring its ecological, productive and social functions only. The former is a reproduction in a strict sense, i.e., a restoration using original materials and current prices; in the latter, the reproduction generates a good which may be different from the original one while performing the same services (replacement cost).

For example, consider a wetland reclamation project. The social loss may be the cost for restoring the wetland to what it was prior to the wetland conversion (reproduction cost in the strict sense), or the production and maintenance cost of a new wetland even if it is located in a different site (substitution or replacement cost).

The cost value approach may be applied in valuing reproducible environmental resources without market or resources whose market value does not represents collective needs. It should be clear that the cost value approach can be used in valuing both positive and negative externalities. For example, the damages of polluted water may be assessed through the expenses incurred for cleaning up the water, plus the (temporary) costs of supplying clean water from other sources.

The Substitution Value

The substitution value is the cost of replacing the good with others giving the same utility. This criterion is very useful when:

1. the market for the good does not exist,
2. but the good can be substituted with others (substitutes), and
3. the substitutes have a market value or can be produced.

This method can be applied for valuing environmental resources without a market but where substitution is possible and reasonable. This method is well suited for valuing certain qualitative aspects of the environment. For example, the pollution of a river may be valued through the functions performed by the water: its use for irrigation purposes would be proxied with the cost of getting groundwater; its drinking use with the price of alternative drinking water supplies; its use for swimming with the admission fee to a swimming pool; and its use for recreational fishing with the additional cost required to reach another river.

One problem with this approach is many environmental resources have a low degree of the 'substitutability' or partial 'functional replaceability'. Indeed, the valuation process reliability depends on the extent of the substitution, i.e., the ability of substitutes to replace the functions, often very complex, performed by an environmental resource.

The Transformation Value

The transformation value, or net realizable value (Appraisal Institute, 1993), is defined as the discounted market value of the transformed good less the transformation cost. This criterion is applied to resources without significant market prices which may be transformed or processed into market good or services.

In valuing environmental resources, the transformation value may be useful for public goods used as inputs in production processes. For example, the stream water exploited for agricultural purposes could be assessed as the difference between the market value of the irrigated crop production less irrigation costs. When bottled, the same water could be valued as the transformation value of bottled water.

The transformation value may also be chosen in the case of events that affect real estate values. For example, the damage on a plot of land whose potential building capacity is impaired by a mining operation may be assessed as the difference between the market value of the building and construction costs.

The Hedonic Value

The hedonic, or complementary (Medici, 1953), value is applied when portions or attributes of a good are split up or separated. This allows one to estimate the change occurred in the value of the original good. The hedonic value is defined as difference between the market value of the good in its unimpaired state and the market value of the same good after the change.

The criterion of the hedonic value is applied for attributes or portions of goods having a complementary relationship with the residual parts, so that separating them reduces or vanishes the value of the original good, i.e., the value of a good as a whole is different from the sum of values of independent portions.[8]

The hedonic criterion may be applied when the following conditions occur:

1. there is a complementarity between the environmental and market goods;
2. the environmental good cannot be easily restored.[9]

Complementarities between market goods and environmental resources are seen, for example, when environmental externalities affect real estate. For example, a property located close to a forest, a park or a pleasant natural area acquires advantages from positive externalities (clean air, pleasant landscape, quietness, etc.) which increase its market value. Similarly, the presence of polluted industrial areas, or decaying environments/landscapes lowers the value of the surrounding properties.

This approach assumes that the market can capture the environmental quality changes, i.e., the market of a real estate internalizes the positive and/or negative externalities.

3.4   THE LIMITATIONS OF THE APPRAISAL APPROACH

All of the approaches discussed in Section 3.3 assume that the welfare change caused by an environmental resource change can be assessed through market prices. The market price should represent the value that society is willing to pay for having an additional unit of a specific good. However, policies and market failures may affect the price, creating a gap between private and social value.[10] In particular, the following situations can be recognized:

1. the market works and the price reflects the value (utility) placed on the good by society;
2. the market exists but is incomplete or affected by distorsions, and the price should be corrected to represent the social value;
3. the market does not exist, but there are reliable market signals for estimating the social value;
4. the market does not exist and market signals do not exist either.

Appraisal approaches may be usefully adopted in situations 1–3, but when the market does not provide any information for estimating the social value of the environmental resource, direct valuation methods (e.g., contingent valuation) should be used (Mitchell and Carson, 1989).

Table 3.2 reports a suggested framework that reconciles environmental resources, market features and appraisal methods.

Valuing environmental resources may involve different appraisal methods. For example, if a good can be reproduced its value can be considered as a reproduction or replacement cost. Conversely, if a good cannot be replicated, but it generates an income, the criterion of the capitalization value may be the best.

Likewise, if the resource is processed into a good actively exchanged in the market, its value can be assessed through the transformation value. If an environmental good affects a real estate property, this effect can be estimated through the hedonic pricing approach. Finally, if the utility produced by a good can also be generated by a substitute, its value can be assessed through the substitution cost ('resource for resource' or 'service for service') (US Federal Register, 1996).

Appraisal methods do not lend themselves to a resource that is not replaceable and has significant non-use values, in which case they tend to give trivial results. Indeed, the non-use components can be captured only by direct methods.

3.5   FROM THEORY TO PRACTICE

In valuing environmental resources using appraisal methods, both direct and indirect effects should be taken into account. The latter are induced economic effects and their magnitude depend on both the type and size of the good, and on its interrelations with the economic system.

When a valuation through appraisal procedures is done by adding single components, a 'double counting error' may occur, especially when indirect effects are included. Because of the multiple utility produced by an environmental resource and the different valuing procedures proposed, methods that measure the value of any single component may overlap.[11] This

Table 3.2   Classification of criteria according to resource feature and market performance

Resource	Market	Criterion	Market information	Values considered
PURE PRIVATE	It works	Market value	Purchase and sale prices	Use value
WITH PUBLIC AND PRIVATE COMPONENTS (e.g., tropical forest)	The market exists but the price does not represent the social value	Market value	Corrected market prices	At least the use value
		Capitalization value	Discounted income	Use value
		Cost value	Input prices	All [a]
		Substitution value	Substitute prices	Use value [b]
		Transformation value	Prices of goods processed and processing costs	Use value
		Hedonic value	Value good as a whole and residual value	Use value
PURE PUBLIC	Market does not exist	Capitalization value	Discounted income	Use value
		Cost value	Input market prices	All [a]
		Substitution value	Substitute market prices	Use value [b]
		Transformation value	Market price of good processed and processing costs	Use value
		Hedonic value	Market value of good as a whole and residual value	Use value

Notes: (a) Use and non-use values.
(b) Depends on substitutability degree between environmental resource and the substitute.

mistake must be avoided when single components are aggregated. Generally, the risk of double counting increases as the magnitude of the environmental resource becomes greater, and/or when the resource is used for multiple purpose (Howe, 1990).

Valuing an environmental resource through appraisal methods often requires discounting monetized costs or benefits that are incurred in the future. The discounted value depends crucially on the discount rate, and there is still a considerable amount of disagreement on the choice of the appropriate discount factor; indeed, some 'perceived-as-precarious' resources and sustainable development[12] approach have recently reignited the debate on the discount rate choice. The choice of an 'appropriate' discount rate, ranging from zero (no-discounting) to higher positive values, is still controversial (Fisher and Krutilla, 1974; Pearce et al., 2003; Markandya and Pearce, 1994).

Many researchers agree on a discount rate lower than the current market interest rate. In particular, intertemporal efficiency and intergenerational ethics force to a market discount rate adjustment (Page, 1997).

The social discount rate should be lower than real market interest rates, for several reasons: i) as a whole, society's time horizon in cost–benefit analyses is longer than the length of time considered by individuals when expressing their preferences over time; and ii) lower risk and uncertainty from the society's point of view (with respect to an individual), when risk on future results is taken into account. The literature recommends that the discount rate should depend on the resource being estimated and it should decline as the time horizon increases. The latter point is motivated by the fact that the social discount rate can be shown to be equal to the sum of two components (Ramsey, 1928):

$$s = \rho + \mu \cdot g \tag{3.5}$$

The first term (ρ) is positive and represents the pure rate of time preference, which reflects people's impatience, and the second is the rate of growth (g) of future consumption (or income) times the elasticity (μ) of utility with respect to consumption (or income). If it is foreseen that people will be richer in the future $g > 1$, the second term is positive and $\mu < 1$ because the marginal utility of a euro will be lower than it is now (Pearce et al., 2004).

Formal approaches to support a time declining discount rate have been developed by Weitzman (1998) and Gollier (2002). Briefly, Weitzman focuses his attention on the uncertainty about future interest rates and demonstrates that the certainty-equivalent discount rate declines as the time horizon increases (see Pearce et al., 2004 for a simple numerical example). In Gollier, discount rates are lowered by uncertainty about future economic growth: a risk averse individual tends to react to increasing uncertainty on future economic growth by increasing savings (prudence effect) which lower the discount rate. Therefore, observing that risk presents a cumulative effects over time, is reasonable to assume a time declining discount rate.

The results of these formal models, the empirical observation that often people discount the future 'hyperbolically' and, last but not least, the ethical consideration that neither 'present' nor 'future' should not dictate in social choices (Pearce et al., 2004) support the choice of a time declining discount rate at least following an approximated step schedule of rates (Oxera, 2002; NOAA, 1999). The discount rates suggested by H.M. Treasury (2003) are summarized in Table 3.3.

Table 3.3   Social Discount Rates

	Period of years					
	0–30	31–75	76–125	126–200	201–300	> 300
Discount rate (%)	3.5	3.0	2.5	2.0	1.5	1.0

Notes: Suggested by the UK Treasury.

3.6   CONCLUDING REMARKS

This chapter highlights how appraisal methods can be used in valuing environmental resources. Appraisal methods rely on the relationships between the utility flow produced by environmental resources and market consumer behaviour. This relationship may be investigated through the 'dual approach' which assesses an environmental resource value as a change in the consumer expenditure function. Indeed, the appraisal methods can be considered among the operating procedures of this theoretical approach. At this time, even if the published economic literature reports only few examples of the application of appraisal methods for valuing environmental resources, they are widely used in cost–benefit analyses and in litigation on environmental damage assessment.

However, values produced by appraisal methods are reliable only when the consumer behaviour is unbiased and easily observed, and when non-use values are negligible. In order to capture the full value of the change in environmental quality, appraisal methods may have to be combined (or even replaced entirely) with approaches that are capable of capturing other components of TEV (such as contingent valuation) and benefit transfer techniques.

NOTES

1. This concern has pervaded the Italian economic-appraisal literature, generating a lively debate on the nature and theoretical foundations of appraisal science.
2. It should be noted that the adjustment does not necessarily influence the market equilibrium as it can take the shape of change in the use of other environmental resources.
3. Often, with reference to situations in which it is necessary to assess a change, the terms ante/post are used as synonyms of with/without. The use of the terms with/without is more correct, however, as the valuation is not performed before and after the event.
4. In this chapter, the market 'price' is defined as an historical bargain that happened in the past (Medici, 1972) whereas the market 'value' is a forecast.
5. In a competitive market, the price tends to be equal to the production cost. Similarly, if two goods are equivalent and can therefore substitute for each other, no operator will pay a higher price than another or sell at a lower price than another. This argument implies that the substitution value is equal to the market price and that the transformation value is equal to the market value, since no one is willing to pay for buying a good an amount of money greater than the income he can get from it (Medici, 1972).
6. Among different capitalization rates, there is one making the capitalization value equal to the market value.
7. In particular, the production cost includes direct expenses plus the income lost during the production process.
8. Di Cocco (1960) discriminates between use complementarity and production complementarity. The former occurs when the utility coming from a joint good consumption is greater than the sum of utilities of two separate ones. Production complementarity is found when the joint input use generates a higher production than the separate one.
9. When the good can be somewhat restored, its complementary value is similar or equal to the cost supported for substitution or reproduction.
10. These include, for example, price support policies, domestic market protection policies, trade-union wage agreements, abuse of market power, taxes, consumers' information asymmetries, etc.
11. To further elaborate on this, suppose that a deterioration in environmental quality affected the health of individuals and impacted adversely ecological systems. If both of these effects are reflected in property values, hedonic pricing values should capture the willingness to pay to avoid all of these effects. This would overlap with values estimated separately for each of these effects, so simply adding these two values to estimate the damages would be inappropriate.
12. The concept of sustainable development is rather elusive. The most popular definition states that the sustainable development is 'the development that satisfies the needs of the present generations while preserving needs of future ones' (World Commission on the Environment and Development, 1987).

REFERENCES

Appraisal Institute (1993), *The Dictionary of Real Estate Appraisal*, Chicago: Appraisal Institute.

Cochrane, H. (1993), 'La valutazione dei danni dovuti a disastri naturali e procurati dall'uomo', in L. Fusco Girard (ed.), *Estimo ed economia ambientale: le nuove frontiere nel campo della valutazione. Studi in onore di Carlo Forte*, Milano: Franco Angeli.

Di Cocco, E. (1960), *La valutazione dei beni economici*, Bologna: Calderini.

EU Commission (1993), *Green Book on Remedying Environmental Damage*, CB-CO-93-147-IT-C. Bruxelles.

EU Commission (2000), *White Book on Environmental Liability*, COM (2000) 66 final, Bruxelles.

Famularo, N. (1943), 'Della variabilità del valore con lo scopo della stima di un possibile sesto criterio di stima', *Rivista del Catasto e dei Servizi Tecnici Erariali*, **3**.

Fisher, A.C. and V. Krutilla (1974), 'Resources Conservation, Environmental Preservation and the Rate of Discount', *Quarterly Journal of Economics*, **89**(3), 358–70.

Forte, C. (1970), 'Piano economico per il rinnovamento del centro antico di Napoli', in A.A.V.V., *Il Centro Storico di Napoli*, Napoli.

Fusco Girard, L. (1993), 'Estimo, economia ambientale e sviluppo sostenibile', in *Le Nuove Frontiere nel Campo della Valutazione tra Conservazione e Qualità dello Sviluppo*, Milano: Franco Angeli.

Gollier, C. (2002), 'Discounting an uncertain future', *Journal of Public Economics*, **85**, 149–66.

H.M. Treasury, (2003), *The Green Book, Appraisal and Evaluation in Central Government*, London.

Howe, C. (1990), 'Damage Handbook: a Uniform Framework and Measurement Guidelines for Damages from Natural and Related Man-made Hazards', in Draft report to the National Science Foundation.

Krutilla, J. (1967), 'Conservation Reconsidered', *American Economic Review*, **57**, 777–86.

Markandya, A. and D. Pearce (1994), 'Natural Environments and the Social Rate of Discount', in J. Weiss (ed.), *The Economics of Project Appraisal and the Environment*, Aldershot, UK and Brookfield, USA: Edward Elgar.

Medici, G. (1953), *Principles of Appraisal*, Bologna: Edizioni Agricole.

Medici, G. (1972), *Principi di Estimo*, Bologna: Calderini.

Merlo, M. (1990), 'Sui criteri di stima delle esternalità', *Genio Rurale*, **7/8**, 82–9.

Merlo, M. (1991), *Elementi di economia ed estimo forestale-ambientale*, Bologna: Patron.

Mitchell, R.C. and R.I. Carson (1989), *Using Surveys to Value Public Good: The Contingent Valuation Method*, Washington, DC: Resource for the Nature.

Molesti, R. (1988), *Economia dell'ambiente*, Pisa: Ipem edizioni.

Nicholson, W. (1995), *Microeconomic Theory: Basic Principles and Extensions*, 6th edition, New York: The Dryden Press.

National Oceanic and Atmospheric Administration (NOAA), (1999), *Discounting and the treatment of uncertainty in natural resource damage assessment*, NOAA Technical paper 99–1, Silver Spring, Maryland.

Oxera, D. (2002), *A Social Time Preference Rate for use in Long-term Discounting*, The office of the Deputy Prime Minister, Department for Transport, and Department for the Environment, Food and Rural Affairs, London.

Page, T. (1997), 'On the Problem of Achieving Efficiency and Equity, Intergenerationally', *Land Economics*, **73**(4), 580–96

Pearce, D., Groom, B., Hepburn, C. and P. Koundoury (2003), 'Valuing the future. Recent Advances in Social Discounting', *World Economics*, **4**(2), 121–41.

Pearce, D., Mourato S. and G. Atkinson (2004), *Recent Developments in Environmental Cost Benefit Analysis*, OECD Report.

Ramsey, F.P., (1928), 'A Mathematical Theory of Saving', *Economic Journal*, **38**, 543–59.

Simonotti, M. (1982), *Introduzione alla valutazione del danno da inquinanti all'agrosistema*, Catania: Università degli Studi di Catania, pp.115–17.

US Federal Register, 15 CFR part 990 (1996), *Natural Resource Damage Assessment*,

Final rule, Department of Commerce.

Weitzman, M. (1998), 'Why the Far Distant Future Should be Discounted at its Lowest Possible Rate', *Journal of Environmental Economics and Management*, **36**, 201–8.

World Commission on the Environment and Development (1987), *Our Common Future*, Oxford: Oxford University Press.

PART II

Applications of Non-Market Valuation Methods
in the Lagoon of Venice

4. Using Contingent Valuation to Value the Island of S. Erasmo in the Lagoon of Venice

Anna Alberini, Paolo Rosato, Alberto Longo and Valentina Zanatta

4.1 INTRODUCTION

This chapter reports on a contingent valuation study eliciting willingness to pay (WTP) for a public programme to improve environmental quality, both directly and indirectly, via construction of infrastructure on and around the island of S. Erasmo in the Lagoon of Venice. S. Erasmo, one of the largest islands in the Lagoon of Venice, is affected by severe coastal erosion problems, degraded environmental quality, and a lack of infrastructure and services. We wish to elicit willingness to pay for the population of (broadly defined) beneficiaries of the programme, so our survey was administered over the telephone to a sample of residents of the Veneto Region.

Information about willingness to pay for the programme was elicited using dichotomous-choice questions in a referendum format. Our survey respondents were told about a hypothetical public programme that would, if passed by a majority vote, restore beaches, implement erosion control, and improve infrastructure on the island. They were subsequently asked whether they would vote for or against the proposition on a ballot, if establishing the programme would imply a cost of €X to their household. Statistical modelling of the responses to this and to follow-up questions allows us to compute mean and median WTP for the programme, and hence its benefits.

Mean WTP for the S. Erasmo public works is €67 per household. Median WTP provides a robust lower bound equal to €20. We estimate the total benefits for the Veneto Region to range between €41 million and €107 million, which suggests that the benefits of the programme exceed its cost. The study suggests that non-use values may account for a large share of the total benefits of preserving S. Erasmo, and that ignoring this component of value may have dramatic effects on the policy benefit-cost calculus.

The reminder of this chapter is organized as follows. Section 4.2 provides background information. Section 4.3 describes the survey questionnaire. Section 4.4 describes the sampling plan. Section 4.5 reports the results of the study and the estimates of willingness to pay. Section 4.6 presents the calculations of the benefits of the public programme, and Section 4.7 provides concluding remarks.[1]

4.2   BACKGROUND AND MOTIVATION

In the early 1970s, the Italian legislature passed a statute designed to address flooding and erosion in the Venice Lagoon System (Law April 16, 1973, N. 171, *Interventi per la salvaguardia di Venezia*). The law covers high tides ('acque alte'), storms, erosion, and pollution, and states that protection of the Lagoon of Venice is a matter of 'pre-eminent national interest'.

The statute does not explicitly require that consideration be given to costs and benefits in the selection of remedies and interventions,[2] and some observers have recently questioned the wisdom of expensive public works on scarcely populated islands of the Lagoon. For example, the cost of the public works on the island of S. Erasmo is €40 million, but the resident population is only 800. This implies that it is important to estimate the benefits associated with some of these initiatives and public works.

What is reported here is one such effort. We use the method of contingent valuation to estimate the benefits of public works on and around the island of S. Erasmo in the lagoon of Venice, focusing on beneficiaries other than its residents. Like other islands in the lagoon, S. Erasmo (shown in Figure 4.1) experiences severe coastal erosion problems, lagoon and beach degradation, and a lack of adequate infrastructure and services. S. Erasmo has very few historical or architectural features, is not a popular tourist destination, and is well-known only to local Lagoon excursionists.

Even people who do not visit S. Erasmo and use its resources, however, may well hold positive values for its conservation. This implies that a contingent valuation study eliciting willingness to pay for public works for improving environmental quality and reducing coastal erosion on and around S. Erasmo should survey both users and non-users of the island.

We employ contingent valuation because other non-market valuation methods are unsuitable and/or fail to capture potentially important components of value. For example, since the housing stock in S. Erasmo is very small and transactions are extremely infrequent, hedonic pricing methods based on property values cannot be applied here. The travel cost method is appropriate for S. Erasmo, but only contingent valuation can capture non-use values, which we are particularly interested in.

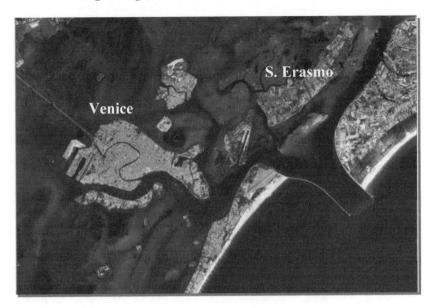

Figure 4.1   The Island of S. Erasmo in the Lagoon of Venice

Earlier applications of contingent valuation on coastal environments include McConnell (1977) (beach use and congestion public beaches in Rhode Island), Bell (1986) (recreational benefits of a beach nourishment programme), and Lindsay et al. (1992) (beach protection programmes in Maine and New Hampshire).

Silberman et al. (1992) elicit willingness to pay for beach nourishment from Sea Bright to Ocean Township, New Jersey, by intercepting users on site and by survey non-users over the telephone. Kontogianni et al. (2001) reports on an effort to compare willingness to pay for wetland protection at Kalloni Bay on the island of Lesvos, Greece, with qualitative information obtained from focus groups of local stakeholders about their priorities for both conservation and development. These studies share some common limitations, in that they are based on relatively small sample sizes and do not use the most recent innovations in the method of contingent valuation. At least some of them, however, recognize that non-use values are likely to be an important component of willingness to pay for beach erosion control programmes.

In addition, contingent valuation has also been employed to value improvements in surface water quality delivered by infrastructure, such as publicly-owned water treatment works (Choe et al., 1996). Construction of wastewater treatment infrastructure is one of the proposed works for S. Erasmo.

Our CV questionnaire was administered over the telephone to a random sample of residents of the Veneto Region stratified by distance from the Lagoon of Venice. This sample includes both people who are currently visiting S. Erasmo or using it in any other way, and people who do not normally visit the island.

4.3   STRUCTURE OF THE QUESTIONNAIRE

Our survey questionnaire is comprised of five sections. Section 1 inquires about the respondent's knowledge and use of the Lagoon of Venice and of the island of S. Erasmo. This section also presents a brief description of the island and its current environmental degradation and erosion problems. In section 2, respondents are queried about their recreational use of the Lagoon of Venice, and are asked questions about number of trips, destinations within the Lagoon, equipment, and cost per trip. Section 3 inquires specifically about the number of visits to S. Erasmo in the last 12 months, if any, and asks respondents to estimate their travel cost to the island.

Section 4 presents the valuation scenario, which consists of a public programme that would implement beach nourishment to offset erosion, drainage of inner canals, construction of a wastewater treatment facility, refurbishment of sewage lines and water ducts, and restoration of the ancient Torre Massimiliana (Maximilian's Tower). The programme would be run by the Veneto Region.

Respondents were told that additional taxes would be needed to raise the revenue necessary to fund the programme. The payment question is phrased as a referendum on the ballot. Should the referendum result in a majority of 'yes' votes, the programme would be implemented and funded with a one-time income tax to be paid by the residents of the Veneto Region; otherwise the proposal would be abandoned, and no additional tax would be imposed on the residents of the Region.

The tax amount is varied across households, and respondents are asked whether they would vote against or in favour of the programme at that cost to their household. In a follow up question, a respondent who has accepted to pay the initial tax amount is asked whether he would be willing to pay 50 percent more. The follow-up bid is 50 percent less than the initial bid for those respondents who declined to pay the initial bid. (The exact bid amounts are reported in Table 4.2 below.)

We also inquire about reasons for each of the possible response sequences ('Yes–Yes', 'Yes–No', 'No–Yes' and 'No–No'), as recommended by the NOAA Panel on Contingent Valuation. Finally, we ask respondents whether they would visit S. Erasmo after the public works, and how many times they expect to do so.

The fifth and last section of the instrument asks questions about the usual individual characteristics (age, gender, education, income, and so on). These will be used in regression models to test the internal validity of willingness to pay.

4.4   SAMPLING FRAME

An important step in any CV study is to define the population of beneficiaries of the programme being valued. In theory, a preservation programme that concerns the Venice lagoon system may potentially produce benefits to all Italians (and perhaps all Europeans or even the entire world). However, S. Erasmo is a relatively little-known destination that does not attract tourists visiting Venice.

If we exclude the value of housing and land on the island, the total economic value of S. Erasmo should be comprised primarily of local recreational use (for example daily beach use during the Summer season) and non-use values.[3] These considerations suggest that use values are likely to be limited to the residents of Venice and neighbouring areas, whereas the residents of other areas are likely to experience primarily non-use values (if any).[4]

In addition, the size of the island and the scale of the public works suggest that the most appropriate programme to improve the island's environment is a Region programme, and not a national one.[5] We felt that the scope of the public works would be too small for a national programme, and too large for a municipal or provincial programme. Accordingly, the survey sample was randomly drawn from the population of residents of the Veneto Region, stratified by distance from the Lagoon of Venice. Table 4.1 describes the stratification areas and their respective sample sizes.

As shown in Table 4.1, 2100 families were initially contacted for the survey. They were sent a letter from the University of Padua, announcing that their household had been selected for participation in the survey. These families were subsequently contacted by telephone in March–June 2002. A total of 729 refused to participate, and 41 could not be found, resulting in 1330 completed interviews.

As always with dichotomous choice CV surveys, the bid amount was varied to the respondents. Initial and follow-up amounts are shown in Table 4.2. There were a total of 10 bid sets. Initial bid levels ranged from €10 to €100; follow-up bids were 50 percent more or less than the initial bid. Respondents were randomly assigned to the bid sets.

Table 4.1   Sampling frame

Zone	Approximate distance from the Venice Lagoon (km)	Planned number of interviews	Actual interviews
Venice (Venice Historical Centre and Lagoon Islands)	0	700	507
A (e.g. Mira, Chioggia, Mestre)	from 0 to 5	500	342
B (e.g. Dolo, Fossalta di P., Mogliano V.to)	from 5 to 15	300	189
C (e.g. Noale, Vigonza, Taglio di Po)	from 15 to 30	250	141
D (e.g. Asolo, Tombolo, Vittorio V.to)	from 30 to 50	200	85
E (e.g. Soave, Valdagno, Feltre)	> 50	150	66

Table 4.2   Bid design in the S. Erasmo survey. All bids in EUR (€)

1st bid (EUR)	10	20	30	40	50	60	70	80	90	100
Follow-up bid if YES	15	30	45	60	75	90	105	120	135	150
Follow-up bid if NO	5	10	15	20	25	30	35	40	45	50
Number of respondents	137	128	139	130	134	140	134	124	128	136

4.5   RESULTS

A. The Data

Our first order of business is to examine the characteristics of our respondents. Descriptive statistics for the respondents' characteristics are reported in Table 4.3. The average respondent is about 50 years old, and has completed two years of high school. The average household income is roughly €21 000 a year.[6] The average household size is 2.84 persons.

Over two-thirds of our respondents are women (69.55 percent), and 41 percent are employed. About 23 percent are retired, and an additional 32 percent do not work outside of the home. This includes homemakers (25 percent), students (4 percent), or unemployed persons (2 percent). The remaining 4 percent did not report their occupation status. Finally, 4 percent of the respondents belong to an environmental organization.

Table 4.4 reports information about use of and familiarity with S. Erasmo.

In the last year, roughly one-fourth of the respondents have visited the Venice lagoon by public or private boats (LAGOONUSER), and 8 percent have been to S. Erasmo (ERASMOUSER).[7] About 14 percent of the respondents have been to S. Erasmo at least once in his/her life (ERASMOVISITOR). About two-thirds of

Table 4.3   Descriptive statistics of the respondents

Variable	Sample average	Standard deviation
Income		
Mean	€21 132	€15 196
Median	€21 000	
Income per member of the household (PCAPINC)		
Mean	€5 990	€6 988
Median	€4 500	
Did not answer the income question dummy (PCAPINCMISS)	0.31	0.46
Years of schooling (EDUCATION)	10.19	4.22
AGE	49.70	16.01
Household size	2.84	1.14
MALE dummy	0.30	0.46
Employed dummy (EMPLOYMENT)	0.41	0.49
RETIRED dummy	0.23	0.42
NONWORKER dummy (unemployed/student/homemaker)	0.32	0.47
Did not report employment status	0.04	0.20
Environmentalist dummy (ENVATT)	0.04	0.20

Notes: $n = 1330$.

Table 4.4   Use and knowledge of S. Erasmo

Variable	Percent
Has visited the lagoon in the last 12 months (LAGOONUSER)	23.31
Has been to S. Erasmo in the last 12 months (ERASMOUSER)	7.59
Has been to S. Erasmo at least once in his or her life (ERASMOVISITOR)	14.51
Will visit S. Erasmo after the public programme is carried out (POTENTIALUSER)	41.88
Knows S. Erasmo (KNOWS)	64.74

the respondents already knew of S. Erasmo before taking the survey (KNOWS), while the remainder learned about the island only through the survey.[8] When those who had never been to S. Erasmo were asked if they would visit the island after the completion of the public works, 42 percent of the respondents said that they would (POTENTIALUSER).

B. Willingness to Pay

The percentage of 'yes' responses to the payment questions is about 58 percent for the lowest bid we used (€10), declining to 23.5 percent when the bid is €100. To estimate mean and median WTP, we combine the responses to the initial and follow-up payment questions to form intervals around the respondent's (unobserved) WTP amount. We then assume that willingness to pay is a Weibull variate with scale σ and shape parameter θ, and estimate these parameters using the method of maximum likelihood.

The log likelihood function is:

$$\log L = \sum_{i=1}^{n} \log \left[\exp\left(-(WTP_i^L/\sigma)^\theta\right) - \exp\left(-(WTP_i^U/\sigma)^\theta\right) \right] \qquad (4.1)$$

where WTP^L and WTP^U denote the lower and upper bounds of the interval around the respondent's WTP amount, and i denotes the individual respondent. Mean WTP is equal to $\sigma \cdot \Gamma(1/\theta + 1)$, whereas median WTP is $\sigma[-\ln(0.5)]^{1/\theta}$.

Using the complete sample, we estimate mean WTP to be €66.61 (s.e. 5.42), whereas median WTP is a much lower figure, €20.39 (s.e. 1.52).[9]

Economic theory holds that the total economic value of an environmental resource is comprised of its use and non-use value:

$$\text{Total Economic Value} = \text{Use value} + \text{Non-use value} \qquad (4.2)$$

To identify use and non-use values, we partition our sample into three groups: (i) current visitors,[10] (ii) respondents who do not currently visit but plan to after the public works,[11] and (iii) non-users. We fit a separate Weibull likelihood function to each of these groups, obtaining that mean WTP is €92 for current users, €71 for potential users, and €36 for non-users.

We interpret the €36 to be the non-use value of the resource. Wald tests show that users and potential users hold mean WTP and median figures that are not statistically different from one another (Wald statistic = 1.55 and 0.30), but are statistically different from the WTP of non-users (Wald statistic = 11.03).[12]

Netting out the non-use values, we obtain €(92 − 36) = €56 as the use value for those subjects that are current users, and €(71 − 36) = €35 to be the potential use values for those subjects who do not visit S. Erasmo now but say that they will once its quality has been improved.

C. Internal Validity of the WTP Responses

To test internal validity of the WTP responses, we estimate accelerated-life Weibull models that let $\sigma_i = \exp(\mathbf{x}_i\beta)$, where $\mathbf{x}$ is a $1 \times k$ vector of individual characteristics and β is a $k \times 1$ vector of unknown parameters.

The vector $\mathbf{x}$ includes dummy variables that capture current and potential use patterns, and the indicator KNOWS, which takes on a value of one if the respondent had heard of S. Erasmo before the survey. It also includes dummies for the area of residence of the respondent, a dummy for whether the respondent contributes to environmental organizations, income per member of the household, age, a gender dummy (MALE), and missing value indicators for the latter three variables.[13] Because some respondents may hold a positive value for the resource, but feel that they cannot commit their household's finances, we created an indicator, NONWORKER, for individuals who are not gainfully employed, such as homemakers, students, and the unemployed.

Table 4.5 presents several specifications of the WTP regression based on various subsets of these regressors. In columns (I)–(III) we include various combinations of current use dummies, where we attempt to distinguish for recent users of the Lagoon who did not visit S. Erasmo and recent visitors to S. Erasmo, and the future use dummy. The coefficients on the dummies for current use of the Lagoon and potential future use of S. Erasmo are positively and significantly associated with WTP. Recent visitors to S. Erasmo, however, do not have significantly higher WTP. This is probably due to the fact that there are too few respondents in our sample who report having taken trips to the island in the past year.

In column (IV), we add dummies for the area of residence of the respondent. We find that these dummies do not improve the fit of the model, and that they do not alter the coefficients of the use dummies. A likelihood ratio test of the null that the coefficients of the geographical variables are all equal to zero fails to reject the null hypothesis at the conventional significance levels.

By contrast, column (V) shows that membership in an environmental organization is significantly associated with WTP. All else the same, both mean and median WTP figures are 66 percent higher for a member of an environmental organization. This effect, however, becomes insignificant in column (VI), where we include additional individual characteristics, such as income, age, gender, education, and (lack of) gainful employment status (plus

Table 4.5 Double bounded estimates for the Weibull distribution

	Model I		Model II		Model III		Model IV		Model V		Model VI	
Loglik	-1569.69	.	-1530.12	.	-1528.03	.	-1514.40	.	-1513.76	.	-1458.66	.
Intercept	3.5236	(52.04)	2.8544	(28.04)	2.8572	(28.14)	2.4092	(9.12)	2.4086	(9.13)	2.8434	(6.68)
LAGOONUSER	0.5339	(3.29)	1.3163	(8.37)	1.2018	(6.89)	1.0758	(6.18)	1.0575	(6.09)	0.616	(3.63)
ERASMOUSER	0.3784	(1.4)			0.3693	(1.41)	0.2921	(1.12)	0.2816	(1.08)	0.2047	(0.81)
POTENTIALUSER			1.1614	(8.68)	1.1587	(8.68)	1.1764	(8.75)	1.17	(8.71)	0.7591	(5.78)
KNOWS							0.6097	(4.58)	0.6081	(4.55)	0.4587	(3.54)
VENEZIA							0.0361	(0.13)	0.0129	(0.08)	0.0253	(0.1)
FASCIA A							0.1536	(0.57)	0.1535	(0.57)	0.1913	(0.71)
FASCIA B							-0.0472	(0.16)	-0.0696	(0.24)	-0.079	(0.25)
FASCIA C							0.0531	(0.18)	0.0289	(0.1)	0.0161	(0.05)
FASCIA D							0.3147	(0.96)	0.297	(0.9)	0.155	(0.48)
ENVATT									0.5131	(1.73)	0.2435	(0.86)
PCAPINC (in thou. euro)											0.0325	(2.6)
PCAPINCMISS											0.0958	(0.62)
EDUCATION											0.0697	(4.26)
EDUCMISS											-0.3322	(1.01)
AGE											-0.0198	(4.86)
AGEMISS											-0.4098	(0.66)
NONWORKER											0.0962	(0.74)
NONWORKMISS											0.0063	(0.01)
MALE											0.03	(0.23)
MALEMISS											-0.137	(0.22)

Notes: N = 1325; T-statistics in parentheses.

the dummies indicating missing values for these variables).

Column (VI) indeed shows that income per household member is positively and significantly associated with willingness to pay. The coefficient on the dummy denoting a missing income value is insignificant, implying that, all else the same, the willingness to pay of those respondents who did not report their income is not different from that of those who did.

To assess the magnitude of the coefficient on income, consider a 30-year-old female resident of the city of Venice who does not belong to environmental organization, has completed high school, is neither a current nor a future user of the Lagoon of Venice, and knows S. Erasmo. Mean and median WTP for an individual with these characteristics are €65 and €25 respectively, at the average income per family member (€6000). If income increases by €1000, mean and median WTP would increase to €67 and €26, and if it were to double to €12 000, they would rise to €87 and €29, respectively. For this respondent, the income elasticity of WTP is 0.192.

The coefficient on education is positive and significant, implying that a more highly educated person is willing to pay more for the preservation of S. Erasmo. Failure to report schooling information is not systematically associated with WTP. In the above example at the average income level, adding 4 years of education (college degree) raises mean WTP from €65 to €86 (roughly €2.50 per additional year of schooling), and median WTP from €25 to €34 (a little less than €2 per additional year of schooling).

Age is negatively and significantly associated with WTP: the coefficient on this variable implies that adding 10 years to the age of the respondent in the above example reduces mean WTP from €65 to €53 and median WTP from €25 to €21. Once again, those respondents who did not report their ages are not significantly different from those who did. Finally, once we control for income, education, and age, we find that the employment status and gender of the respondent do not further explain his or her willingness to pay.

4.6   THE BENEFITS OF THE PROGRAMME

To compute the benefits of the programme, it is necessary to distinguish between use and non-use values. We proceed as follows. First, we note that current and future visitors to S. Erasmo hold WTP values that are statistically indiscernible from one another, which implies that they can be pooled, and that models of the WTP responses can be fit for the pooled group. Using this approach, and the usual assumption that the latent WTP is distributed following the Weibull distribution, we obtain an estimate of mean WTP of €77.37 (standard error 6.29), and median WTP of 34.22 (s.e. 2.34) for current/future visitors. A Weibull model of the WTP responses by those respondents who do not currently visit S. Erasmo nor plan to in the future produces mean and median WTP figures of 36.21 (s.e. 7.89) and 4.80 (s.e. 1.24), respectively.

We then assume that the population percentages of visitors/potential users and non-users in each zone are the same as those observed in the sample, and compute the total number of households with actual or potential visitors, and without users, for each zone.[14] We sum the households of each type over the zones to compute the expected total of households with and without users in the Veneto Region, which we denote as N^U and N^{NU}, respectively. The total benefits are $(N^U \times 77.37 + N^{NU} \times 36.21)$, when mean WTP is used, and $(N^U \times 34.22 + N^{NU} \times 4.80)$ when median WTP is used.

Our calculations show that $N^U = 1\,107\,696.80$ and $N^{NU} = 591\,538.20$, resulting in total benefits of €107 122 100 (s.e. 11 634 649) when mean WTP is used, and €40 744 768 (s.e. 992 518) when median WTP is used. These estimates suggest that the benefits greatly exceed the cost of the public works when mean WTP is used, and barely exceed them when median WTP – a robust, conservative estimate of WTP – is used.

4.7 DISCUSSION AND CONCLUSIONS

This chapter reports the results of a contingent valuation survey that elicits willingness to pay for a public programme for erosion control and infrastructure improvement on the island of S. Erasmo in the Lagoon of Venice. Residents of the Veneto Region were surveyed over the telephone using dichotomous choice payment questions.

Our statistical analyses show that people are willing to pay for S. Erasmo. Mean WTP is about €66 per household, whereas median WTP – a robust lower bound for mean WTP – is roughly €20. Our WTP responses show internal consistency, in that WTP increases with knowledge of the island, current use of the lagoon, and expected use of S. Erasmo after the works have been completed. Willingness to pay depends in predictable ways on income, educational attainment of the respondents, and age.

Given the internal validity of our results, we conclude that contingent valuation is a reasonable and promising approach to estimating WTP for publicly policies for erosion control and environmental quality improvement in island/coastal areas, and might be usefully employed in similar contexts at other locales. For example, recent global climate change protocols have emphasized coastal and island erosion as a potentially serious consequence of climate change (see, for example, the discussion in Yohe and Schlesinger, 2002), which begs for estimating the benefits of offsetting policies at these locales.

Finally, we compute the total benefits of the public works by distinguishing between current and potential visitors, and non-users. Total benefits from the programme range between €41 million (using median WTP) and €107 million (using mean WTP). Both exceed the costs of the programme. We regard the former figure as a robust lower bound for the benefits accruing to the residents of the Veneto Region.

NOTES

1. The authors are grateful to Andrea Galvan, Richard Carson and Luigi Fabbris for their invaluable help and comments. We also wish to thank the participants of the workshop on 'Information and Technology' held in Copenhagen, Denmark, April 2003, and of the Session on Contingent Valuation III at the 12th Annual EAERE Conference, Bilbao, Spain, June 2003, for their helpful comments.
2. No benefit–cost analyses have been conducted for public works of limited scope, but some rudimentary benefit–cost work has been conducted for public works and engineering feats with broader, system-wide impacts. For example, efforts have been made to list the possible *categories* of benefits associated with the construction and operation of MOSE (MOdulo Sperimentale Elettromeccanico, originally the prototype mobile barrier against high tides used for experimental and study purposes between 1988 and 1992, and later the name of the entire project for mobile barriers at the lagoon inlets; see http://www.salve.it – last access: November 2005), but we are not aware of actual benefit estimates. At any rate, the results of this study are unpublished.
3. Use values refer to the utility from direct consumption of the good. Non-use values are generally classified into existence, option, and bequest. In particular, existence is due to the utility an individual derives from the awareness that a good exists, even though the individual does not use it and will not do so in the future. Option value derives from the possibility to use the good in the future, as individuals cannot forecast their future preferences. Finally, bequest value is about the utility from preserving the good for future generations. See Freeman (1993).
4. Two hundred pre-test interviews confirmed that S. Erasmo is virtually unknown to people living 50 km or farther from the Lagoon of Venice, but that these persons nevertheless hold positive values for the public programme.
5. The Region is a jurisdiction similar to the State in the US and the Province in Canada.
6. About one-third of the respondents do not report his or her family income. The average household income of €21 000 is calculated for those respondents who did report their household income.
7. The proportion of users is as high as 39 percent among those respondents who live in the city of Venice, and as low as 3 percent among those respondents who live in areas farther than 50 km. from the Lagoon.
8. The percentage of respondents who know of S. Erasmo is about 88 percent among residents of Venice, and about 23 percent among those respondents who live over 50 km from the Lagoon.
9. The standard errors are computed using a simulation-based approach (see Alberini and Cooper, 2000).
10. Since only about 8 percent of the respondents have visited S. Erasmo in the 12 months before the survey, we include in this group both those persons who had visited the island in the previous year and those persons who had taken trips to the Lagoon of Venice during this period, even though they had not necessarily visited S. Erasmo. This means that group (i) is comprised of those individuals with LAGOONUSER = 1.
11. The correct way to disentangle use and non-use values is to identify users and non-users after the environmental programme has been implemented. Group (ii) is comprised of those

respondents with POTENTIALUSER = 1.

12. The Wald statistics for comparison of users and non-users are 10.26 for mean WTP and 46.09 for median WTP. The Wald statistics for comparison of potential users and non-users are 11.03 for mean WTP 101.51 for median WTP. Under the null hypothesis of no difference in mean WTP across each pair, the Wald statistic is distributed as a chi square with one degree of freedom. The critical limit at the 5 percent significance level is 3.84.

13. We created a dummy variable, PCAPINCMISS that takes on a value of 1 when the respondent did not answer the income question. Missing values in the income variable were then replaced with zeros, and both the income variable and PCAPINCMISS were included in the right-hand side of the WTP equation. A similar procedure was followed for MALE and AGE.

14. To illustrate, if 20 percent of the households in zone A in our sample were users or potential users, and N_j is the number of households residing in this zone as per the most recent Census, the total number of households with users or potential users in zone A is computed to be $N_j^U = N_j \times (0.20)$. The total number of households in zone A without users would be $N_j^{NU} = N_j \times (0.80)$.

REFERENCES

Alberini, A. and J. Cooper (2000), 'Applications of the Contingent Valuation Method in Developing Countries: A Survey', *FAO Economic and Social Development Paper*, **146**, FAO, Rome.

Bell, F.W. (1986), 'Economic Policy Issues Associated with Beach Nourishment', *Policy Studies Review,* **6** (2), 374–81.

Choe, K., D. Whittington and D.T. Lauria (1996), 'The Economic Benefits of Surface Water Quality Improvements in Developing Countries: A Case Study of Davao, Philippines', *Land Economics*, **72**(4), 519–37.

Freeman, A.M. III (1993), *The Measurement of Environmental and Resource Values: Theory and Method*, Washington, DC: Resources for the Future.

Kontogianni, A., M. Skourtos, I.H. Langford, I.J. Bateman and S. Georgiou (2001), 'Integrating Stakeholder Analysis in Non-market Valuation of Environmental Assets', *Ecological Economics*, **37**, 123–38.

Lindsay, B.E., J.M. Halstead, H.C. Tupper and J.J. Vaske (1992), 'Factors Influencing the Willingness to Pay for Coastal Beach Protection', *Coastal Management*, **20**, 191–230.

McConnell, K.E. (1977), 'Congestion and Willingness to Pay: A Study of Beach Use', *Land Economics*, **53**(2), 185–95.

Silberman, J., D.A. Gerlowski and N.A. Williams (1992), 'Estimating Existence Value for Users and Nonusers of New Jersey Beaches', *Land Economics*, **68**(2), 225–36.

Yohe, G. and M. Schlesinger (2002), 'The Economic Geography of the Impacts of Climate Change', *Journal of Economic Geography*, **2**, 311–41.

5. Evaluation of Urban Improvement on the Islands of the Venice Lagoon: A Spatially-Distributed Hedonic–Hierarchical Approach

Paolo Rosato, Carlo Giupponi, Margaretha Breil and Anita Fassio

5.1 INTRODUCTION

The economic evaluation of the environmental and urban improvement is a topical subject and has seen an impressive number of methodological and operational contributions in the last decades. In this chapter, we use methods that estimate the monetary value of the utility produced by public interventions using changes in the market value of private goods, especially residential properties. Dwellings are complex goods whose value depends on many factors, including the quality of the environment and services in the area. Immobility renders the value of housing extremely sensitive to externalities (Curto, 1993; Rosato and Stellin, 2000), so by analysing the factors that influence value it is possible to identify and quantify the social appreciation for the protection of public goods and services (Garrod and Willis, 1992; Scarpa, 1995; Chattopadhyay, 1999). Changes in property values – surveyed or estimated by a simulation of the property market – thus become an indicator for estimating the value of an urban improvement.

The model developed in this chapter is the result of a collaboration between scientists in different disciplines and integrating two different approaches: a simplified procedure developed for the economic valuation of environmental improvement (Rosato et al., 2002) and an ecological evaluation model in a Geographical Information System (GIS) environment developed to analyse the relations between land use and biodiversity (Giupponi and Coletto, 2003). These are, clearly, very different contexts, which however present good synergies, the former in providing tools for economic analysis and valuation, and the latter in providing the methodology for setting up, interpreting and modelling functional relationships between georeferenced information about prices of residential properties and their current or future/possible local context, by exploiting the spatial data processing capabilities offered by GIS.

The idea behind this work is that of examining how advanced methods of geographical modelling can be integrated with economic valuation methods to produce synergies that can improve and simplify the economic valuation of public investments.

The economic model used in this chapter is based on a 'hybrid' value function developed using multi-criteria analysis and is sufficiently precise to evaluate the impact on property value of small variations in environmental quality. The model requires that we identify all of the elements that influence the market value and their weights in the specific local situation. To identify these elements and their weights, local property market experts were asked for their opinions.[1]

The evaluation model was encoded in a Geographical Information System (GIS) that manages the spatial relations between objects (for example buildings, public works, environmental goods) and a set of digital maps of the northern part of the Venice Lagoon created specifically for this purpose.[2] On this basis it is possible to analyse and simulate the interactions between the territorial system and market realities, that is, in this case, to analyse the effect of environmental variations induced by public works on the value of the property stock. The integration of GIS and valuation model is particularly useful for analysing the real estate market because property values depend a great deal on location. The above described model was applied to testing a number of hypotheses about the effects of urban and environmental improvement works on the main inhabited islands in the Lagoon of Venice: Burano, Murano and S. Erasmo.

The chapter is organized as follows. Section 5.2 gives a brief overview of the geographical context within which the model was implemented, the major islands of the northern part of the Venetian Lagoon. Section 5.3 is dedicated to methodological aspects of the hierarchical model. A description of the GIS model realised follows in Section 5.4. Section 5.5 describes the simulations and the results, leading to our conclusions in Section 5.6.

5.2   THE CASE STUDY

The three islands considered within this research project – Murano, Burano and S. Erasmo – are situated north of the historical centre of Venice (see Figure 5.1). They differ greatly from one another in terms of physical location in the Lagoon, property characteristics and services. Murano is very close to the city of Venice, while Burano is much farther away. S. Erasmo is

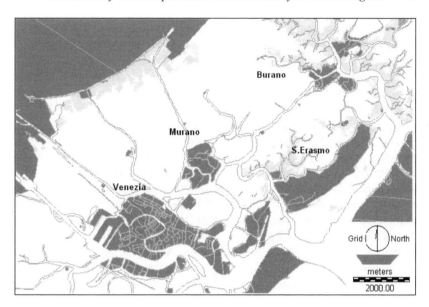

Notes: Dark grey: mainland and islands, light grey: canals and marshes.

Figure 5.1   Map of the Northern Lagoon

in an intermediate position, but is rather isolated. Access from the mainland to Murano is from Tessera, using the airport link, whereas connections from the mainland of Burano and S. Erasmo are situated on the Cavallino coast, with boats departing from and arriving at Treporti and Punta Sabbioni.

A second distinguishing element of the three islands is their property characteristics and land use. S. Erasmo is essentially a farming island with a very small population and its dwellings are scattered between the cultivated fields, as is usually seen in rural environments. In the centre of the island there are few buildings and minimal public and private services: the church, a bank, one shop. For other services, the residents of S. Erasmo depend on other islands and the mainland (Treporti and Cavallino). Murano bears many signs of its glass industry: there are large factories, now almost entirely abandoned, and residential buildings, a few of which date back to pre-industrial times. Burano has maintained the characteristics of an old fishermen's settlement, with the traditional Lagoon morphology along the canals and fields, and with fairly small buildings. Services are much better on Murano and Burano, where daily needs, both private (shops, banks, etc.) and public (schools, primary health care, local council offices), are met.

The real estate market of Murano is in a certain way linked to that of the city of Venice: it follows the same trends but has lower prices. The residential market of the island of S. Erasmo and, to a lesser degree, that of Burano are instead almost exclusively limited to the resident community. Especially on S. Erasmo, where sales are rare, real estate agents seldom learn about transactions among islanders. But there is also some demand coming from outside of the island, mainly from residents of the historic centre of Venice searching for a second home for weekends or short holidays, and for indulging in hobbies linked with nature (gardening, horticulture, small animal or fish rearing). This segment of the demand is particularly interesting for the purposes of this chapter as it places much importance on the quality of the environment surrounding the buildings. These transactions are more transparent because professional help is frequently requested, so that real estate agents are able to depict the situation more precisely. Because it is tied to local demand, real estate agents generally believe that this market, unlike that of Murano, has not been substantially involved in the recent boom in property values that has occurred in the city of Venice.

The two types of demand reflect different factors. The residential demand considers the ease of reaching the island from the city of Venice and the mainland, and the location within the island, whereas for the demand for second homes, which is less dependent on regular transfers and commuting, these aspects are less important. In contexts like S. Erasmo the availability of a private boat berth also appears to be important, as boats compensate for scarce connections of public transport and can be used for leisure trips around the Lagoon. Public transport from the city of Venice connects the islands with the Fondamente Nuove area, with services varying a great deal from island to island: Murano has more than 200 daily connections with the city of Venice, while this figure drops to 43 for Burano and 26 for S. Erasmo. Travelling times are 15 minutes for Murano, 30 for S. Erasmo and 40 for Burano. The islands are also connected to the long-term parking facilities at Treporti (for Burano and S. Erasmo) and the International Airport (for Murano). Given the size of S. Erasmo, central locations within the island and the proximity to its three landing docks are of greater importance than on Burano and Murano, where distances are fairly short and all parts of the islands are within walking distance.

The experts point out that another important factor is the size of the property: given that the demand for property on the islands aims at relatively low prices, the properties that are easily sold on the market tend to be quite small,[3] the optimal size being generally around 60–70 m^2. On S. Erasmo, this arouses interest in rustic outbuildings or other small buildings that can be renovated and adapted for residential use. Land suitable for vegetable gardens, channels for fish farming, the proximity to hunting or natural areas also appear to be much appreciated. For Burano and Murano the historical– architectural context and open spaces that can be used as gardens or vegetable patches are highly appreciated. The residential demand also gives much weight to the availability of services such as shops, banks, schools, health services, etc. Last but not least, exposure to high water events is an important factor for residential demand, penalising buildings located in frequently flooded areas.

5.3 THE ECONOMIC VALUATION MODEL

The economic valuation model developed in this chapter builds on a prototype previously set up to evaluate ex ante the impacts of improvement works planned for the island of S. Erasmo (Rosato et al., 2002). In that case, the estimate of the value was based on a function that generates the value of the properties, using the pairwise comparison approach for determining the weights of each characteristic on the market value and subsequently calibrating the model on the local property market data. In this chapter we use a similar approach, revising the variables and parameters of the value function on the basis of new and more precise information gathered from experts and in relation to the specific characteristics of the islands of Murano, Burano and S. Erasmo.

Residential property values depend on many characteristics, each of which is appreciated in a different way on the market (Rosen, 1974). Changes in any of these characteristics produce changes in the market value. The market prices of the properties can therefore be analysed by breaking them down into the specific characteristics of each dwelling and corresponding prices. This analysis of the 'composition' of the properties and prices can be used to identify the marginal price of any given characteristic, including those of the area where the dwelling is situated.

Having said that, the change in values induced by an upgrading intervention on a given site is equal to the sum of the changes in value experienced by each of the buildings on that site, that is:

$$\Delta V = \sum_j \Delta V_j \qquad (5.1)$$

where ΔV is the difference in value on the site induced by the investment; ΔV_j is the difference in value of building j before and after the public works.

The difference in value of each building j can be expressed in euro per m^2, thus allowing a comparison with other buildings. The difference in value is the product of building size and the difference between the value per m^2 with and without the public investment:

$$\Delta V_j = D_j \left(V_{ujc} - V_{ujs} \right) \tag{5.2}$$

where D_j is the size of property unit j (m^2), V_{ujc} represents the value per m^2 of property j with the investment, and V_{ujs} represents the value per m^2 of property j without the investment.

As mentioned above, this procedure is based on the hypothesis that the value per m^2 of properties can be expressed as a function of their characteristics. Formally,

$$Vu_j = f(x_{ij}) \tag{5.3}$$

where Vu_j is the estimated value of the j-th good and x_{ij} is the state of the ith characteristic of the jth good.

Now the basic problem is the construction of the value function $f(x_{ij})$. The approach proposed here uses a multiple criteria evaluation model, fed by judgements from experts, and calibrated on the basis of available market data. The estimate of the value function is done in two steps: the first estimates a cardinal indicator function, I_j, of the characteristics of the good, through which we create a ranking of the goods being evaluated: $I_j = g(x_{ij})$; the second estimates a function $h(I_j)$ which gives a monetary measure of the value:

$$Vu_j = h(I_j). \tag{5.4}$$

The cardinal indicator I_j was estimated using a procedure of hierarchical decomposition and re-composition of real estate characteristics that includes:

1. identification of all the i characteristics (x_{ij}) that influence the value of the jth good considered;
2. classification of the characteristics and aggregation in criteria and/or families of criteria (A);
3. elicitation of the weights (w) which express the relative importance of the various characteristics at each level of hierarchical breakdown.[4]

Steps 1 and 2 were addressed by drawing on the literature on property valuation (Curto, 1993, 1994), which has established and classified the characteristics affecting property value, especially residential. All of the elements affecting the value were analysed and organised hierarchically. This approach permits the identification of relationships between the basic characteristics and the value, representing the way in which the market summarises and appreciates the various aspects of the considered goods.

The structure of the hierarchy model can thus be represented by a tree diagram (see Figure 5.2).

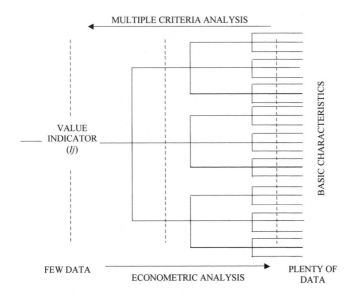

Figure 5.2   The structure of the value function

The third point was addressed using the pairwise comparison technique (Saaty, 1980) with the collaboration of a panel of experts who expressed judgements on the relative importance of the various elements in the hierarchy model (see Rosato et al., 2002, for details).

An initial telephone survey of all agents affiliated with the Federazione Italiana Agenti Immobiliari Professionisti (Italian Federation of Professional Real Estate Agents) and operating in Venice allowed us to select those real estate agents who were familiar with the real estate market of the islands in the northern Lagoon, especially Murano, Burano and S. Erasmo. Our final panel was comprised of five experts. Semi-structured interviews were then conducted with the aim of obtaining a description of the market and the specific factors relevant to the local context.

On the basis of the information gleaned from the real estate agents, the characteristics influencing the value were listed in a hierarchical way, grouping them into four broad categories: 1) location; 2) typology; 3) technical, and 4) economic.

The location characteristics include accessibility to the property from outside the island (distinguishing for access from the mainland and from the city of Venice) and on the island itself; the presence or absence of both public and private services; the frequency with which the property is exposed to high water; environmental attributes, such as overall environmental quality and scenic views.

The typology factors include the type of building, its size, view, exposure and outbuildings. The technical factors summarise the finishes and state of repair of the living area (floors, fixtures, heating, plumbing and lighting) and building (roof, walls, attics, foundations and common parts). Finally, the economic characteristics include any restrictions on the use of the properties (residential, commercial, etc.) and on whether maintenance, restoration, renovation works, etc. are allowed.

The result of this procedure is a value function $g(\cdot)$ which, when applied to the characteristics (x_{ij}) of each property, estimates the corresponding indicator I_j. Given the logic of the method, the value function takes the following form:

$$I_j = \sum_{i=1}^{n} x_{ij} c_i \quad \text{with} \quad c_i = \prod_{k=1}^{l} w_{ki} \quad (5.5)$$

where k is the hierarchical level considered in evaluating the contribution of characteristic i to the value, x_{ij} is the performance of the jth good with respect to the ith characteristic, w_{ki} is the weight of the ith characteristic at the kth hierarchical levels, and c_i is the aggregate weight of the ith characteristic.

The panel of experts provided the fact-finding elements for the assignment of weights using the pairwise comparison technique, expressing the relative importance according to a nine-point Saaty scale (equally, moderately, strongly, very strongly, extremely more/less important; and an intermediate level between each of these values). The location characteristics were evaluated first as these were considered central to the evaluation of changes in the values associated with the environment changes. The weights of location, typology and economic characteristics were then defined (see Figure 5.3).[5]

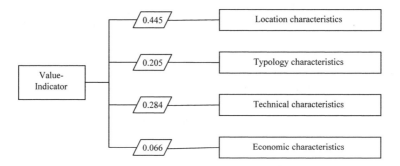

Figure 5.3   Hierarchy model for the estimate of value on the islands in the Venice Lagoon: main categories

The experts estimated that the location characteristics (see Figure 5.4) which include both elements of environmental quality and other context elements like services, accessibility and exposure to high water, contribute about 44.5 percent of the value per m², the typological characteristics (type, aspect/exposure, size, view and outbuildings) approximately 20.5 percent (see Figure 5.5), the technical ones 28.4 percent (see Figure 5.6), while only 6.6 percent is attributed to flexibility with respect to restrictions on use and structural interventions (see Figure 5.7). Within the typology characteristics category, the relative weights were similar for all three contexts, with 17.3 percent attributed to accessibility, 2.9 percent to the frequency of high water events, 9.7 percent to the availability of services and 14.5 percent to environmental quality.

Consistent with previous research on S. Erasmo alone, exposure to high water has a relatively minor role, taking less than 3 percent of the total weight of the elements that form the location component of the value. Once the value indicator (I_j) has been determined for each property, its monetary equivalent must be estimated.

To do this it is necessary to gather market prices for some of the *j*th goods for calibrating function (5.4). The value function can be calibrated in different ways according to the number of known market prices: the estimate can be made by interpolation with linear or polynomial functions (for example *weighted sum*) or by introducing functions of increasing complexity.

The complexity of the function that transforms the value index into sums of money also depends on the size of the sample of market transaction data available. With few data points, mono-parametric procedures can be used (sample averages and simple regression), while multi-parametric techniques can be used when more data points are available (multiple regression).

It should be noted that the use of multi-parametric techniques allows us to shift the weights evaluation from the experts' judgement to the econometric analysis, moving from technical analysis methods towards economic analyses (see Figure 5.2). Therefore the more market data available, the more aspects can be evaluated with statistical analysis. In this way a fairly flexible hybrid model was created that incorporates aspects that are difficult to account for in a statistical analysis and, at the same time, uses appropriately the available market information.

The model calibration on the market value was carried out starting from the information (prices and descriptions) collected on the sales recorded in the last year on the islands of the northern Lagoon. These properties were evaluated with the hierarchical model, translating the description of their characteristics into scores using the weights given to the characteristics in the hierarchical model. In this way an overall 'scoring' was estimated, which can be correlated with the price per m² registered in market transactions. Due to

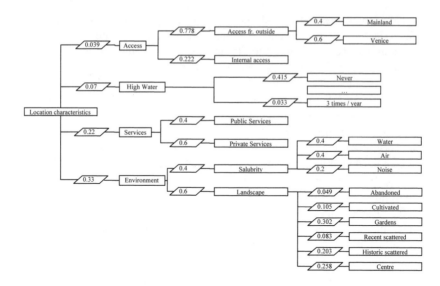

Figure 5.4   Location characteristics, a schematic representation

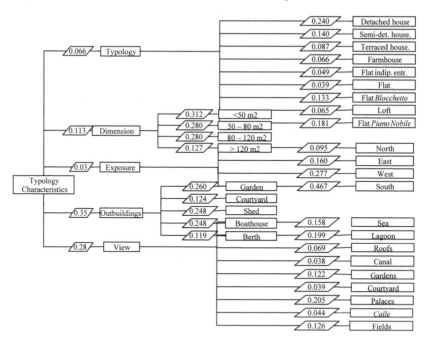

Figure 5.5   Typology characteristics, schematic representation

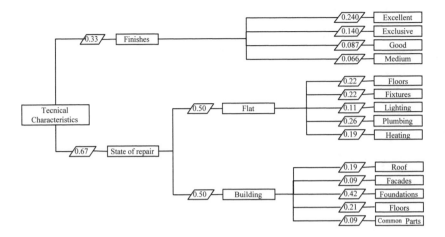

Figure 5.6   Technical characteristics, schematic representation

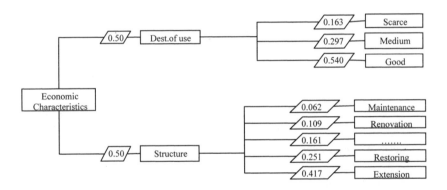

Figure 5.7   Economic characteristics, schematic representation

the dearth of transactions, we specify a simple linear interpolation of prices per m² and indicators calculated by the model:

$$V_u = a + bI \qquad (5.6)$$

The parameters of the equation are reported in Table 5.1.

The value function provides reasonable results (see Figure 5.8): the market values range from €900/m² for properties in the hypothetically poorest condition on S. Erasmo to almost €4200/m² for the hypothetically best apartments on Murano (2003 prices).

Valuing Complex Natural Resource Systems

Table 5.1   Calibration of the hierarchy model

Parameter	Coefficient	Standard Error	t-stat
a	375.99	145.93	2.577
b	7094.38	2002.92	3.542

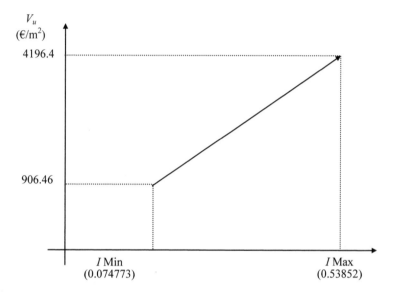

Figure 5.8   From value indicator to market value

Based on equation (5.6) the difference in overall value is equal to the product of the differences in value per m² of the buildings *j* times the size of the buildings, i.e.:

$$\Delta V = \sum_j D_j \cdot b\left(I_{jc} - I_{js}\right) \tag{5.7}$$

where D_j is the size of the property *j*, I_{jc} the value indicator at *j* with the intervention, and I_{js} the value indicator at *j* without the intervention.

5.4 THE IMPLEMENTATION OF THE ECONOMIC MODEL IN A GIS ENVIRONMENT

The model described in the previous sections was implemented in a Geographical Information System that mapped the distribution of values in the islands and simulated the spatial distribution of changes caused by the hypothetical improvements. The GIS was used for mapping functions and for the analysis and interpretation of the data processed by the spatial model. The following functions were used:

1. query and filtering using Structured Query Language (SQL);
2. manipulation with mathematical operators to build simple territorial models through the application of functions to the database;
3. context analyses with distance operators, which generate buffer areas, least-cost pathways and spatially interpolated data;
4. statistical analyses for efficient processing of the input data to produce general results and summary indicators of distribution, variability, etc.

Using these procedures, the hierarchical structure of the value function was implemented into a GIS that geographically locates the relevant factors for the real estate values. The overlay of layers was implemented using the weights determined within the hierarchical model.

The implementation of the evaluation model in a GIS environment faced a number of problems. First, the study involved the management and processing of a large amount of data, in part because it looked at different environmental attributes. Second, data limitations required much preliminary database construction work in order to create the missing thematic layers and to provide the interoperability necessary for spatial analysis. Third, the high resolution of the maps (1 m) resulted in long processing times and produced large amounts of data.

The GIS evaluation procedure was organised in four basic stages: in the first the model inputs, i.e., the thematic maps of technical parameters of the evaluation, were created. In the second stage the evaluation procedures of the 'weighted linear combination' type were structured and solved. The third stage consisted in simulating the two scenarios that represent possible future environmental changes and their effects on the property value on the three islands as a whole. In the last stage, the changes in the value of the residential properties induced by the improvement scenarios were calculated.

The procedures were created within the *Macro Modeler* function of the GIS Idrisi Kilimanjaro software, a graphical modelling environment in which it is possible to assemble and run multi-step analyses (Figure 5.9). The entire logical procedure for analysing the problem and solving it can thus be

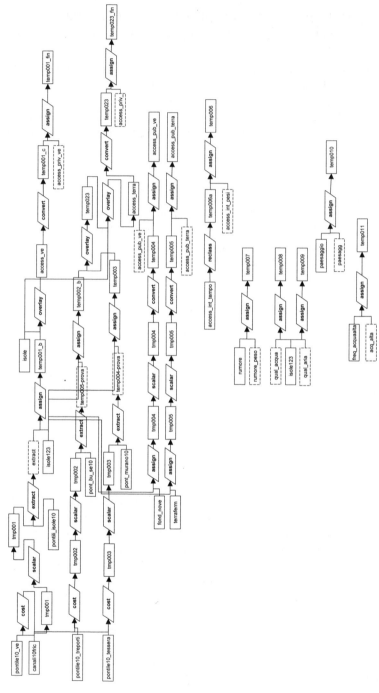

Figure 5.9   The Macro Model used for the creation of the maps

visualised and edited and re-processed at any step, in a consistent and transparent way.

Creating the input maps involved an onerous preliminary phase of acquisition of the basic data and data pre-processing, which led to the formation of a GIS structured according to the evaluation model.

The maps representing the location factors created were: (1) internal accessibility (time); (2) external public and private accessibility (time); (3) landscape (classes); (4) noise (classes); (5) air quality (classes); (6) water quality (classes); (7) frequency of high water (events per year); and (8) availability of public and private services (dummy variable).

The thematic layers created for the analysis phase are (1) value per m^2 for each island; (2) residential housing (binary map and map of built-up areas); and (3) net surface area of the residential properties.

The database was built using existing digital maps and/or by digitising directly information directly from several sources, as in the case of the landscape layer.[6] For example, information on elevation and frequency of high water were integrated to create the layer for flooding frequency. The Local Council Noise Classification Plan[7] was used to identify the classes of exposure to noise on S. Erasmo and Burano, while for the island of Murano we constructed similar buffers along the main canal banks (with decreasing levels of noise as one moves from the banks inland).

The Idrisi module 'Cost Analysis' was used to produce accessibility maps. We began with identifying reference points for the external and internal access to each island: the main landing docks of each island (Fondamente Nuove, Murano Museo, S. Erasmo Capannone and Burano ACTV landing dock) were used for this purpose. Travel times from the official public transport timetables were combined with travel times on foot on the islands into a single 'travel cost' layer. Similarly, the maps of private internal and external accessibility were created with a model of spatial movement in terms of progress along a route, taking into account travel times along the navigable canals at the speed limit of each stretch.[8] External accessibility by private transport was calculated as follows: for simplicity, we used the Fondamente Nuove landing as the reference for trips to and from Venice for all three islands; for trips to the mainland, the reference points were the Treporti landing for S. Erasmo and Burano, and Marco Polo Airport at Tessera for Murano.

Direct on-site measurements and direct digitization were necessary in some cases, such as for surveying the presence and location of specific public and private services for Murano, Burano and S. Erasmo.

The construction of the thematic maps described in the previous section led to creating factor maps. These maps are produced in a raster grid format with a resolution of 1 metre. As already mentioned, these maps represent the quantitative parameters referring to the current status or the possible future situations according to the different hypothesised scenarios.

In order to be used in the evaluation these maps must be re-elaborated using functions that convert, for each cell of the raster grid, the parameters into the corresponding monetary value (in euro per m^2) expressed by scores deriving from the economic evaluation model. For this, an approach based on the creation of look-up tables was adopted, the values of which express the one-to-one relationship between the values of the factor maps and those of the evaluation criteria, in terms of scores to be assigned on the basis of continuous or discrete value functions. This approach represents an advantage of the methodology in terms of facilitating the simulations as the tables can be edited or substituted to simulate the effect of different scenarios, to implement any future developments in the evaluation model or to update the currently available data.

The hierarchical multicriteria combination of the factor maps was done, as mentioned above, with the simplest approach, that is the weighted sum of factor maps (criteria) on a pixel-by-pixel basis, implementing the weights determined within the economic valuation model. The global index value *I* was thus obtained for each cell of the analysed territory,[9] that is all the 1×1 m cells lying within residential buildings, and applying calibration formula (6) to obtain average property values per m^2 (Figure 5.10). The values obtained with the evaluation vary from approximately €1300/m^2 in the island of S. Erasmo to approximately €4200/m^2 in some parts of Murano. The real estate agents operating in Venice have confirmed these values.

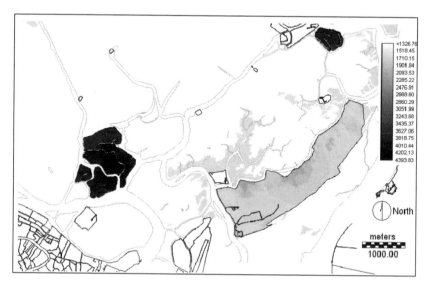

Figure 5.10   Map of current market values in €/m^2

Average values amount to about €4050/m^2 on Murano, €3802/m^2 on Burano and €1812/m^2 on S. Erasmo. The highest values observed for Murano occur in an inner area of the island undisturbed by water traffic but close to the ACTV 'Museo' landing dock, which was used as a reference for evaluating the criterion of internal accessibility. The variation of the values within the island mainly reflects different susceptibility to high water: the area with the maximum values corresponds to an area where the probability of flooding is less than one event every 100 years. Likewise, a second area with high – but not quite as high – values is seen southwest of the first area, in a relatively high part of the island (around the church of S. Pietro). For the same reason relatively high values are generated in the strip of open land in the northwest of the island (Sacca Serenella). This area does not have very good internal accessibility or spectacular views, but has little exposure to high water (less than one event every 100 years).

Burano has a more uniform distribution of values. In this case exposure to high water did not result in any appreciable differences in values, in that the very few data points available place the whole island below the level where at least three floods per year would be expected, thus imputing the worst value for this criterion to the whole island. The differences in values within the island are due to varying degrees of accessibility to the ACTV landing, landscape–urban characteristics and, finally, exposure to noise, with the highest values in the western part of the island.

There is an analogous distribution, albeit with much lower values, on S. Erasmo. The highest values are found not in the village, but rather in the northwest because of the splendid view, good accessibility and elevation above sea level. Against this, the lowest values are recorded at the northern and southern tips of the island, with the exception of the area around the Torre Massimiliana and the beach, because of the higher urban and landscape value.

Finally, the final value map and built-up area map were combined to obtain the map of average values for each building (Figure 5.11) and distribution of the stock of housing.

5.5   THE EVALUATION OF THE IMPROVEMENT SCENARIOS

The model was used to estimate the effects of different public investment projects for the northern Lagoon of Venice. We examined two public investment scenarios currently under discussion or construction that may have an impact on property values on the islands. The first alters the current modes of access to the islands through the construction of a 'subway' under the bottom of the Lagoon; the second eliminates all flooding problems with

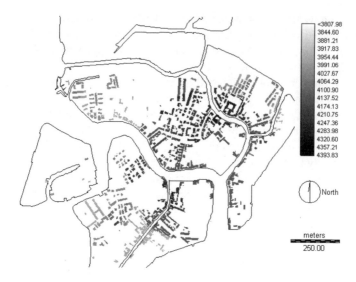

Figure 5.11   Map of average values of residential buildings: prices in €/m²
            (Murano)

water levels of 120 cm or less on all three islands by requiring that all ground
floors be raised.

The changes brought by the public investment scenarios were estimated
for each indicator. These changes affect mainly the location factors. Table 5.2
displays the factors taken into account and the ways in which the scenarios
affect the island contexts. Factors that are unaffected by the public works are
indicated with a '–', and those that slightly or significantly improve, with a
'+' or a '++', respectively.

Our model computes, for the whole area, absolute values and changes in
values associated with the public works. The spatial distribution of changes
and absolute values can be represented in two ways: by showing either
average values per m², or the value of the entire existing building.

First Scenario: A Subway Under the Lagoon

The first scenario changes dramatically the current accessibility system and
implies the regeneration of the Arsenale area with the creation of the so-
called *Città Bipolare* (Bipolar City).[10] Most likely, a 'subway' will connect
the Arsenale with Tessera and Mestre town centre, via the Fondamente
Nuove and Murano. Access to Murano would therefore be facilitated; the
island would become easily and quickly reachable from the mainland and
from Venice (Fondamente Nuove), and from the developing area of the

Table 5.2   Indicators considered in the outlining of the scenarios

Factors		Scenario 1 Subway under the Lagoon	Scenario 2 Protection from high waters < 120 cm
Access to Venice			
	Murano	+	−
	Burano	−	−
	S. Erasmo	−	−
Access to the mainland			
	Murano	++	−
	Burano	−	−
	S. Erasmo	−	−
Internal access			
	Murano	−	+
	Burano	−	+
	S. Erasmo	−	+
Exposure to high water		−	++
Public services		−	−
Private services		−	−
Air quality		+	−
Water quality		+	−
Level of noise		++	−

Notes: − unvaried, + slight improvement, ++ significant improvement.

Arsenale. The impacts of this new access route on the other islands of the northern Lagoon would be positive and override the current access modes: the point of arrival of the subway at Murano and that of the water transport system to Burano and S. Erasmo would be integrated within a multimodal system, and this would change the current orientation of these islands towards the mainland of Cavallino and make access to the Mestre town centre or Tessera more important. From the geographical modelling point of view, this scenario can be considered as the effect of a 'point perturbation' on the territory, that is, directly focussed on the access to Murano, given that external access to the island will change significantly. Within the model of the formation of property values these transformations would affect the following attributes of Murano:[11]

1.   Access:
   •   from the mainland: the increased number of trips and shortened travel times justify an 'optimal' judgement in place of the current 'good'.

- from Venice: the current judgement, in comparison with the other islands, is already 'optimal' and would therefore not change.
2. Noise: the strip along the Murano Grand Canal and along the west coast of the island, which currently experience high noise levels due to private and public transport, would receive a better judgement, being upgraded from 'bad' to 'average'.

The subway project produces a clear effect on the values on Murano due to the improvement in accessibility from the outside. The 'optimal' level is therefore reached for links with both Venice and the mainland, thanks to the more frequent and rapid connections. Estimated values also increase in the strips along the major canals of the island, which benefit from the reduction in boat traffic in terms of reduced noise levels. The value increases generated in the first scenario, for Murano, range from 5 to 6 percent, with higher values in the areas along the southern (Colonna area) and northern canals (Sacca Serenella) of the island where initial values were lower.

Second Scenario: Protection from Low to Medium High Water

The second scenario hypothesises a generalised defence of the whole Lagoon from high water, and simulates interventions that raise the banks and/or defence of low-lying land on the three islands to prevent flooding. In the model, these were captured into the attribute measuring the frequency with which a site is exposed to flooding. Since it involves the three islands, this scenario represents a general perturbation effect.

Based on projects and work underway on the islands, we assumed that the effects of the interventions at Murano and Burano these would be experienced in areas lower than 120 cm above sea level, whereas for S. Erasmo we assumed that all areas below 160 cm above sea level would be affected by the interventions. Based on these assumptions, the estimate of flooding frequency is reduced to once per year for Murano and Burano and once every 10 years for S. Erasmo.

The differences in values generated with this simulation are quite small for the islands of Burano and Murano (0.1 percent). The effect is uniform over the entire island of Burano, whereas in Murano the effects are limited to some areas which lie below 120 cm above sea level. On S. Erasmo, where on the one hand the improvement is greater and, on the other, the initial property values were much lower, increases in value vary between 5.5 and 7 percent, with an average of 5.9 percent.

The relatively small effects on property values estimated with the evaluation model on Murano and Burano are due to several reasons. First, the simulated improvement does not reduce the number of floods drastically: at

120 cm above sea level there is still a probability of flooding once per year. Second, the effect is slight because the model was applied to the values of entire buildings and not just to the ground floors: high water has an obviously greater effect on the value of ground floor properties. Therefore higher increases would be obtained if ground floors alone had been taken into account. Third and last, it should be remembered that this study only considered residential properties, so the economic effects on businesses are excluded.

5.6   CONCLUSIONS

Our evaluation model for estimating property assets based on the hierarchical decomposition and recomposition of the characteristics determining the value gives reasonable results for the main islands of the Venice Lagoon. We consider the results encouraging for future operational applications and refining of the methodology.

The most important advantage of the model is the possibility of obtaining rapid evaluations of the economic effects of policies for urban regeneration and protection from flooding and erosion and showing their distribution over

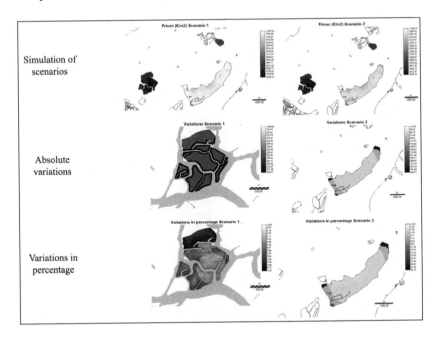

Figure 5.12   Maps of scenarios and differences in values generated

the territory. The integration of the economic evaluation and geographical models offers interesting synergies. The prices and their changes predicted by our value function are realistic, and their spatial distribution realistically mirrors the differences observed in the islands of the Venice Lagoon. Furthermore, the simulation of the interventions provides realistic estimates of the economic value of the benefits of urban improvement interventions.

The procedure is also transparent and intuitive, fully uses all the information available, both qualitative and quantitative, and rigorously incorporates the expertise of those familiar with the socio-economic reality studied here. Of particular interest is the possibility of continuously refining the hierarchical model as new market information and/or new expert judgements become available, via the recalibration of the value functions and new simulations of the spatial model. At the same time, the GIS information here used may be improved through the integration of new databases and, where necessary, more specific surveys. The synergies between a more accurate value function and more detailed location data will definitively improve the quality of the output of the proposed procedure.

Obviously this approach has certain limitations which can in part be attributed to the hierarchical approach to the property evaluations, as already expressed by Rosato et al. (2002). Specifically, it is somewhat subjective, in the sense that it is based on the judgements of experts, who, despite careful selection of the panel, .may be not entirely representative of the market. The model could, therefore, be improved if we were able to interview more experts and cover the market more widely, and if we were able to acquire more market data. This would permit a more precise estimate of the value function, moving the evaluation from the expert judgement base to the econometric one. In this regard, it must be remembered that the model used in this chapter should not be considered, in general, a substitute for the more accurate classic hedonic model, but that it can provide useful support when the low availability of market data does not permit any other type of value function appraisal.

NOTES

1.   Interviews were conducted with real estate agents operating in Venice who are familiar with the specific situation of the islands. The authors would like to express special gratitude to each of them, and especially to Riccardo Maione.
2.   The authors are grateful to the Urban Planning Board, and the Tidal Forecast and Signalling Office of the Venice City Council, CORILA and INSULA for making their digital elaborations available.
3.   This is confirmed by the fact that in recent years large houses (which tend to be higher priced than normal) have remained unsold.

4. The weights, in an additive multiple criteria model, represent the *trade-off* between the different evaluation parameters. In the case of models of the *weighted sum* type, which assume independence of preferences, the weights can be considered scale factors (Bouyssou et al., 2000).
5. The initial attempt to find homogeneous value judgements for all three islands (Murano, Burano and S. Erasmo) met some resistance from the panel, who denied the possibility of reaching uniform weights for such different contexts. The preferences were therefore expressed relative to each island, leading to three separate 'prototypes' of the value model. However, at the end of the evaluations it was argued that the differences between the three contexts did not translate into the weights assigned to the different categories of criteria, which resulted as being practically identical in the three models. These were therefore re-aggregated in a single hierarchy model.
6. For the landscape layer we used aerial photographs of the Lagoon provided by CORILA and the Regional Technical Numerical Map, which we digitized ourselves. We worked with six landscape categories: historical centre, recent scattered buildings, historic scattered buildings, fallow land, gardens and farmland.
7. The plan can be consulted on the Venice City Council website at http://194.243.104.176/website/rumore/viewer.htm (last access: November 2005).
8. The following travel speed factors were adopted: 11 km/h for private boats (average speed limit on the channels in the lagoon), 5 km/h for the walking speed on the islands, and 12 km/h for travel by bicycle on S. Erasmo.
9. The Weighted Linear Combination was done using a mathematical model built with the modulus *Image Calculator* in which the summation notation operations of the products of the factor maps and relative weights were combined.
10. The project '*Città Bipolare*' intends to connect the area of the Arsenale in the historic centre of Venice with the International Airport on the mainland. The connection will consist of a subway line running under the Lagoon for transport of persons and goods. See http://www.comune.venezia.it/urbanistica/home.asp (last access: November 2005).
11. The effects on the other islands are not considered because the available projects do not permit an adequate evaluation of the impacts.

REFERENCES

Bouyssou, D., Th. Marchant, P. Perny, M. Pirlot and Ph. Tsoukiàs Vincke (2000), *Evaluation and Decision Models: a Critical Perspective*, Dordrecht: Kluwer Academic Publishers.

Chattopadhyay, S. (1999), 'Demand for Air Quality in Chicago', *Land Economics*, **75**(1), 22–38.

Curto, R. (1993), 'Qualità edilizia, qualità ambientale e mercato immobiliare: un'applicazione della Multiple Regression Analysis (MRA) al caso della città storica', XIV Conferenza Italiana di Scienze Regionali, Bologna 4–5 October 1993.

Curto, R. (1994), 'La quantificazione e costruzione di variabili qualitative stratificate nella Multiple Regression Analysis (MRA) applicata ai mercati immobiliari', *Aestimum*, special number, Florence, June–December.

Garrod, G.D. and K.G. Willis (1992), 'Valuing Goods Characteristics: an Application of the Hedonic Price Method to Environmental Attributes', *Journal of Environmental Management*, **34**(1), 59–76.

Giupponi, C. and L. Coletto (1993), 'Creazione di mappe di "suitability" e rilievi sperimentali in ambiente GIS per il re di quaglie (Crex crex L.) in provincia di Belluno. L'informazione territoriale e la dimensione tempo', 7a Conferenza Nazionale ASITA, II, 1209–14.

Rosato, P. and G. Stellin (2000), 'A Multiparametric Model for Evaluating the Weight of Externalities on the Formation of Property Value', in P. Brandon, P. Lombardi and S. Perera (eds), *Cities and Sustainability: Sustaining our Cultural Heritage*, The Millennium Conference, University of Moratuwa: Katubedda, Sri Lanka.

Rosato, P., C. D'Apaos, G. Marella and G. Stellin (2002), 'La valutazione ex-ante degli effetti sul valore immobiliare di interventi di salvaguardia ambientale: un approccio edonico-gerarchico', *La Valutazione degli Investimenti sul Territorio*, Atti del XXXII Incontro di studio del Ce.S.E.T,Venice, 11 October.

Rosen, S. (1974), 'Hedonic Prices and Implicit Markets: Product Differentiation in Pure Competition', *Journal of Political Economy*, **82**(1), 34–55.

Saaty, T. (1980), *The Analytic Hierarchy Process*, New York: McGraw Hill.

Scarpa, R. (1995), 'Metodo del prezzo edonico per la stima delle variazioni di benessere per beni pubblici: lo stato dell'arte e l'applicabilità in Italia', *Aestimum*, **33**, 93–121.

6. Valuing the Implementation Costs of Ecosystem Friendly Clam Fishing Practices in the Venice Lagoon: Results from a Conjoint Choice Survey

Paulo A.L.D. Nunes, Luca Rossetto and Arianne de Blaeij

6.1 INTRODUCTION

The Lagoon of Venice is a complex wetland coastal zone characterized by the presence of dynamic and open systems, involving terrestrial and aquatic, freshwater and marine ecosystems. The introduction of exotic marine species into the Lagoon has resulted in significant environmental damage to the lagoon ecosystem. In this chapter we focus on the environmental damages associated with the introduction of the exotic clam species *Tapes philippinarum*.

Many of these environmental damages are associated with the fact that this exotic clam species has a very high commercial value relative to other Lagoon native species. Such a market price incentive brought important changes in clam management practices. These include the abandon of the traditional, manual rakes system in favor of fishing management practices based on the use of mechanical rakes systems, such as the use of suction dredgers and vibrating rakes for harvesting clams. The latter is responsible for important environmental damages, including the erosion of the Lagoon bottom the reduction of the clam and native fish stocks in the Lagoon. In this chapter we focus on measuring the monetary costs of clam management policies that impose reverting to traditional, and hence less environmental damaging technologies.

The organization of the chapter is as follows. Section 6.2 describes recent clam fishing practices and the associated environmental damages. Section 6.3 explores the use of an economic model to study fishermen's behavior in general and the choice of fish management practices in particular. Section 6.4 links the selected theoretical model to an empirical exercise, using a contingent choice questionnaire to conduct an economic valuation exercise. Section 6.5 discusses the range of the economic estimates and evaluates these for different policy scenarios. Section 6.6 concludes.[1]

6.2   STATEMENT OF THE NATURAL RESOURCE PROBLEM

Clam Fish Management Practices in the Lagoon of Venice

Clam fishing takes place in Lagoon canals as well as in water areas of the Lagoon dedicated to fish farming. The clam fishing activity involves two native species: *Tapes decussatus*, and *Scrobicularia plana*. Originally, clam fishing relied on manual rakes and triangular iron dredges, also known by the local fishermen population as 'cassa'. Such a traditional fishing practice goes back to the *Serenissima Republic* and was accompanied by many restrictions. For example, nets had to conform to pre-determined models, their mesh needed to be of a certain dimension, and fishing was absolutely forbidden in some periods of the year (see Ninni, 1940; Pellizzato and Giorgiutti, 1997). Until recently, clam fishing activity in the Lagoon continued to be heavily regulated. The local authority together with fishing cooperatives controlled the fishing activity by fixing prices and amounts of catch, as well as defining and managing specific areas in the lagoon (Bevilacqua, 1998). Furthermore, until the end of World War II motorboats were limited to the port of Chioggia. Only rowing and sailing boats were allowed elsewhere in the Lagoon. Their main fishing systems were limited to trawl nets, fyke nets, gillnets, seine nets, and other manual equipment (Brunelli, 1940; Zolezzi, 1944).

Today more than 2000 people are employed in the clam fishery sector. The current clam fishing practice is characterized by an open access situation. In other words, in order to fish in the Lagoon, it is necessary to buy a license but there is no limit on the total licenses issued per fishing season or the quantity harvested. This, together with the high revenues associated with clam fishing, has encouraged an increasing fishing effort, resulting in the adoption of technological intensive equipment and the progressive abandon of the traditional fishing practices (Pellizzato and Giorgiutti, 1997). Mechanical and vibrating fishing equipment, including the use of suction dredgers and vibrant rakes for harvesting clams (see Figure 6.1), has become increasingly used in the Lagoon.

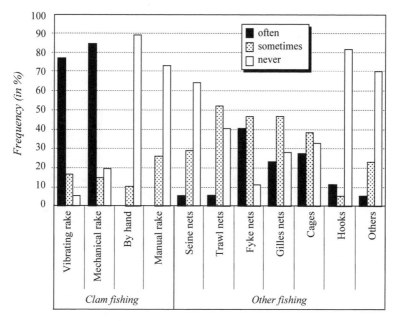

Source: Boatto et al. (2002)

Figure 6.1   Diffusion of fishing equipments in the Lagoon of Venice

The Introduction of the Exotic Clam Species

The clam fishing effort in the Lagoon has strongly increased since 1983, after the introduction of *Tapes philippinarum*, also called the Manila clam, an Asian species that has rapidly adapted to the Lagoon environment. It is now responsible for colonising large shallow areas and competing directly in the ecological niche with the native clam species. The relatively high market price of this species, ranging from €4.06 to €7.15 a kilogram, has contributed to an increase of the Manila clam fishing profitability. Because of the open access situation, many operators have recently entered the clam fishing sector. Most of them have adopted mechanical equipment, such as the vibrating rake technology, which is used exclusively for harvesting of this shellfish. This has led to a significant increase in the clam fishing effort. For example, in 1998, the fishing fleet was comprised of about 600 vessels, 84 of which used the vibrating rake technology. A vibrating rake is equipped with an electrical cage that shakes and filters sediment, harvesting 150 to 200 kg of clam shellfish a day (Solidoro, 2000). Manila clams live on the bottom of the Lagoon and for this reason they are very sensitive to water movement and to the deposit and accumulation of sediments (Orel et al., 1997). Harvesting this shellfish requires moving sediment, and mechanical and vibrating fishing equipment has greatly increased these sediment movements. The adoption of these vibrating technologies has, therefore, brought unavoidable negative environmental impacts on the morphology processes and marine life functions of the Lagoon (ICRAM, 1994; Pranovi and Giovanardi, 1994; Sfriso, 2000). This has reduced the stock of fish and clams. For example, market data shows that the supply has decreased by approximately 40 percent between 2000 and 2001 due to a reduction in clam stocks (see Granzotto et al., 2002, for additional details).

In this context, the economic valuation of alternative clam management practices is of central importance since it sheds light on the involved welfare changes. These can be compared with the benefits derived from protecting the lagoon from environmental damage across alternative policy scenarios (see van den Bergh et al., 2002; Nunes and van den Bergh, 2002). Modeling fishermen behavior, the cornerstone for any welfare assessment, will be discussed in detail in the next section.

6.3   MODELING FISHERMAN BEHAVIOR

Random Utility Model

In this section, we provide a framework for modeling the responses to our conjoint choice questions. The underlying assumption when assessing the economic valuation of alternative clam management practices is that the monetary value reflects fishermen's behavior. In other words, the economic valuation exercise reflects fishermen preferences regarding the choice of alternative clam fishing management practices. Let U_{ij} be the utility of the ith fishing alternative for the jth individual fisherman. Furthermore, we assume that each utility value can be partitioned into two components: a systematic component, V_{ij}, and a random component, ε_{ij}. Formally,

$$U_{ij} = V_{ij} + \varepsilon_{ij} \qquad (6.1)$$

In addition, we assume that fishermen will choose the clam management practice that yields the highest utility. In other words, the individual fisherman j will choose fishing alternative i if and only if:

$$U_{ij} > U_{hj} \quad \forall i, h \in A \text{ with } i \neq h \qquad (6.2)$$

Combining equations (6.1) and (6.2), we know that a management practice i is chosen if and only if

$$\left(V_{ij} + \varepsilon_{ij}\right) > \left(V_{hj} + \varepsilon_{hj}\right), \text{ or } \left(V_{ij} - V_{hj}\right) > \left(\varepsilon_{hj} - \varepsilon_{ij}\right) \tag{6.3}$$

Since we cannot observe $(\varepsilon_{hj} - \varepsilon_{ij})$, we cannot exactly assess if $(V_{ij} - V_{hj}) > (\varepsilon_{hj} - \varepsilon_{ij})$. Therefore, we only can make statements about a choice of a fish management practice up to a certain point. In other words, we need to calculate the probability that $(\varepsilon_{hj} - \varepsilon_{ij})$ will be less than $(V_{ij} - V_{hj})$:

$$\text{Prob}\left(x_{ij} \mid s_j, A\right) = \text{Prob}_{ij} =$$
$$= \text{Prob}\left[\left\{\varepsilon(s, x_{hj}) - \varepsilon(s, x_{ij})\right\} < \left\{V(s, x_{hj}) - V(s, x_{ij})\right\}\right] \forall i, h \in A \tag{6.4}$$

that is the probability that a fisherman will choose x_i, i clam management practice, equals the probability that the difference between the random component of the utility function is less than the difference between the systematic component of the utility function across the two clam management practices under consideration. In other words, we set up a random utility model formulation (see MacFadden, 1974).

We do not know the actual distribution of $(\varepsilon_{hj} - \varepsilon_{ij})$ across the population. However, we assume that this unobserved distribution is related to a particular statistical distribution. There are many statistical distributions available, but the one most frequently used in random utility modeling is the extreme-value type I distribution. With the help of this family distribution we will able to translate the unobserved random index $(\varepsilon_{hj} - \varepsilon_{ij})$ into a probability that helps understand fisherman's utility (see MacFadden, 1984; Hanemann, 1984). Formally, we can express the probability of choosing clam management practice i as follows

$$\text{Prob}_i = \frac{1}{\sum_{h=1}^{H} \exp\left(V_h - V_i\right)} \tag{6.5}$$

In other words, equation (6.5) that defines the basic empirical specification regarding fisherman's behavior that is consistent with the random utility model. This is referred to in this chapter as the Conditional Logit (CLM) model (see Louviere et al., 2000, for more details). The task is now to proceed with the estimation of the utility parameters as described in equation (6.5). This task will be discussed in the following sub-section.

Estimation of the Parameters of Fisherman's Utility

The first step refers to the specification of a functional form of the utility expression $V(\cdot)$, i.e., the relationship between the various attributes of the fishing management practice and observed fishermen choices. We work with a linear, additive form that maps the multidimensional X attribute vector into a unidimensional V utility (rating). Formally,

$$V_{ij} \left(= \sum_k \beta_{ik} X_{ikj} \right) \tag{6.6}$$

Given estimates of the utility parameters β an estimate of V_{ij} is computed by taking the β_s and the X_s for individual j and alternative i.

We use the maximum likelihood estimation method to estimate the utility parameters of the closed-form CLM model. We find the $\hat{\beta}$ that maximize

$$L = \prod_{j=1}^{J} \prod_{h=1}^{H} \text{Prob}_{hj}^{d_{hj}} \tag{6.7}$$

with d_{hj} defining a dummy variable such that $d_{hj} = 1$ if alternative h is chosen by individual j and equal zero otherwise, or the log likelihood function

$$\underset{\beta}{\text{Max}}\, L^* = \sum_{j=1}^{J} \sum_{h=1}^{H} d_{hj} \log\left(\text{Prob}_{hj}\right) \tag{6.8}$$

Combining equations (6.5), (6.6) and (6.8) we have,

$$\underset{\beta}{\text{Max}}\, L^* = \sum_{j=1}^{J} \sum_{h=1}^{H} d_{hj} \log \left(\dfrac{1}{\displaystyle\sum_{h=1}^{H} \sum_{k} \beta_{ik} X_{ikj}} \right) \tag{6.9}$$

Where the β estimates are interpreted as the weight of the each attribute in the utility expression. This theoretical model allows us to compare expected maximum utility levels across different fish management practices and thus rank them. Therefore, according to the CLM model formulation the expected utility of a particular alternative i is

$$\log \sum_i e^{V_i} \tag{6.10}$$

Bearing equation (6.10) in mind, one can express the expected value from an initial management condition, denoted by 0, to a new management condition, denoted by 1, as follows,

$$\text{WTP} = \frac{1}{\lambda}\left[\log \sum_i e^{V_i^0} - \log \sum_i e^{V_i^1}\right] \qquad (6.11)$$

where WTP (willingness to pay) denotes the economic welfare impact of the management change, or income compensating variation, that makes the individual as well off in the original situation, V_i^0, as he will be under the new management situation, V_i^1. λ is the marginal utility expressed in monetary terms, or simply marginal utility of money. In the present valuation exercise, λ is derived from the CLM linear model as the price of the fishing permit coefficient estimate. However, the price of the fishing permit has negative coefficient, which reflects that a higher cost of the fishing permit results in lower utilities. In order to change this into the marginal utility of money we need to multiply this price CLM coefficient estimate by -1, that is

$$\text{WTP} = -\frac{1}{\beta_{price}}\left[\log \sum_i e^{V_i^0} - \log \sum_i e^{V_i^1}\right] \qquad (6.12)$$

Now are we ready to apply this model to predict fishermen choice behavior. We need, however, to identify other fishing-related attributes that together with the price of the fishing permit characterize the utility function of the fishermen. This constitutes an important task in our empirical work and it will be discussed in detail in the next section.

6.4   PRELIMINARY SURVEY DESIGN AND QUESTIONNAIRE FORMULATION

Identification of the Attributes and Measured Levels

The alternatives in the conjoint choice questions are described by three attributes: (1) fishing system; (2) size of the fishable area, and (3) the cost of the annual fishing permit. We arrived at these attributes after discussions with biologists, economists, policy makers and the local fishermen. The discussion also provided valuable information on possible different levels of the attributes, which are reported in Table 6.1. These attributes are interpreted as major determinants entering in the fishermen utility function and are thus the components of any policy package for regulating clam fishing practices and their environmental damage in the Lagoon.

Three fishing regimes were considered for analysis. We refer to the

Table 6.1   List of the attributes used in the clam fishing stated choice value
            application

---

1. Fishing area:
    *   3.5 hectares
    *   10 hectares
2. Fishing systems:
    *   Traditional: manual rake and fyke nets
    *   Medium intensive (as today): mechanical rake + fyke nets
    *   Intensive: vibrant rake
3. Price of annual permit (originally stated in the survey in Italian Lira):
    *   258 euro
    *   517 euro
    *   775 euro
    *   4649 euro
    *   5165 euro
    *   5682 euro

'traditional' system, the 'present situation' system, and the 'vibrating and scraper' system. The traditional system is characterized by the use of small boats and the exclusive use of manual fishing nets. For this reason, it is not associated with important environmental damage, but it is not very attractive to fishermen since its profitability is low, due to low clam catch rates. Alternatively, the vibrating and scrapers fishing system, as the name suggests, makes intensive use of mechanical suction, vibrating and scraper equipment. This equipment allows fishermen to have very high catch rates, at least in the short term, and is thus associated with the highest profitability. However this system is also associated with the highest environmental damage to the Lagoon due to scraping the lagoon bottom, which causes significant damage to the marine ecosystem, such as destruction of clam nurseries. The fishery system that is identified as the 'present situation' is characterized by a mix of both regimes, and therefore interpreted as an intermediate system, both from the fishermen's profitability and the environmental damage perspective (see Boatto et al., 2002, for a further analysis).

In addition, the size and the location of fishing areas play an important role on the fishermen choice behavior. We consider two levels for the size of the fishing area: 3.5 hectares and an area of 10 hectares. Finally, we consider a price vector for the fishing permits that range from €258 to €5682 a year. We arrived at this price vector after discussions with experts and authorities, following the current price of a fishing permit and indications on the important profitability gap that would emerge across the different clam fishing technologies under consideration. In other words, we need to be sure that the proposed price range is in accordance with the changes involved so as to ensure the credibility of the stated choice valuation question.

Conjoint Choice Questionnaire

In our questionnaire, we describe two alternative fishing management practices and ask respondents to state which one they prefer (see Table 6.2 for an example of a contingent choice question). Each respondent faces one such pair of fishing management practices. The respondent is informed that the two fishing practices presented in the scenario are the only possibilities available for the next fishing season and he is asked to choose one, including also the option to choose 'neither' as an answer.

We elected not to ask several conjoint questions to each respondent because this type of questionnaire was a novelty, both for the fishermen and for the interviewers. Furthermore, we were told by the interviewers that in this particular survey, where the full questionnaire coincides with the conjoint question, an additional conjoint choice question would not be fully understood by the fisherman since doing so would depict another 'fishing possibility set' and create comprehension or credibility problems for the entire valuation exercise. Finally, since we decided to administer the survey to fishermen intercepted on site, it was important to keep the questionnaire as short as possible. Therefore, we increased the number of observations not by asking several conjoint choice questions to each respondent, but by interviewing more fishermen.

Our goal is to use the data about the respondent's choices to value the attributes of the fishing management practices. The coefficients of the attributes are the implicit marginal prices of the attributes themselves. To study the degree in which preferences for fishing management practices differ between segments in the fishermen population, we define two fishing

Table 6.2   Example of a stated choice question

Assuming that the following fishing management practices were the only practices available, which one of the two listed below would you consider more attractive for you, if either?

	Practice A	Practice B
Fishing area (ha)	3.5	3.5
Fishing system	Mechanical rake + fyke nets	Vibrant rake
Price of annual permit	258 euro	4649 euro
	Neither □	

segments corresponding to two types of ownership regimes in the Venice Lagoon. The first consists of vessels jointly managed by cooperatives. The second consists of smaller and individually owned vessels. While the former are currently subject to a set of cooperative managing rules, the latter are often managed by private individuals, who predominantly fish to supplement their income. In addition, some of these individuals are unauthorized or illegal fishermen. By creating interactions between the dummy for the fishing regime of the individual and the attributes, we hope to elicit the preferences of fishermen who operate in collective areas and who operate in individual areas. Valuation results are presented and discussed in the next section.

6.5   SURVEY VALUATION RESULTS

The survey was carried out in summer 2001. Our sample selection rule was to intercept fishermen returning from a fishing outing in various parts of Lagoon, namely the northern area, including Burano, and the southern area. We elected this sampling frame because it allows us to obtain a sample of respondents that represents as close as possible the total universe of Lagoon's fishermen, and its distribution across collective and individual al fishing regimes. (We declined to use a sampling frame based on a list of the operators with a license because (i) the licenses are not issued for exclusive fishing in the Lagoon (and thus the universe of fishermen would also include open-sea fishermen), and (ii) doing so would fail to capture those who fish without a permit.)

The questionnaire was administered in person. The interviewers were researchers with good knowledge of local fishing conditions and practices. The interviewers contacted 193 fishermen, 114 of which completed the questionnaire. The participation rate is therefore about 60 percent. Figure 6.2 shows the descriptive statistics of the surveys responses.

Our questionnaire contains only one section, the conjoint choice question. The empirical specification of the random utility model assumes that the systematic utility component is a linear function of the price of the permit, area of fishing concession, and the type of fishing system. The estimation results are presented in Table 6.3a. First, all explanatory variables estimates are statistically significant at the 10 percent level or better. Second, the probability of choosing a management practice is positively related to the dimension of the fishing concession area. Third, the choice of a management practice is negatively related to the price of the license. Finally, the choice of a management practice reveals it is positively related to its degree of technology, measured in a three-level attribute. In other words, any policy

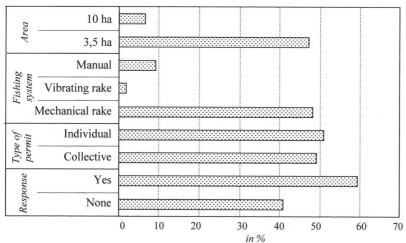

Source: Boatto et al. (2002)

Figure 6.2 Descriptive statistics of contingent choice questionnaire

Table 6.3a Stated preferences model estimates

Variable	Estimate	p-value
Price of the permit	−0.0006	0.000 [*]
Area [(a)]	0.3340	0.005 [*]
Fishing system [(b)]	−0.6017	0.085 [**]
Adjusted R^2	0.1911	.

Table 6.3b Economic welfare measurement

WTP for	Point estimate	95% confidence interval [(d)]
Area	568 € (1.70) [(c)]	[125 € ; 1732 €]
Fishing system [(b)]	1005 € (1.36) [(c)]	[−119 € ; 3236 €]

Notes: Calculations are performed using the multinomial logit procedure in *LIMDEP*[®].
   [*] [(**)] Statistically significant at 5% (10%).
   [(a)] Coded as a dummy variable.
   [(b)] Ordinal categorical variable with 0 = today (benchmark), 1 = manual, and −1 = vibrant.
   [(c)] t-values are computed using the delta method.
   [(d)] CI is estimated using the asymptotic t-test method as described by Armstrong et al. (2001).

option that is characterized by the exclusive use of a vibrant rake is, ceteris paribus, associated with a positive impact in fishermen's welfare and thus connected with a higher probability of choice.

The amount of money that an individual fisherman would be willing to pay for a change in the dimension of the fishing concession is €568 per year. In addition, Table 6.3b shows that the economic welfare impact of a change in the clam management practice, due to a change in the fishing system amounts to €1005. In other words, an individual fisherman would be willing to pay €1005 for a change from today's fishing situation towards a fishing practice exclusively based on the vibrant rake system.

In Table 6.4a we report an additional model specification, which includes interactions of operations in collective regime and operations in individual

Table 6.4a   Stated preferences model estimates with cross effects for the fishing regime

Variable	Estimate	p-value
Price of the permit	−0.0007	0.008[*]
Area [a]	0.5814	0.008[*]
Fishing system [b]	−1.7661	0.013
Regime [c] × price	−0.0011	0.316
Regime [c] × area	0.5856	0.492
Regime [c] × system	4.2996	0.052[*]
Adjusted R^2	0.3023	.

Table 6.4b   Economic welfare measurement

WTP for	Point estimate	95% confidence interval [e]
Area	811 € (1.97) [d]	[225 € ; 2917 €]
Fishing system [b]	2456 € (1.84) [d]	[403 € ; 8340 €]

Notes: Calculations are performed using the multinomial logit procedure in *LIMDEP*®.
[*] [**] Statistically significant at 5% (10%).
[a]   Coded as a dummy variable.
[b]   Ordinal categorical variable (0 = today, 1 = manual, −1 = vibrant).
[c]   Regime is a dummy variable with 1 denoting regime cooperative and 0 regime individual.
[d]   t-values are computed using the delta method.
[e]   CI is estimated using the asymptotic t-test method as described by Armstrong et al. (2001).

regime (individual characteristics) with the attributes of the stated preferences model. As before, estimation results show that as the price of the permit increases, utility decreases. Similarly, as the concession area increases, utility increases. In addition, regime interactions coefficients are added to the main effects for fishermen who operate in the cooperative regime. Since fishermen who operate in the individual regime are coded as zero, the result indicate that fishermen who operate in the cooperative regime are more sensitive to the price of the permits. For the population that operates in the individual regime, a price increase negatively impacts utility and the coefficient is -0.0007. In contrast, the fishermen population who operate in the cooperative regime this impact decreases to -0.0028 ($= -0.0007 - 0.0011$). Independently of the type of fishermen, price estimates are statistically significant indicating that, everything else held constant, fishermen continue to receive more utility from lower prices.

We can also observe that a change in the dimension of the concession area has a stronger impact on the utility of the population of the fishermen who operate in the cooperative regime than on fishermen who operate in the individual regime, 1.167 and 0.5814 respectively. Finally, estimation results show that the welfare impact of a change in the fishing system differs substantially across the two fishermen populations, and is particularly strong for the fishermen who operate in the cooperative regime. Such parameter estimates are reflected in the economic welfare measurements – see Table 6.4b. In fact, when comparing these valuation results with the ones presented in Table 6.3b, which represents the pooled fisherman population, we can observe that the population of fishermen who operate in the cooperative regime present higher monetary valuation for an increase in the dimension of the fishing concession, which is now valued at €811. In addition, this population is characterized by a stronger willingness to pay for a change from today's fishing situation towards a fishing practice exclusively based on the vibrant rake system, which is now estimated at €2456.

Finally we address the following policy question: How much would it cost to pay all fishermen, independently of their current fishing equipment, to adopt such an environmental friendly clam fishing technology? According to our calculations – see Table 6.5a and 6.5b – the financial costs associated with the adoption of such a policy is estimated to be €5904 per fisherman per year, ranging up to a maximum of €80 160 per fisherman per year, depending on the type of fishermen population and current management practice. Combining this value with the total number of fishermen currently operating in the Lagoon of Venice, the total welfare loss associated with the adoption of the manual clam fishing technology is estimated to be at €11.8 million per year. This information is crucial for the evaluation of the costs due to the adoption of a clam fishing system based on the use of manual rakes. In this

Table 6.5a　Model estimation with cross effects for the fishing regime (a)

Variable	Estimate	p-value
Price of the permit	−0.0003	0.030 [*]
Area	0.2787	0.031 [*]
Fishing system = manual	−1.8644	0.013 [*]
Regime [(b)] × Price	−0.0015	0.170
Regime [(b)] × area	0.8888	0.292
Regime [(b)] × manual	4.4041	0.048 [*]
Adjusted R^2	0.3023	.

Table 6.5b　Economic welfare measurement

WTP for	Point estimate	95% Confidence Interval [(d)]
Fishing system = Manual	−5904 € (1.66) [(c)]	[−80 160 € ; −953 €]

Notes: [*] Statistically significant at 5%.
　　[(a)] Calculations are performed using the MULTINOMIAL LOGIT procedure in *LIMDEP*®.
　　[(b)] Regime is a dummy variable with 1 denoting regime cooperative and 0 regime individual.
　　[(c)] t-values are computed using the delta method.
　　[(d)] CI is estimated using the asymptotic t-test method as described by Armstrong et al. (2001).

context, this figure can be regarded as a lower bound to the benefits of implementation of a clam fishing system associated with the lowest environmental damage in the Lagoon.

6.6　CONCLUSIONS

This chapter focused on the economic valuation of alternative clam management practices in the Lagoon of Venice, which we do by gathering information through a survey of commercial fisherman. The estimation results show that: (1) fishermen bear a utility change whenever the price of the annual permit, the fishing technological system and the dimension of the fishing area change; (2) the probability of the choice of a management practice is positively related to the dimension of the fishing concession area and the level of technology. In other words, any policy option that is characterized by the exclusive use of the vibrating and scrapers fishery system is associated with a positive impact on the fishermen's welfare. Furthermore, (3) the choice of a management practice reveals to be negatively related to its associated costs, reflecting the fact that higher prices of the annual permit result in lower utilities.

In addition, monetary valuation results show that fishermen's willingness to pay for a larger fishing area is approximately €568 per year. Second, an individual fisherman is willing to accept €1005 for a change from the present fishing practice situation towards a fishing practice exclusively based on the manual rake system. Third, the welfare impact of a change in clam management practices differs substantially across the population of fishermen that operates in the cooperative regime and the population of fishermen that operates in the individual regime. The former hold a higher monetary valuation for an increase in the dimension of the fishing concession, which is now valued at €811, and a greater willingness to accept for a change from today's fishing situation towards a fishing practice exclusively based on manual rake systems, which is now estimated at €2456. Finally, we estimate the welfare loss associated with the adoption of a clam management policy based exclusively on manual rakes to be to €11.8 million per year. This figure can be regarded as a lower bound to the benefits from the implementation of a clam system anchored in the use of manual, ecosystem-friendly rakes. In other words, from a cost–benefit perspective, any environmental policy protection measure is justified if the associated benefits, in terms of forgone environmental damages, are €11.8 million or more per year.

NOTE

1.   Anna Alberini has provided valuable comments on an earlier draft of this chapter.

REFERENCES

Armstrong, P., R. Garrido and J.D. Ortùzar (2001) 'Confidence intervals to bound the value of time', *Transportation Research*, **37E**(2–3), 143–61.
Bevilacqua, P. (1998), *Venezia e La Acque*, Venice, Italy: Donzelli Press.
Boatto, V., L. Galletto, G. Orel, M. Pellizzato, L. Rossetto, A. Sfriso, S. Silvestri and A. Zentilin (2002), 'Evaluation of alternative scenarios for alieutic resources management in the Lagoon of Venice', Working Paper presented at 1st Corila Conference, Isola di San Servolo, Venice.
Brunelli, G. (1940), 'La pesca nella laguna: parte generale e introduttiva', in G. Brunelli, G. Magrini, L. Milani and P. Orsi, *La laguna di Venezia*, Venice, Italy: Essay, Vol. III, section IV, tome IX, par. LII.

Granzotto, A., P. Franzoi, A. Longo, F. Pranovi and P. Torricelli (2002), 'La pesca nella laguna di Venezia: un percorso di sostenibilità nel recupero delle tradizioni – Lo stato dell'arte', Working Paper, Venice, Italy: Fondazione Eni Enrico Mattei.

Hanemann, W.M. (1984), 'Discrete/continuous models of consumer demand', *Econometrica*, **52**, 541–61.

Louviere, J.J., D.A. Hensher and J.D. Swaat (2000), *Stated Choices Methods: Analysis and Applications*, Cambridge, UK: University Press.

ICRAM (1994), 'Indagine preliminare sull'utilizzo della draga idraulica (turbosoffiante) per la pesca dei bivalvi in ambiente lagunare', *Quaderni*, 7.

MacFadden, D. (1974), 'Conditional logit analysis of qualitative choice behavior', in P. Zarembka (ed.), *Frontiers in Econometrics*, New York, US: Academic Press.

MacFadden, D. (1984), 'Econometric analysis of qualitative response models', in Z. Griliches and M.D. Intriligator (eds), vol. 2, Amsterdam, The Netherlands: North-Holland.

Ninni, E. (1940), 'Attrezzi e sistemi di pesca nella Laguna', in G. Brunelli, G. Magrini, L. Milani and P. Orsi, *La laguna di Venezia*, Venice, Italy: Essay, Vol. III section IV, tome IX, par. LII.

Nunes, P.A.L.D. and J.C.J.M. van den Bergh (2002), 'Measuring the economic value of a marine protection program against the introduction of non-indigenous species in the Netherlands', Tinbergen Institute Discussion Paper 057/3, 54 pages, Tinbergen Institute, The Netherlands.

Orel, G., G. Di Silvio and G. Pessa (1997), 'Effetti della Draga e del Rastrello sul Sistema Lagunare', Report for the judicial act n. 20729/96 R.G.N., Venice, Italy.

Pellizzato, M. and E. Giorgiutti (1997), 'Attrezzi e Sistemi di Pesca nella Provincia di Venezia', Provincia di Venezia, Venice, Italy.

Pranovi, F. and O. Giovanardi (1994) 'The impact of hydraulic dredging for short-necked clams on an infaunal community in the lagoon of Venice', *Science Marine*, **58**, 345–53.

Sfriso, A. (2000), 'Eutrofizzazione e inquinamento delle acque e dei sedimenti nella parte centrale della laguna di Venezia', in CVN, MAV, LLPP (eds), *Nuovi Interventi per la Salvaguardia di Venezia*, vol. 3, Venice, Italy.

Solidoro, C., M. Pellizzato, R. Rossi, R. Pastres and C.D. Melaku (2000) 'Modelling the growth of Tapes philippinarum in Northern Adriatic lagoons', *Marine Ecology Series*, **199**, 137–48.

Van den Bergh, J.C.J.M., P.A.L.D. Nunes, H.M. Dotinga, W.H.C.F. Kooistra, E.G. Vrieling and L. Peperzak (2002), 'Exotic harmful algae in marine ecosystems: an integrated biological–economic–legal analysis of impacts and policies', *Marine Policy*, **26**(1), 59–74.

Zolezzi, G. (1944), 'La pesca nella provincia di Venezia', *Bollettino Pesca, Piscicoltura e Idrobiologia*, **22**(2), 155–231.

7. The Value of Recreational Sport Fishing in the Lagoon of Venice

Valentina Zanatta, Anna Alberini, Paolo Rosato and Alberto Longo

7.1 INTRODUCTION

The Lagoon of Venice is a site of exceptional interest, due to its distinctive environmental features and unique cultural and social significance.[1] It is regarded as a unique hydrological resource and its ecosystem is rich in native plants, animals and marine organisms. As one of the most important wetland sites in the Mediterranean region, the Lagoon of Venice is covered by the European Union's policy for wetlands preservation. Moreover, conservation of the Lagoon is a priority for the local economy.

At this time, however, the Lagoon of Venice is environmentally degraded, due to the industrial pollution from chemical plants and refineries in nearby Porto Marghera, and its fish stocks have been depleted by excessive commercial fishing, an important economic activity for the Venice area and the Veneto region. In addition, biodiversity is endangered by an exotic clam species that was artificially introduced for commercial fishing during the 1980s. The introduction of the *tapes philippinarum* clam has been blamed for serious changes in the natural lagoon environment, as harvesting this species involves the use of invasive (and illegal) fishing techniques, such as mechanical scrapers, which were eventually prohibited in the lagoon (Pranovi and Giovanardi, 1994; ICRAM, 1999).

Public programs are currently under consideration that would seek to restore environmental balance in the Lagoon of Venice by removing pollution and implementing and managing sustainable commercial fishing practices. When examining these programs, economists would suggest that at least some consideration be given to their costs and benefits. One category of possible beneficiaries of improved environmental quality in the Lagoon is recreational anglers.

We are interested in estimating the value of sport fishing in the Lagoon for two reasons. First, this is a popular activity suggesting that the benefits of environmental quality conservation in the Lagoon may be large. Second, much recent attention has been dedicated to the issue of sustainable use of the Lagoon of Venice and traditional commercial fishing practices that are compatible with ecosystem and fish stock maintenance. Presumably, restoring fish stocks benefits recreational anglers as well, raising the question of exactly how large such benefits are.

This chapter reports the results of a Travel Cost Method (TCM) study about the recreational use of the Lagoon of Venice for sport fishing. We use the TCM to estimate the value of sport fishing in the Lagoon under the current and improved catch rate conditions. Briefly, the TCM uses information about the number of fishing trips and their cost to anglers to place a value on the Lagoon as a fishing site. The method relies on the fact that travel costs vary across visitors, allowing one to estimate the demand function for trips at different trip prices. The TCM assumes that, all else the same, trips are an increasing function of environmental quality.

In April–July 2002, we conducted a mail survey of anglers with valid fishing licenses for the Lagoon of Venice to gather data on their fishing trips to the Lagoon and expenditures over the previous year. We also asked questions about trips that would be undertaken under hypothetical changes in the price of a trip and in catch rate. The answers to these hypothetical questions refine our information about the demand for trips at the current catch rate, and allow us to estimate the shift in the trip demand curve in the presence of improved catch rates. This shift in the demand function is crucial for estimating the benefits of fish stock maintenance to sports anglers.

The reminder of this chapter is organized as follows. Section 7.2 describes our TCM methodology. Section 7.3 describes the questionnaire used in our study, the sampling frame, and the mode of administration of the survey. Section 7.4 describes the econometric model. Section 7.5 describes the data. Section 7.6 presents the results from the econometric model and the calculation of the welfare statistics for the sample and the population. We provide concluding remarks in Section 7.7.[2]

7.2   A TRAVEL COST MODEL OF FISHING TRIPS TO THE LAGOON

The purpose of this study is to estimate the value of recreational sport fishing and the welfare change associated with changes in the environmental quality of the Lagoon. We estimate an individual angler's demand function for sport fishing in the Lagoon, and then calculate the individual surplus from this activity under both the current and improved fishing conditions.

We use a single-site TCM of sport fishing in the Lagoon of Venice. We assume that an individual's utility depends on aggregate consumption, X, leisure, L and fishing trips, r:

$$U = U(X, L, r) \tag{7.1}$$

We further assume weak complementarity between trips and quality at the site, q. In other words, the individual does not care about quality at the site if he or she does not visit the site, and r is an increasing function of q. The individual chooses X, L and r to maximize utility subject to the budget constraint:

$$y + w \cdot \left[\overline{T} - L - r(t_1 + t_2) \right] = X + (f + P_d \cdot d) \cdot r \tag{7.2}$$

where y is non-work income, w is the wage rate, $\overline{T}$ is total time, t_1 is travel time to the site, t_2 is time spent at the site, f is the access fee (if any), P_d is the cost per kilometer, and d is the distance to the fishing site.[3]

This yields the demand function for trips:

$$r^* = r^*(y, w, p_r, q) \tag{7.3}$$

where $p_r = w(t_1 + t_2) + f + p_d \cdot d$ is the full price of a trip.

In our empirical work, we assume that the demand function is linear in its arguments:

$$r^* = \beta_0 + \beta_1 w + \beta_2 p_r + \beta_3 q \tag{7.4}$$

To estimate equation (7.4), we collect data on p_r and r^*, plus w, y, and other individual characteristics, through a survey of anglers. Our survey questionnaire also includes additional questions that elicit the number of trips that would be undertaken by the respondent under hypothetical changes in quality q, which here is the catch rate, and price per trip. Varying the catch rate to the respondents allows us to estimate the effect β_3 of environmental quality improvements brought by public programs currently under consideration, while varying the price per trip within respondents, combined with the variation in price per trip across respondents, should result in more efficient estimates of β_2.

7.3 STRUCTURE OF THE QUESTIONNAIRE AND SURVEY ADMINISTRATION

The questionnaire (reported in Appendix A in the English translation) is divided into four sections. The first section inquires about the respondents' sport fishing habits in the Lagoon of Venice. For example, we ask them how many fishing trips they take per year, what means of transportation they use for their fishing trips, what type of boat they own, if any, and so on.

In section 2 respondents are asked to report their fishing trip expenses in the last 12 months, broken down by category. In section 3, respondents are invited to pinpoint their specific fishing sites, and the place(s) from which they usually launch, on a map. They are also asked to check on a list which species they generally fish.

Questions 22–27 query the respondents about their fishing behaviors under hypothetical conditions. We begin by asking them how many trips they would take if the price per trip increased by a specified percentage. This percentage is varied to the respondent, and is selected at random from five possible values (20 percent, 40 percent, 60 percent, 80 percent and 100 percent). Next, we ask respondents how many additional trips they would take (i) if there were a 50 percent increase in the catch rate, and (ii) for a simultaneous increase in the price per trip and in the catch rate.

Two questions ask the respondents for their opinions about environmental quality in the lagoon, focusing specifically on the problem of the *tapes philippinarum* clam and on pollution. Finally, the fourth and last section of the questionnaire asks questions about individual and socio-economic characteristics of the respondents (for example age, gender, income, education, and so on).

The survey was administered by mail in April–July 2002. In a first wave of mailings, we sent questionnaires to 3000 anglers. This sample was drawn from the universe of all holders of fishing licenses in the Province of Venice, stratified by distance of the angler's place of residence from the Lagoon and age.[4] The survey packet included a participation notice card, which was filled out and returned by about 500 anglers.

In our second wave of mailings, we sent a reminder card to the remaining 2500 anglers. We received about 500 more participation cards after this reminder. In sum, the participation notice card was filled and returned to us by 1048 anglers. Of these, 605 stated that they did not intend to participate in the survey, while the remaining 443 filled out the questionnaire. Out of the latter 443, 269 had gone fishing in the Venice Lagoon in the previous 12 months. In this chapter, attention is restricted to these 269 individuals.

7.4 THE ECONOMETRIC MODEL

A. Econometric Model and Welfare Calculation

Two types of welfare measures are of interest in this study: (i) the value of access to the Lagoon of Venice, and (ii) the value of changes in the environmental quality in the Lagoon of Venice.

Our survey questionnaire asks questions about actual trips and travel costs to the Lagoon, as well as intended number of trips at alternative prices and catch rates. By varying the catch rate, our measure of quality of the fishing site, and price per trip we gather multiple responses from the same individual. We have a total of four scenarios, with as many observations on the number of trips for each respondent.

The first scenario is the current one, which is defined as the current price per trip (pt_{i0}) and catch rate (cr_{i0}) for individual. The remaining three scenarios are hypothetical. In scenario 2, we keep catch rate at the current level (cr_{i0}) but posit that there is a hypothetical increase in the price of a trip ($pt_{i1} = (1 + X)\,pt_{i0}$). X is selected at random among five possible values: 0.20, 0.40, 0.60, 0.80 and 1.00, implying an increase of 20 percent, 40 percent and so on in the cost of a fishing trip.

In scenario 3, we keep the price per trip at its current level (pt_{i0}) but hypothetically increase the catch rate by 50 percent: $cr_{i1} = cr_{i0} \cdot (1 + 0.5)$. Finally, in scenario 4 we alter both price per trip ($pt_{i1} = (1 + X)\,pt_{i0}$) and catch rate ($cr_{i1} = cr_{i0} \cdot (1 + 0.5)$). The four scenarios are summarized in Table 7.1. Respondents are told that the change in catch rates is delivered by programs for improving environmental quality and policies for managing fishing activities in the Lagoon. For simplicity, in this chapter we assume that catch rates are the same for all respondents, which implies that $cr_{i0} = cr_0$ and $cr_{i1} = cr_1$ for $i = 1, 2, \ldots, n$.

Clearly, using four scenarios results in a dataset that has the structure of a panel. Our regression equation is:

$$TRIPS_{ij}^* = \mathbf{x}_i \beta + price_{ij} \gamma + catch_j \delta + price_i^A \lambda + \varepsilon_{ij} \qquad (7.5)$$

Table 7.1   Survey Design

Scenario	Type	Price per trip	Catch rate
1	Actual	Actual price per trip (pt_{i0})	Current conditions (cr_{i0})
2	Hypothetical	Higher price: ($pt_{i1} = (1+X)pt_{i0}$), where X is selected at random out of {0.20, 0.40, 0.60, 0.80, 1.00}	Current conditions (cr_{i0})
3	Hypothetical	Actual price per trip (pt_{i0})	Increase of 50% over current conditions: $cr_{i1} = cr_{i0} \cdot (1 + 0.5)$
4	Hypothetical	Higher price: ($pt_{i1} = (1+X)pt_{i0}$), where X is selected at random out of {0.20, 0.40, 0.60, 0.80, 1.00}	Increase of 50% over current conditions: $cr_{i1} = cr_{i0} \cdot (1 + 0.5)$

where $i = 1, 2, \ldots, n$ denotes the respondent, and $j = 1, \ldots, 4$ denotes the scenario. *TRIPS** is the underlying number of trips per year, **x** is a vector of individual characteristics, *price* is a continuous variable measuring the cost per fishing trip to the Lagoon, and *catch* is a dummy indicator that takes on a value of one for those scenarios that posit an improved catch rate. *Price^A* is a continuous variable that measures price per trip to an alternative fishing destination. β, γ, δ and λ are unknown coefficients, and ε_{ij} is an error term.

Because under scenarios 2 and 4, which involve higher prices per trip, some respondents may forgo fishing altogether, we specify the following mapping between latent trips (*TRIPS**) and the number of trips, *TRIPS*, reported by the respondent in the survey:

$$TRIPS_{ij} = TRIPS_{ij}^* \text{ iff } TRIPS_{ij}^* > 0$$
$$\text{and} \tag{7.6}$$
$$TRIPS_{ij} = 0 \text{ iff } TRIPS_{ij}^* \leq 0.$$

This mapping results in a Tobit model (see Greene, 2003).

Another caveat is in order. The observations on fishing trips under the four scenarios are correlated within an individual if unobservable angler characteristics influence both current fishing trips and the announced number of trips under the hypothetical scenarios.

To account for unobserved heterogeneity, we assume that $\varepsilon_{ij} = v_i + \eta_{ij}$, where v_i is a respondent-specific, zero-mean component, and η_{ij} is an i.i.d. error term. v_i and η_{ij} are uncorrelated with each other, across individuals, and with the regressors in the right-hand side of equation (7.5). The presence of the individual-specific component of the error term (v_i) result in correlated error terms ε within a respondent.[5] We account for this within-individual correlation by estimating a random-effect tobit model.

We use the estimated coefficients to calculate two welfare measures. The first is the consumer surplus associated with current fishing conditions and prices, which is equal to:

$$CS_i(p_{0i}, cr_{0i}) = -\frac{1}{2\gamma}[\mathbf{x}_i\beta + p_{0i}\gamma]^2 \tag{7.7}$$

The second is the change in surplus due to an improvement in catch rate (holding the prices the same). This is equal to:

$$\Delta CS_i = CS_i(p_{0i}, cr_{i1}) - CS_i(p_{0i}, cr_{i0}) = -\frac{1}{2\gamma}[\delta^2 + 2\delta(\mathbf{x}_i\beta + p_{0i}\gamma)] \tag{7.8}$$

B. The Choice of Regressors in the Econometric Model

Economic theory suggests that the demand for a fishing trip should depend on the full price of a trip, which includes the opportunity cost of time (see section 7.2). Earlier literature (since Cesario, 1976) has suggested that the opportunity cost of time should be about one-third of the market wage rate, and McConnell and Strand (1981) have suggested an approach for estimating this fraction directly from the data reported by the respondent in a TCM survey. Recently, Feather and Shaw (1999, 2000) have proposed approaches for computing the value of time for individuals who are employed but do not choose the number of hours they work, and for individuals who choose not to work.

Rather than computing a price per trip inclusive of the opportunity cost of time, in this chapter we choose to enter in the regression model four variables that capture the full cost of a fishing trip. The first is PRICEE, the sum of boat fuel costs, the cost of the car trip (fuel, wear-and-tear, and highway toll), the fee for launching the boat from a boat ramp, the cost of bait, and food and beverages. The second is household income divided by the number of household members, along with a dummy – our third variable – that takes on a value of one if the respondent did not answer the question about household income.[6] The fourth variable is a dummy indicating whether the respondent is retired from the workforce, which captures time constraints, among other things.

When estimating a single-site TCM model, it is important to control for the price of a trip to an alternative site. Due to the extension of the Lagoon of Venice, its location, nature and species, there are very few sites that may serve as substitutes for it for sport fishing. Only the Po River Delta, the Lagoon of Caorle and the Lagoon of Marano are comparable to the Lagoon of Venice in terms of fish species and catch rates. In practice, the Lagoons of Caorle and Marano are generally judged to be closer substitutes for the Lagoon of Venice than the Po Delta. For this reason, we compute the price of a trip to the Lagoon of Marano and use this cost as our *price^A*.

Additional variables thought to influence the demand for fishing trips to the Lagoon of Venice include (i) a dummy denoting use of the angler's own boat to go fishing (BOAT), (ii) a dummy indicating whether the angler is a resident of Venice (FASCIAA), and (iii) several dummies for the species normally caught by the angler (BRANZI, SOGL, VONGOLA, CEFALO). To elaborate on (iii), we create the variable BRANZI (a short for *branzino*, a local variety of seabass) because this is a highly prized species that, unlike others, is caught year round. SOGL is equal to one if the respondent catches sole (*sogliola* in Italian) and/or flounder, which tend to attract highly skilled anglers. VONGOLA means that the anglers catches clams, and CEFALO is the Italian for mullet, a species that is generally regarded as very difficult to catch, and hence a challenge to the angler.

Finally, we wish to see if the frequency of fishing trips is influenced by the angler's opinions about pollution in the Lagoon and the impact of *tapes philippinarum* on catch rates. In addition to two dummy variables that capture the angler's beliefs about these factors, we also create a dummy accounting for behavioral responses to these factors.

7.5   THE DATA

A. Characteristics of the Respondents and Current Fishing Behavior

Our first objective is to examine the descriptive statistics of the sample, which we report in Table 7.2. We remind the reader that our sample is comprised of those anglers who returned the questionnaire and reported having gone sport fishing in the Lagoon of Venice at least once in the 12 months prior to the time of the survey.

As shown in Table 7.2, virtually all of the anglers in our sample are males. The average respondent is about 50 years old, has had about 10 years of schooling, and has an annual household income of €20 000. Retired persons account for about one-third of the sample.[7]

Regarding fishing behavior and experience, the average respondent reports taking about 30 trips a year in the Lagoon, for a total expenditure of about €765 a year. The average cost per trip is €31. On average, our anglers have been fishing in the Lagoon for 26 years, and more than 50 percent use their own boat on their Lagoon fishing trips.

We also wish to examine whether the individual characteristics of our respondents and their fishing behaviors and experience vary with their area of residence. Table 7.3 reports descriptive statistics by zone.

As shown in Table 7.3, the average cost of a fishing trip is similar across zones, but respondents who live in the city of Venice or on the islands of the Lagoon (Zone 1) take more fishing trips than the others. As expected, the average number of fishing trips declines with distance from the Lagoon. The other individual characteristics are similar across zones, although the anglers from Zone 1 tend to be a little older than the residents of the other zones. The Zone 1 subsample also includes a higher proportion of retired persons.

B. Fishing Trips by Scenario

As previously explained, in scenarios 2, 3 and 4 we alter the cost of a trip and the catch rate to the respondent. Descriptive statistics about the number of trips announced by the respondents under these hypothetical scenarios are shown in Table 7.4.

Table 7.2   Descriptive statistics for the sample (n=269)

Variable	Sample average°
Individual characteristics of the respondent	
Age (ETA) (years)	51.22 (14.74)
Male (SEX) (dummy)	0.985 (0.12)
Annual Household income* (INCOME)	€20 524 (€15 389)
Does not report INCOME (PCAPINCM) (dummy)	0.078 (0.26)
Annual Income per member of the household* (PCAPINC)	€7920.64 (6351.51)
Retired person (RETIRED) (dummy)	0.334 (0.47)
Years of schooling (EDUCATION)	9.80 (3.83)
Fishing behavior and experience	
Price per trip to the Lagoon of Venice (PRICEE)	€31.23 (37.89)
Number of fishing trips in the Lagoon in the last 12 months (QVPLA)	30.28 (35.30)
Total fishing expenditure in the last year	€765.57 (1612.08)
Uses own boat to go fishing (BOAT) (dummy)	0.580 (0.49)
Uses friends' boat to go fishing (FRBOAT) (dummy)	0.078 (0.26)
Numbers of years the respondent has been fishing in the Lagoon (DQAP)	26.37 (16.76)
Price per trip to the Lagoon of Marano** (MARANO)	€5.76 (2.62)

Notes: ° standard deviation in parentheses.
   * Calculated for those respondents who do report household income.
   ** Proportional to the distance from the respondent's home to the Lagoon of Marano. Does not include the cost of bait, boat fuel, and launching fee.

Under the current conditions, our subjects reported an average of 30 trips to the Lagoon in the 12 months prior to the survey. About 39 percent of the respondent took 1–12 trips, 35 percent took 13–30 trips, and 26 percent took more than 30.

Valuing Complex Natural Resource Systems

Table 7.3   Characteristics of the sample by zone*

	Zone 1 (n = 131)	Zone 2 (n = 84)	Zone 3 (n = 40)	Zone 4 (n = 13)
Individual characteristics of the respondent				
Age (ETA) (years)	54.9 (13.86)	48.8 (14.25)	45.2 (15.05)	46.8 (17.15)
Annual household income** (INCOME)	€21 061 (15 226)	€19 726 (14 474)	€21 100 (19 260.0)	€18 642 (8023.6)
Does not report INCOME (PCAPINCM) (dummy)	0.061 (0.23)	0.059 (0.23)	0.200 (0.40)	0.00
Retired person (RETIRED) (dummy)	0.396 (0.48)	0.321 (0.46)	0.150 (0.35)	0.357 (0.48)
Years of schooling (EDUCATION)	10.24 (4.43)	9.16 (3.14)	9.95 (3.38)	8.76 (1.87)
Fishing behavior and experience				
Price per trip to the Lagoon of Venice (PRICEE)	€32.9 (44.57)	€31.7 (34.56)	€23.5 (15.12)	€32.2 (33.72)
Number of fishing trips to the Lagoon in the last 12 months (QVPLA)	39.9 (43.6)	21.9 (20.6)	20.42 (23.3)	15.7 (15.8)
Total fishing expenditure in the last year	827.13 (910.23)	613.77 (1001.96)	427.23 (491.93)	471.16 (603.26)
Uses own boat to go fishing (BOAT) (dummy)	0.748 (0.43)	0.476 (0.50)	0.400 (0.49)	0.142 (0.35)
Uses friends' boat to go fishing (FRBOAT) (dummy)	0.04 (0.20)	0.107 (0.30)	0.075 (0.26)	0.214 (0.41)
Years fishing in the Lagoon (DQAP)	28.79 (18.01)	23.9 (15.59)	23.4 (14.50)	28.0 (15.91)

Notes: Sample average (standard deviation in parentheses).
* Zone 1 = city of Venice and islands of the Lagoon; Zone 2 = population centers on the shores; Zone 3 = population centers 5 to 10 kilometers from the Lagoon; Zone 4 = population centers 10 or more kilometers from the Lagoon.
** Calculated for those respondents who do report income.

When asked to consider a hypothetical situation with higher prices per outing, respondents announced that they would either keep the number of trips the same, or that they would take fewer trips. The average number of trips per year under scenario 2 is 14, with 38 percent of the respondents stating that they would no longer go fishing.

Under scenario 3, people generally told us that they would take more trips, for an average of almost 39 per year. Under scenario 4, which posits higher prices and a higher catch rate, the average number of announced trips is 21, with 28 percent of the respondents reporting an intended number of trips

Table 7.4   Descriptive statistics for the number of fishing trips by scenario

Scenario	Number of trips			
	Mean	Standard Deviation	Minimum	Maximum
1 (current conditions)	30.28	35.27	1	200
2 (higher price per trip)	14.18	26.59	0	200
3 (higher catch rate)	38.76	42.13	1	250
4 (higher price and catch rate)	21.21	32.54	0	200

Notes: n = 268 for each scenario.

equal to zero. These figures suggest that the responses to the hypothetical trip questions are well behaved, and confirm that the demand for trips should be estimated using a (random-effects) Tobit model.

C. Perception of Environmental Quality in the Lagoon of Venice

Our questionnaire also queries anglers about their perception of environmental quality in the Lagoon. We use three questions to explore this matter. The first asks whether the presence of chemical pollutants and industrial waste in the Lagoon is thought to affect catch rates. The second question asks the respondents if they feel that catch rates have been negatively affected by the introduction of the *tapes philippinarum* clam. The third question asks the respondent if he has changed his own fishing behavior as a result of these negative events: the sediment pollution and the introduction of this species. Two response categories (yes and no) are provided for each of these questions.

The distribution of the responses to these three questions is displayed in Table 7.5. As shown in this table, the majority of our respondents clearly feel that pollution influences catch rates in the Lagoon. Over 82 percent of our anglers felt that catch rates had been negatively impacted by the introduction of the *tapes philippinarum* clam, and 78 percent of them have actually changed their own fishing behavior as a result of pollution and exotic species. These response patterns suggest that anglers are aware of the potential effects of water quality and exotic species on catch rate, and they should accept hypothetical scenarios where improvements in catch rates are delivered by water quality and fishing management policies.

Table 7.5   Frequencies of yes/no responses about the environmental quality of the Lagoon of Venice

Question	Percentage YES
Do you think that sediment pollution in the Lagoon of Venice has affected the catch rate of a fishing trip? (dummy variable INQUI)	91.87%
Do you think that the commercial fishing of the *tapes philippinarum* clam adversely affects the catch rate per fishing trip? (dummy variable VOGO)	82.52%
Have you changed your fishing habits and site choice since the introduction of the *tapes philippinarum* clam, or because of sediment pollution in the Lagoon? (dummy variable CAMBIA)	78.05%

Notes: n = 246.

7.6   RESULTS

A. Random-effects Tobit Models

The demand for fishing trips should depend on price per trip, income, and other individual characteristics that proxy taste for fishing and/or the value of time. We work with a linear demand function, which we estimate using a random-effects Tobit model. We exclude from the usable sample two anglers who reported spending less than €5 or more than €9000 a year on fishing trips to the Lagoon of Venice, and one angler who failed to answer the fishing trip questions, which brings the total number of individuals with usable responses from 269 to 266, and the total number of usable observations from 1076 to 1064.

Specification (A) in Table 7.6 is our basic specification of the random-effects Tobit model of trips, which includes *price* (price of a trip), the dummy *catch*, the price of a trip to the alternative site, the Lagoon of Marano (MARANO), and the two income variables. As shown in column (A) of Table 7.6, the demand for trips is negatively and significantly related to the price of a trip. The coefficient on own trip price indicates that a 10-euro increase in price would result in about 1.2 fewer trips per year. Improving the catch rate by 50 percent would increase the number of fishing trips by almost eight, an effect that is statistically significant at the 1 percent level.

It is interesting that the coefficient on the price of a trip to the Lagoon of Marano is not statistically significant, which casts doubts on our conjecture that Marano serves as a substitute site for the Lagoon of Venice. The income

Table 7.6   Results of the random-coefficient Tobit

Variable	(A)	(B)	(C)	(D)	(E)	(F)
Intercept	29.900**	26.198**	26.199**	22.940**	3.185	6.983
	(5.94)	(5.16)	(6.03)	(4.33)	(0.53)	(0.89)
Price per trip (price)	−0.122**	−0.122**	−0.121**	−0.128**	−0.121**	−0.121**
	(−4.60)	(−4.51)	(−6.21)	(−4.20)	(−4.83)	(−4.29)
Improved catch rate (dummy)	7.787**	7.787**	7.787**	7.787**	7.787**	7.787**
	(6.05)	(6.02)	(6.05)	(5.97)	(5.96)	(5.95)
Price per trip to alternative site	−0.178	−0.057	0.120	−0.436	−1.113^	−0.909
	(−0.33)	(−0.09)	(0.23)	(−0.64)	(−1.70)	(−0.86)
Income per household member	−0.00023	−0.00043	−0.0002	−0.0005^	−0.0005	−0.0005
	(−0.92)	(−1.25)	(−0.93)	(−1.79)	(−1.62)	(−1.55)
Income missing (dummy)	−6.105	−8.103	−5.464	−7.281	−2.265	−2.302
	(−1.38)	(−1.16)	(−1.27)	(−0.88)	(−0.36)	(−0.36)
Retired	.	.	5.644^	6.113^	3.676	3.879
			(1.83)	(1.85)	(0.94)	(0.95)
Resident of Zone A (FASCIAA) (dummy)	.	11.237**	.	12.337**	11.151**	11.226**
		(2.63)		(3.23)	(3.33)	(3.30)
Uses own boat to go fishing (BOAT) (dummy)	.	.	.	6.581	9.775**	9.461**
				(1.62)	(2.65)	(2.53)
Years of fishing experience	.	.	.	.	0.312**	0.333**
					(2.97)	(2.97)
BRANZINO (dummy)	.	.	.	.	14.183**	14.43**
					(4.29)	(4.13)
SOGLIOLA (dummy)	.	.	.	.	3.711	3.561
					(1.10)	(1.02)
VONGOLA (dummy)	.	.	.	.	1.647	1.744
					(0.48)	(0.49)
CEFALO (dummy)	.	.	.	.	10.654**	10.911**
					(3.21)	(3.14)
VOGO (dummy)	.	.	.	.	.	−0.799
						(−0.18)
INQUI (dummy)	.	.	.	.	.	−4.668
						(−0.76)
CAMBIA (dummy)	.	.	.	.	.	−0.877
						(−0.14)
Log likelihood	−5036.90	−5029.22	−5035.09	−5026.05	−5005.59	−5005.23

Notes: T statistics in parentheses. Number of anglers = 266, total number of observations = 1064.
** = significant at the 1% level;
* = significant at the 5% level;
^ = significant at the 10% level.

variables are not statistically significant either. Despite the lack of significance of the coefficient on the latter three variables, a Wald test suggests that this model as a whole is significant at the 1 percent level or better.

In specification (B), we wish to see whether proximity of the angler's place of residence to the Lagoon exerts an independent effect on the demand for fishing trips above and beyond that already captured into the price of a trip. To answer this question, we add a dummy variable, FASCIAA, taking on a value of one if the respondent is a resident of Venice.

As shown in Table 7.6, column (B), the coefficients on price per trip and catch are virtually the same as their counterparts in column (A), but those on the income variables are rather different. Despite the differences, the coefficients on the income variables remain statistically insignificant. The results of this run also show that those respondents who live in Venice do report more frequent fishing trips. All else the same, they take 11 more Lagoon fishing trips than the other respondents in our sample.

In specification (C), we drop FASCIAA, preferring to control, instead, for whether the angler is a retired person. Doing so does not change the coefficients on price per trip and catch rate, and brings the coefficients on the income variables close to their respective values in (A). The latter two coefficients, however, remain statistically insignificant. Finally, the coefficient on the retired person dummy suggests that retirees take, on average, six more Lagoon fishing trips than the other respondents in the sample, but this effect is significant only at the 10 percent level.

Column (D) differs from (C) in that it adds back the dummy for Zone 1, and further controls for whether the respondent uses his own boat to go fishing. The results for this run suggest that the residents of the city of Venice and persons who use their own boat to go fishing do tend to take more numerous fishing trips to the Lagoon. Adding these variables improves the fit of the model, but leaves the coefficients on the other regressors in the model virtually unchanged.[8]

In specification (E), we further add the species dummies, and control for fishing experience. Specification (E) suggests that fishing experience does influence the number of annual fishing trips to the Lagoon, as do dummies for the species caught. A likelihood ratio test rejects the null that the coefficients on the new variables are jointly zero, the LR statistic being equal to 40.92. Again, the coefficients on all other variables are affected very little by the inclusion of these regressors.

Finally, in (F), we wish to check whether fishing trip frequency reflects opinions about pollution and exotic species. We therefore include the dummies capturing the respondent's beliefs about environmental quality in the Lagoon and the effect on catch rates of introducing exotic species, plus a dummy for behavioral responses to the introduction of the Philippine clam, but find no evidence of an effect on the part of these variables (LRstatistic=0.52, p-value=0.91).

In all of the specifications we attempted, there was evidence of random effects, and the coefficient of correlation between the error terms within an individual was roughly 0.55–0.69, depending on the specification. We experimented with further dummies for the area of residence of the respondent, but to no avail.

B. Surplus

We use the simplest specification of our random-effects Tobit model (column (A), Table 7.6) to predict angler surplus at the current conditions and the surplus change for a 50 percent improvement in catch rates. Results are reported for the average respondent in our sample in the first row of Table 7.7. To perform these calculations, we use the average price per trip in our sample (€31.23) and income per household member (€7920.64 a year). As shown in the first row of Table 7.7, surplus at current conditions is pegged at €2214 a year, while the welfare change associated with the catch rate improvement is €1732 a year.

Welfare calculations are specialized to the residents of Venice (FASCIAA=1), and to the residents of the other areas in our sample (FASCIAA=0) in the second and third row, respectively, of Table 7.7. For these calculations, we use specification (B), holding the price per trip the same across these two groups, while income per household member is set to €8474.55 for Venice residents, and €7391.00 for all others. Rows 2 and 3 of Table 7.7 show clearly that surplus at the current conditions is over twice as

Table 7.7   Surplus and surplus changes after 50% catch rate improvement

Anglers	Surplus at current catch rate (€ per year)	Surplus at improved catch rate (€ per year)	Surplus difference (€ per year)
All respondents*	2214.07	3946.13	1732.06
Respondents living in the city of Venice and the islands of the Lagoon (ZONA=1)**	3603.86	5735.11	2141.25
Respondents living in other areas (ZONA=2, 3, or 4)**	1461.02	2914.66	1453.64

Notes: * Based on specification (A), Table 7.6
          ** Based on specification (B), Table 7.6.

large for Venice residents than for all other respondents, and that welfare change is about 50 percent larger for the former.

C. Benefits Calculations

To extrapolate the benefits of improved catch rates to all Lagoon anglers, we begin with dividing our sample into strata and computing the welfare statistics for each stratum k, $k = 1,..., K$. We denote our welfare measure of interest with $S(\mathbf{x}_k, \hat{\beta})$, where $\mathbf{x}_k$ is a vector of regressors and $\hat{\beta}$ is a vector of estimated coefficients. The welfare measure for the population is, therefore, equal to:

$$S = \sum_{k=1}^{K} S(\mathbf{x}_k, \hat{\beta}) \cdot N_k \qquad (7.9)$$

where N_k is the number of Lagoon anglers in stratum k in the population.

In this chapter, K is equal to 2, the two strata being (i) Lagoon anglers who are residents of Venice or the islands of the Lagoon, and (ii) Lagoon anglers who reside in other areas. This implies that we use specification (B) of the random-effects Tobit model in computing 7.9. For simplicity, in this chapter attention is restricted to those anglers who currently go fishing in the Lagoon of Venice, ignoring the possibility that improvements in catch rates might entice other persons to go fishing in the Lagoon. This assumption leads to conservative benefit estimates.

We compute two measures of welfare among current users: surplus from current use of the Lagoon (B^1), and change in surplus associated with changes in catch rates (B^2). Formally,

$$B^1 = CS(\mathbf{x}_1) \cdot N_1 + CS(\mathbf{x}_2) \cdot N_2 \qquad (7.10)$$

where CS is consumer surplus (equation (7.7)), and subscripts 1 and 2 denote anglers who are Venice residents, and all other anglers, respectively. As reported in Table 7.7, $CS_1 = CS(\mathbf{x}_1) = €3604$, while $CS_2 = CS(\mathbf{x}_2) = €1461$ a year.

The welfare change associated with a 50 percent improvement in catch rates in the Lagoon is equal to

$$B^2 = \Delta CS(\mathbf{x}_1) \cdot N_1 + \Delta CS(\mathbf{x}_2) \cdot N_2 \qquad (7.11)$$

where ΔCS denotes the welfare change (equation (7.8)), which is €2141 a year for Venice residents and €1454 a year for all others. Implicit in this calculation is the assumption that our sample is similar to the population of Lagoon anglers in terms of observable characteristics, such as income.

No one knows exactly N_1 and N_2, the populations of Lagoon anglers that reside in Venice and in all other areas, respectively. We offer two alternative estimates of these populations, based on somewhat extreme assumptions. We start with pointing out that the universe of fishing licenses valid in the Province of Venice is comprised of a total of 34 018 persons. Of these, 4415 are residents of Venice and Lagoon islands, while the remaining 29 603 live in other areas (for the most part, the inland portion of the Province of Venice, with some residents of the Provinces of Treviso and Padua).[9]

The first estimate is based on the conservative assumption that only the holders of fishing licenses that actually go fishing in the Lagoon bother to return the completed questionnaire,[10] and that our sample reflects the Lagoon fishing participation rates of the population. Since the questionnaire was returned by 13.4 percent of the recipients with Venice and Lagoon islands addresses, and 7.1 percent of the other recipients, we estimate N_1 to be equal to $(4415 \times 0.134) = 591$ and N_2 to be equal to $(29\ 603 \times 0.071) = 2102$. The surplus associated with current fishing conditions is, therefore, €2 132 080 for Venice residents and €3 070 792 for residents of other areas who go fishing in the Lagoon, for a total of €5 200 945 a year. The welfare change figures associated with a 50 percent improvement in catch rates are €1 226 779 and €3 055 279, for a total of €4 282 058 a year.

Our second estimate is much more generous. According to this second procedure, one would reason that Lagoon fishing participation rates in the population of fishing license holders mirror those seen in our sample of 443 completed questionnaires. Since 90 percent of the residents of Venice in this sample of 443 respondents go fishing in the Lagoon, and 48.3 percent of the residents of other areas in this sample of 443 go fishing in the Lagoon, N_1 is estimated to be $4415 \times 0.90 = 3973$, and N_1 is estimated to be $29\ 603 \times 0.483 = 14\ 298$. Current surplus would, therefore, be €14 321 743 for Venice residents and €20 889 743 for residents of other areas, for a total of €35 211 486 a year, while the change in surplus figures associated with a 50 percent improvement in catch rates are €8 509 288 and €20 784 145, respectively, for a total of €29 293 433 a year. Clearly, these figures are about four times as large than those resulting from the first approach.

7.7   CONCLUSIONS

We have surveyed anglers who go fishing in the Lagoon of Venice to gather information about the frequency of their Lagoon fishing trips and cost incurred. We have then used this information to estimate a single-site TCM equation explaining trips as a function of cost per trip and other factors affecting fishing trip frequency. In doing so, we have augmented our observations on actual trips and costs with the trips our respondents told us they would undertake under hypothetical changes in the cost per trip and in the catch rate. This additional information has allowed us to improve the efficiency of our estimate of the slope of the trip demand function. It has also allowed us to estimate the shift in the demand function associated with a 50 percent improvement in catch rate.

We estimate that for the average angler in our sample the surplus at the current price per trip and catch rate conditions is €2214. The change in surplus associated with a 50 percent improvement in catch rate is €1732. These figures, however, differ dramatically across those anglers who reside in the city Venice and islands of the Lagoon, and those who live elsewhere.

To compute the population surplus and surplus change, it is necessary to multiply the surplus (surplus change) by the number of anglers who do fish in the Lagoon. No one knows exactly how many anglers visit the Lagoon, and how many of these anglers are Venice residents or residents of other areas. We estimate the total numbers of Lagoon anglers under different assumptions, producing estimates of surplus at the current conditions ranging from over €5 million (€4 million) to €35 million (€29 million) a year. Conversations with officials of the Province of Venice suggest that credence should be lent to the more conservative assumptions, and hence to the lower bound of the above range of benefits.

It should be kept in mind, however, that our calculations do not account for persons who do not go fishing in the Lagoon at this time, but could be enticed to do so if catch rates improved. Moreover, any benefit–cost analyses of proposed policies that seek to improve environmental quality and fish stocks in the Lagoon should also examine the benefits brought by these policies to other categories of beneficiaries, in addition to Lagoon anglers.

NOTES

1. In 1987, Venice and the Lagoon of Venice were placed on the UNESCO Cultural Heritage List.
2. We wish to thank Mr. Chiaia of the Province of Venice for providing the database of fishing license holders in the Province of Venice, and Andrea Galvan of FEEM for his help with the administration of the survey.
3. This model further assumes that travel time and time spent at the site are exogenous, that there is no utility or disutility from traveling to the site, and that each trip to the site is undertaken for no other purpose than visiting the site. It also assumes that individuals perceive and respond to changes in travel costs in the same way they would to changes in a fee for being admitted to the site (Freeman, 2003). Finally, the model assumes that work hours are flexible.
4. Specifically, we created four areas. The first area (Zone 1) is the city of Venice, plus the islands of the Lagoon. The second area (Zone 2) is comprised of population centers on the shores. The third area (Zone 3) is population centers 5 to 10 kilometers from the Lagoon,

and the fourth and last (Zone 4) is comprised of population centers 10 kilometers or more from the Lagoon.
5. Specifically, $E(\varepsilon_{ij}\,\varepsilon_{ik})=\sigma_v^2$, where σ_v^2 is the variance of v, for $j\neq k$, whereas the variance of each ε_{ij} is $\sigma_v^2 + \sigma_\eta^2$, where σ_η^2 is the variance of η.
6. Specifically, we create a dummy (PCAPINCMISS) taking on a value of one for those respondents who did not answer the household income question. If PCAPINCMISS = 1, we recode income per household member (PCAPINC) to zero. Both PCAPINC and PCAPINCMISS must be entered in the right-hand side of the regression. The latter variable captures any systematic differences in fishing trips among those respondents who did and did not report information about their incomes.
7. The proportion of retired persons among Lagoon anglers is higher than among all holders of fishing license in the Province of Venice (18.3 percent). The reason is that Lagoon sport fishing is closely related to traditional fishing in the Lagoon and hence requires a lot of time. Consequently, lagoon sport fishing selects older people with a lot of spare time.
8. The likelihood ratio test of the null that the coefficients of BOAT and FASCIAA are jointly zero is equal to 18.08. The null is thus soundly rejected.
9. We remind the reader that N_1 and N_2 are not the same as the number of holders of valid fishing licenses for the Province of Venice that reside in Venice and in other areas, respectively. This is because purchase of the fishing license entitles access to and use of many bodies of water in the Province of Venice, of which the Lagoon of Venice is only one. N_1 and N_2 are, therefore, less than or equal than 4415 and 29 603, respectively.
10. Under this assumption, a person who received the questionnaire but did not fill it out is held to never go fishing in the Lagoon.

REFERENCES

Cesario, F.J. (1976), 'Value of Time and Recreation Benefit Studies', *Land Economics*, **52**(1), 32–41.
Feather, P. and W. Douglass Shaw (1999), 'Estimating the Cost of Leisure Time for Recreation Demand Models', *Journal of Environmental Economics and Management*, **38**, 49–65.
Feather, P. and W. Douglass Shaw (2000), 'The Demand For Leisure Time in the Presence of Constrained Work Hours', *Economic Inquiry*, **38** (4), 651–61.
Freeman, A.M. (2003), *The Measurement of Environmental and Resource Values*, Washington, DC: Resources for the Future.
Greene, W.H. (2003*), Econometric Analysis*, 5th edition, Upper Saddle River, NJ: Prentice Hall
Istituto Centrale per la Ricerca Scientifica e Tecnologica Applicata al Mare (ICRAM) (1999), 'Studio dell'impatto della raccolta delle vongole veraci filippine (Tapes philippinarum) nella Laguna di Venezia per una gestione razionale della risorsa e dell'ambiente', IV Piano Triennale Pesca Acquacoltura. I° Rapporto Intermedio, Università di Trieste.
McConnell, K.E. and I.E. Strand (1981), 'Measuring the Cost of Time in Recreation Demand Analysis: An Application to Sport Fishing', *American Journal of Agricultural Economics*, **63**(1), 153–6.
Pranovi, F. and O. Giovanardi (1994), 'The Impact of Hydraulic Dredging for Short-necked Clams, Tapes sp. p., on an Infaunal Community in the Lagoon of Venice', *Scientia Marina*, **58**(4), 345–53.

APPENDIX A

Translated questionnaire

The Universities of Padua and Venice are conducting a study about the most important aspects of recreational use of the Lagoon of Venice. We would like to ask you to help us by answering a few questions about sport fishing in the Lagoon of Venice. Your opinion is very important for our research. Your answers to our questions are strictly confidential and your name will not be associated with your answers.

1. How many times do you go fishing in a year, on average? ....

2. How many years have you been fishing? .... years.

3. Do you ever go fishing in the Lagoon of Venice?
    ❑   NO (terminate)
    ❑   SI   (continue)

4. How many times a year, on average, do you go fishing in the Lagoon of Venice?
    ....

5. Who do you go fishing with?
    ❑   By myself
    ❑   With my family
    ❑   With friends

6. Do you use a boat to get to your fishing site(s)?
    ❑   YES
    ❑   NO

7. If yes, which of the following best describes most of your fishing trips?
    ❑   Own boat
    ❑   Friends' boat
    ❑   Boat owned by an association
    ❑   Rental boat
    ❑   Public transportation boat (vaporetto)

8. If you use your own boat, please describe it below for us.

Characteristics	Please circle the appropriate type		
Type of boat	Oars	Sail	Motor
Type of skull	Wood	Fiberglass	Dinghy
Length of the boat	....		
Vintage of the boat	....		

9. If your boat has a motor, what are its characteristics?

Characteristics	Please explain	
Strokes	Two	Four
Horsepower		
Vintage of the motor		

10. If you use a boat, where do you keep it?
   - ❏ At home
   - ❏ In a canal. Which canal and where? ....
   - ❏ In a marina. Which marina and where? ....

11. In the last twelve months, how much did you spend to go fishing in the Lagoon of Venice?

Category	Expenditure (lire)
Gear (nets, rods, and so on)	
Boat and motor maintenance	
Boat mooring (marina, insurance, etc.)	
Clothing	
Other (please explain)	

12. What is the average cost per trip to the Lagoon for each of the following categories?

Category	Cost (lire)
Bait (only if you buy bait)	
Boat fuel	
Launching from a boat ramp	
Other (please explain)	

13. If you do not buy bait, how much time do you spend gathering or preparing bait for each fishing trip?
   Number of hours ....

14. If you own a boat, do you believe that your fixed costs* are high, relative to your income?
   - ❏ yes
   - ❏ no

   By fixed costs we mean expenses that are incurred every year regardless of the number of trips (insurance, marina, maintenance, etc.)

15. If you own a boat, what is, in your opinion, the minimum number of trips that should be undertaken to justify the fixed costs of owning a boat?
   - ❏ The minimum number of trips is ....
   - ❏ There is no minimum number of trips, because I use my boat for other purposes as well

16. Please mark on the following map the sites from which you usually access the Lagoon

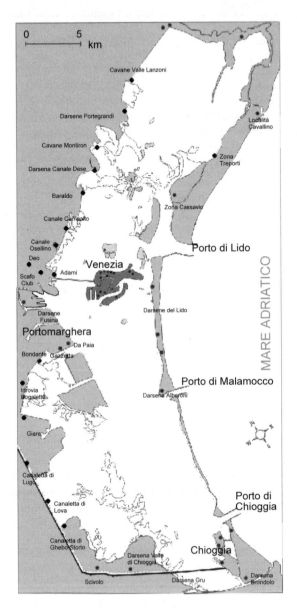

17. Please mark on the following map the sites where you normally go fishing

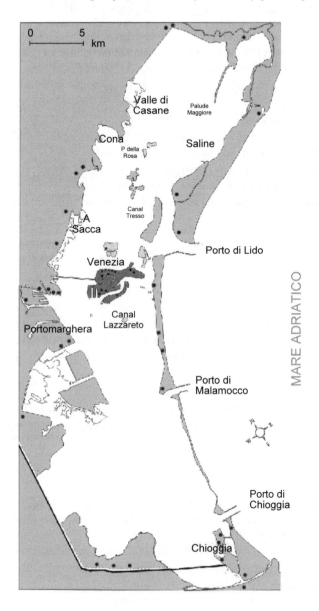

18. Which species do you usually fish? (Please check all applicable species.)
  - ❑ Branzino (seabass)   ❑ Seppie (squid)
  - ❑ Orata (gilthead)   ❑ Vongole (clams)
  - ❑ Sogliola (Sole)   ❑ Go
  - ❑ Mormora   ❑ Cefalo (mullet)
  - ❑ Passera (flounder)   ❑ Other, please explain _____

19. What time of the day do you usually go fishing?
  - ❑ Morning
  - ❑ Afternoon
  - ❑ Evening
  - ❑ Night

20. How many hours do you spend at the fishing site on a typical fishing trip?
  - ❑ Up to 3 hours
  - ❑ 3 to 7 hours
  - ❑ 7 to 12 hours
  - ❑ more than 12 hours

21. Which season do you usually go fishing? (Please check one or more boxes)
  - ❑ Spring
  - ❑ Summer
  - ❑ Fall
  - ❑ Winter

22. If the cost per Lagoon fishing trip increased by **X**%, would you keep your number of fishing trips the same?
  - ❑ Yes
  - ❑ No, I would decrease them to _____ per year
  - ❑ No, I would stop going fishing in the Lagoon of Venice altogether

23. In your experience as a fisherman, would you say that the commercial fishing of *vongola filippina* (caparozzolo) (Philippines clam), as is currently done, has had an adverse effect on catch rates in the Lagoon?
  - ❑ Yes
  - ❑ No

24. In your experience as a fisherman, would you say that polluted sediments have had an adverse effect on catch rates in the Lagoon?
  - ❑ Yes
  - ❑ No

25. Have you changed the number of your fishing trips and your fishing sites in the Lagoon as a result of the pollution of the Lagoon and illegal clam fishing?
  - ❑ Yes
  - ❑ No

26. Suppose that illegal fishing of the Philippines clam were subject to regulation, and that polluted sediments were removed, resulting in a 50% increase in catch rates in the Lagoon. If the cost per trip were the same, would you increase your number of Lagoon fishing trips?
    ❏　Yes. Could you tell us how many more times you would go fishing in the Lagoon per year? ....
    ❏　No. Why? ....

27. Suppose that illegal fishing of the Philippines clam were subject to regulation, and that polluted sediments were removed, resulting in a 50 % increase in catch rates in the Lagoon. If the cost per trip increased by **X**%, would you keep the number of your Lagoon fishing trips the same?
    ❏　Yes, I would keep it the same
    ❏　No, I would increase it by .... times a year
    ❏　No, I would decrease it by .... times a year
    ❏　No, i would stop going fishing in the Lagoon altogether

Individual characteristics of the respondent

28. Gender　　　❏ M　　❏ F

29. Year of birth ....

30. Place of Residence ....

31. Education
    ❏　Elementary school
    ❏　Junior high school diploma
    ❏　High school diploma
    ❏　College degree
    ❏　Other (please explain) ....

32. Occupation
    ❏　Teacher
    ❏　Business owner
    ❏　Professional
    ❏　Self-employed
    ❏　Manager
    ❏　Clerk
    ❏　Factory worker
    ❏　Homemaker
    ❏　Retiree
    ❏　Student
    ❏　Other (please explain) ....

33. How many people is your household comprised of? ....

34. Which of the following categories best describes your pre-tax household income? (Your answers are confidential.)
    - ❑ Less than 15 million lire
    - ❑ 15 to 20 million lire
    - ❑ 20 to 30 million lire
    - ❑ 30 to 50 million lire
    - ❑ 50 to 80 million lire
    - ❑ 80 to 150 million lire
    - ❑ More than 150 million lire

35. Which percentage of total household income do you contribute?
    - ❑ Less than 50%
    - ❑ 50% to 75%
    - ❑ More than 75%

This is the end of the questionnaire!
The Universities of Padua and Venice thank you for your attention and for taking the time to complete the questionnaire.

PART III

Assessing Remediation Options and Policies for
Contaminated Sites in the Venice Area

8. What is the Value of Brownfields? A Review of Possible Approaches

Stefania Tonin

8.1 INTRODUCTION

Brownfield redevelopment is currently considered to be one of the key factors for urban regeneration. According to the United States Environmental Protection Agency (US EPA), the term brownfield site means real property, the expansion, redevelopment, or reuse of which may be complicated by the presence or potential presence of a hazardous substance, pollutant, or contaminant (US EPA, 2001). Implicit in the word brownfield is the need to consider whether the land can be reused. Cleanup and redevelopment of these areas can contribute to creating new employment opportunities, maintaining or enhancing the quality of life, improving recreational opportunities, and enhancing environmental quality and other public goods.

Acquiring, cleaning up and reusing old – and often abandoned – industrial sites can be an expensive and time-consuming undertaking (Bartsch, 2001). In many situations, private developers and financial institutions are not able, or willing, to act on their own to ensure that the full economic potential of site reuse will be achieved. Also, strict liability regimes and the possible adverse effect on human health and on the surrounding economy create hurdles to cleanup and reuse of brownfields.

Contamination may affect the value of a site through three pathways: i) cost of cleaning up or containing the contamination; ii) the stigma factor which may persist even after the area is cleaned up; and iii) liability over future cleanup costs. All of these factors will be broadly examined in the remainder of the paper.

The remainder of the chapter is organized as follows. Section 8.2 outlines the general framework for valuing contaminated land property and the key factors that can influence the economic valuation function. Section 8.3 presents the main valuation techniques applied for contaminated property and some empirical studies. In Section 8.4 we summarize the chapter and discuss which techniques may or may not be applied to study property values and developer preferences for the industrial area at Porto Marghera.

8.2 HOW DO WE VALUE CONTAMINATION?

The economic value of goods or services is generally captured by market price or, more precisely, by how much people are willing to pay to obtain them. Absent markets where certain goods – such as environmental quality and risks to human health – are traded, economists have resorted to a variety of techniques to place a value on them. In general, there are two main approaches for valuing non-market goods: revealed preference and stated preference methods. With revealed preference techniques, preferences for environmental goods are revealed indirectly when individuals purchase market goods that are in some way related to the non-market goods. Examples include the travel cost and the hedonic price methods.

By contrast, stated preference techniques seek to obtain consumers preferences directly through direct questions about their willingness to pay for a specified good (contingent valuation) or by asking people to choose among hypothetical alternatives (conjoint choice). Both of these approaches rely on surveying individuals.

The main question of this chapter is how we place a value on contaminated land. The easiest answer to this question is to subtract the cost of cleanup from the value of uncontaminated property. Chan (2000) warns that consideration should also be given to factors such as marketability, stigma, and possible change of highest and best use. Formally:

$$V_c = V_u - L - C_r - S \tag{8.1}$$

where V_c is the value of the land in its contaminated state, V_u is the value of the land in its uncontaminated state, L is the loss due to reduced income/productivity and/or legal liabilities, C_r measures investigation and remediation costs, and S captures stigma impacts.

Until a few years ago, only specialists attempted to rehabilitate contaminated properties. Today, many developers are interested in brownfield redevelopment because well-located, non-polluted sites have become harder to find, remediation technology is cheaper than ever before and there is more clarity related to liability and government-sponsored incentives (Leon, 2003).

Another reason is the high profit potential in brownfield redevelopment due to the below-market or subsidized pricing for the properties. Private sellers often prefer to lower the price of idle properties than incur the costs associated with possible contamination. In addition, the presence of existing infrastructure at most brownfield sites can save on development costs.

Another way to write equation (8.1) is to recognize that the value of the land is the discounted stream of profits associated with its use. Profit P earned by developers is:

$$P = R - V - C - D - L - AC \qquad (8.2)$$

where R is the revenue from the project, V is the cost of buying the land, C is the cleanup cost, D captures other development costs, L is expected liability, and AC captures other costs incurred due to contamination (e.g., loss of income or higher cost of borrowing). In the remainder of this section we discuss some of the factors included in equation (8.2) and how they can influence the profits resulting from contaminated land redevelopment operations.

The market demand for a contaminated site depends on local/regional economic conditions, and often it is very limited (thin market) or unknown. Those who invest in contaminated sites incur potentially large costs for each phase of the redevelopment project, such as the environmental and risk assessment, and remediation. These costs have to be weighed against the revenue of the project.

Whenever high costs and risks are linked with pollution and the purchase of the property, investor interest often falls off. The ability to attract private funds is one of the critical steps in a successful initiative to restore an abandoned area.

Even if they are less important now than in the past, there are a number of disadvantages associated with the development of contaminated areas: the environmental liability regime, lender reluctance based on uncertainty and impaired collateral, time and complexity of environmental and land use approval processes and delayed return on initial investment are some of the factors that may discourage developers from undertaking brownfield projects. In addition, those who decide to invest in brownfield sites may incur high initial transaction costs, such as the site assessment for identifying the type and extent of the contamination. Other potentially important factors include time delays in the realization of the projects, higher costs for the activation of loans, additional costs caused by change cleanup standards due to subsequent changes in regulations, and other legal expenses.

Wolfe (2000) points out that in the USA, in recent years, a number of factors have combined to improve the regulatory and business climate for redeveloping urban brownfields. As the pressure to reuse urban properties has increased, developers and other stakeholders with substantial economic resources have become interested in brownfields, thanks to increasingly flexible approaches to liability avoidance. Regulatory initiatives have resulted in a business opportunity which can reduce both cleanup and redevelopment costs. Wolfe highlights the fact that a brownfield project can offer certain advantages to both owners and prospective purchasers or developers, such as: i) obtain more favourable cleanup standards which are consistent with future land use, ii) reduce long term care requirements by placing the property into productive use, iii) overcome regulatory inertia by obtaining local support for job creation and increasing the tax base, iv) recover the asset value of the property in the marketplace, and v) address liability concerns.

The purchaser, knowing the physical and chemical characteristics of contaminants and soil, may utilize the best cleanup technology, eliminating less appropriate choices. Many operators work closely with the local authority and the private sector to identify the sites to develop, determine a final end use that is appropriate for the site and the surrounding community, encourage the adoption of more favorable approaches for cleanup, and to ensure the resources necessary for the development are available.

Cost of Cleanup

The cost of cleanup depends on the type and severity of contamination (extent, mobility of contaminants, and health risks of the pollutant) and the characteristics of the site itself (location and historical conditions of the area), the choice of the best available cleanup technology and, finally, the administrative and legal costs relative to the acquisition, cleaning and recovery of contaminated sites.

Impediments to brownfields redevelopment include: i) lack of funding for cleanup; ii) liability concerns for owners and redevelopers arising from the legislation; iii) requirements for expensive environmental assessments; and iv) uncertainty over cleanup standards.

Liability

We have already discussed how liability can hinder contaminated property redevelopment in general. Urban Institute et al. (1997) select a mix of successful and failed redevelopment projects in various cities in the US, and interview developers, consultants, lawyers and public officials involved in them about the hurdles they encountered. Liability concerns were frequently cited by appraisers as obstacles to redevelopment, but almost always in combination with issues of known (or anticipated) costs. Liability refers to the risk that additional costs may be incurred as a result of the discovery of large amounts of unknown contamination, future litigation over damages or cleanup costs, and other highly uncertain events. Liability concerns are compounded by uncertainty over changes in environmental standards and remediation technologies that may require additional outlays for contamination already remediated.

Other Costs Incurred Due to Contamination

Brownfield redevelopment projects pose higher levels of uncertainty to decision-makers than other property investments. The higher risks refer to the site assessments needed to determine the type and extent of the pollutants, remediation planning, the execution of remediation plans, and the environmental damage liability claims associated with the past pollution of a site. Any one of these factors implies higher transaction costs that involve an array of measurement, information, bargaining, and contracting costs other than those associated with acquisition of land.[1]

Another key factor is that for successful brownfield redevelopment, there may be several interested parties or stakeholders and this means that much time and money is needed to identify interests, conflicts and problems. At the very minimum, interested parties will include i) the property owner; ii) the brownfield redeveloper; iii) the lender or financial backer; iv) the regulators; v) local government planning and redevelopment agencies; and vi) representatives from the affected community.

Although many contaminated sites have the potential for becoming profitable business opportunities, generating new activities and new employment opportunities, they often need public investment. The role of the public sector in these projects is to design the cleanup strategy, to pinpoint the appropriate areas for development, to initiate the remediation process, to provide funding and to encourage the participation of the private sector (OECD, 2000).

Other costs incurred due to contamination are related to the difficulties in accessing the necessary funding for development project. According to a study of the International City/County Management Association (2001), financiers are risk averse in issues relating to the environment, but are slowing changing their attitude about projects involving polluted areas. When developers, investors and companies are involved in redevelopment projects, they want to assess risks quickly. The fear of surprises has implied substantial changes in funding practices.

Strachota (1998) surveyed almost 3000 lending institutions across the United States to study the reactions of these institutions to transactions involving contaminated real estate. The survey revealed that over the previous five years lending institutions had become much more involved with the issue of environmental contamination. Approximately 7 percent of loan applications received by the responding institutions in this survey involved properties with some form of contamination. Along with their increased involvement, lending institutions have become much more sensitized to the potential impact of environmental contamination. The respondents indicated that of the loan applications involving contaminated property, over half are rejected based upon the risks associated with this contamination. Strachota (1998) estimates that environmental auditing was required in 67 percent of the applications in his sample. It is worth mentioning that these financial institutions did not express confidence in EPA regulations, considering them the cause of many economic risks, such as potential collateral value losses of the property, inability of those who applied for loans to return the capital, and loss of financial interests.

The Value of Externalities: Other Factors that Can Influence Property Value

Other positive and negative factors can influence the economic value of brownfields. In theory, possible effects on human health, ecological damage, aesthetic damage, as well as the availability of infrastructure and the creation of new employment and production opportunities could be captured into the value of these parcels.

It is sometimes argued that brownfield property values are negatively affected by stigma. Stigma is a market-imposed penalty that can affect a property that is known or suspected to be contaminated, property that was once contaminated but is now considered clean, or a never contaminated property located in proximity to a contaminated property (Patchin, 1988). In a rational market place, once the property has been cleaned up, the value of the property should return to its normal precontaminated market value.

However, there is evidence that suggests that despite cleanup in compliance with the standards, potential buyers are reluctant to purchase previously contaminated properties. The issue of stigma is discussed at length in the section below.

The Stigma Factor: What Does It Mean and How Can We Measure It?

Researchers offer various definitions and interpretations for the stigma effect (Jackson, 2003; Appraisal Institute of Canada, 1998), but generally agree that it is an intangible, abstract element that can influence the property value and is not easily measurable.

Patchin (1991) broadly defines stigma as a loss in value beyond the cost of remediation. He lists the following factors as possible causes of stigma: i) fear of hidden cleanup costs which creates uncertainty in the total cleanup cost; ii) the trouble factor, which refers to the return that should be allocated to an entrepreneurial effort that is required to deal with the contamination;[2] iii) fear of public liability; iv) lack of mortgageability; v) residential vs. commercial, in the sense that market reaction to contamination differs according to whether the property is residential or commercial; vi) uncertainty about the extent of cleanup required by law (how clean is clean?).

The stigma effect can have an impact on the value of contaminated sites before, during and after the cleanup process. Dale et al. (1997) and McCluskey and Rausser (1999) examine temporary or permanent stigma using the hedonic pricing (HP) approach with house sale prices in Dallas, Texas. The empirical evidence suggests that stigma affects only in properties situated in the closest proximity to dangerous sites. By contrast, Hurd (2002) finds that property near hazardous waste sites can recover value over time because of changes in buyer perceptions.

The post-reclamation stigma effect is the residual value loss that is obtained after taking into account recovery, insurance and monitoring costs. Bond (2001) defines it as the difference between the value of a recovered site and the value of a clean site, without any precedent contamination. To estimate the monetary losses due to these factors, Weber (1997) uses a Monte-Carlo technique to estimate the probability of post-recovering stigma effects occurring. Kinnard and Worzala (1999) claim that in the United States the availability of real estate market sale data, and improved and more reliable valuation techniques, allow the estimation of the post-recovery stigma effect. Roddewig (1996, 1999) and Elliot-Jones (1999) rely on market sale data for to identify the loss of value which they attribute to the stigma effect.

Chan (2001) surveyed 500 Australian real estate appraisers with experience in the valuation of contaminated sites. The majority of those interviewed confirmed that there is a stigma effect and that they take it into account during the appraisal process. Chan points out that not all contaminated properties suffer from the stigma effect, and that there are other important factors that should be considered such as the type and stage of contamination, the remediation methods used, the cleanup standards attained, the period of time between the discovery and the assessment of the contamination, the identification of the person responsible or owner of the area, and market conditions. By contrast, Urban Institute (1997), finds little empirical evidence of stigma in transactions of reclaimed properties. In fact, in only one of 48 cases is the stigma effect found to hinder project development.

In sum, the evidence of stigma is not unambiguous. We conclude that the results obtained depend on the different location investigated, on the different methods applied and on the people's perception of the contamination problem. Moreover, the stigma (if any) is likely to be temporary (before and during cleaning up of the site), but there is no strong evidence of the presence of permanent stigma (after site remediation is complete).

In spite of the many studies that have been published, especially in the US and Great Britain, a gap in research remains regarding the type and measurement of the stigma effect, the risk perceived by players in the market and the approach used to isolate its effect.

8.3   FROM THEORY TO PRACTICE: THE ECONOMIC VALUATION OF BROWNFIELDS

In this chapter, we classify valuation techniques for contaminated sites into two main categories depending on whether they refer to traditional appraisal theory (e.g., cost approach, market approach or income approach), or empirically study the effects of contamination and other negative environmental externalities that determine a change in real estate prices (e.g., hedonic pricing). These methods are reviewed in what follows.

Appraisal Method

Chan (2000) distinguishes between two basic approaches to valuing contaminated land. The first is the unimpaired valuation approach (or unaffected approach). The unimpaired value of a property is the value considering all restrictions on use and costs of ownership other than those imposed by the presence of an environmental risk. It requires the appraiser to value the property as if it were clean. The appraiser highlights this assumption in the valuation report and warns the client about the possible impacts of the contamination of the site.

This approach is not particularly helpful to the client, as the valuation does not reflect the real conditions on site. The next approach is known as the impaired valuation approach (or affected value approach). Wilson (1994) points out that in the US the impaired value is derived from the unimpaired value using the formula:

$$I = U - C_{NCP} - C_R - C_F - M_U \qquad (8.3)$$

where I is the impaired value, U is the unimpaired value, C_{NCP} is the cost to implement the remediation plan consistent with the National Oil and Hazardous Substances Pollution Contingency Plan, C_R is the cost of restrictions on use and/or environmental liability prevention, C_F is the impaired financial cost, and M_U captures intangible market factors.

In other words, the impaired value gives due consideration to the impact of environmental risks known or thought to be present. Using this approach, the appraiser first values the property as if it were clean. A deduction is then made for any production (income) loss due to the contamination, and loss due to any investigation and remediation cost and stigma factor.

Clearly, appraisal valuation depends crucially on the choice of the final end use of the real estate property. The traditional appraisal approaches are: 1) market (sales) comparison approach; 2) income method and 3) (replacement) cost approach.

The market comparison approach compares the property under appraisal with recent offerings and sales of similar properties. It is the most common method used to estimate the value of personal, portable, tangible property. By definition, this approach should result in the most accurate representation of fair market value. The basis of this approach is that the estimated value of the property is best determined by gathering market data on previous transactions where identical assets have changed hands and then applying the previous transactions to the property presently being appraised.

The income method is based on the capitalization of the income derived by real estate property. An income approach analysis involves the following steps: i) identification and quantification of revenue sources to estimate gross potential income; ii) deduction of an allowance for vacancy and collection loss to estimate the effective gross income; iii) identification and quantification of operating expenses and potential refunds; iv) estimation of net operating income; v) estimation of appropriate capitalization rate and discount rate; and vi) performance of direct capitalization on discounted cash flow analysis and test of reasonableness (Keating, 1994).

The (replacement) cost approach involves estimating the site value, estimating the improvement value and summing site value and improvement value. Site value and improvement value are not analysed together. This method treats site value as an exogenous variable. It is simply a number that is determined elsewhere and has no part in cost analysis (Ramsett, 1998).

Ramsett (1998) states that the cost approach is an effective method for value estimation, and in some cases the only available method for valuing unique properties or other special situation. The cost approach may be improved by calculating more reliable estimates of cleanup costs, and/or demonstrable market value losses due to the negative effect of stigma factor. The risk in performing that adjustment is that it is necessary to avoid overestimating cleanup cost and stigma.

McLean and Mundy (1998) point out that the traditional valuation techniques for properties are often problematic with contaminated sites. This is due to three reasons. First, the market for real estate properties that have been exposed to short- or long-term contamination is often thin, and the recent or even long-term sales history may be spotty or limited. Second, these may be limited awareness or knowledge among prospective buyers of the extent of the contamination, its risks and current status. Third, knowledge about these factors may spread unevenly throughout the population and changes in property values reflecting contamination may correspondingly occur unevenly over time.

The decrease in property value measured by the traditional techniques reflects any predictable market value loss on the property due to contamination, the longer time needed to sell the property because of the pollution, and the loss of use and enjoyment of the property. In some cases, health problems resulting from pollution are included. It should be borne in mind that all these elements affect the market price only when the potential buyers have complete information about the problem, and as McLean and Mundy (1998) point out, this is unlikely to happen for those operating in the market of contaminated properties.

McLean and Mundy (1998), suggest using compensation measures based upon the cost of cleanup along with the traditional valuation methods. Frequently, those approaches cannot evaluate correctly either the risks for a potential buyer nor the decreased value observed even after the substantial removal of the contamination (stigma effect). The prices of uncontaminated properties, adjusted to reflect the actual value of cleanup costs, may be used as benchmarks.

Jackson (2001) notes that the literature regarding valuation has offered few empirical studies of contaminated real estate, but has focused on how existing appraisal methods can be adapted to estimate the impacts of contamination on market value. One reason for the lack of empirical research about contamination and industrial/commercial properties, compared to the residential property studies, is that contaminated commercial and industrial properties have only recently begun to sell more frequently. In the past, the risks perceived by market participants were such that equity and debt capital were generally unavailable for contaminated properties. This situation appears to be changing, and sales data are becoming more available.

Hedonic Pricing Method

Property is an example of what in economics is termed a differentiated good. Such goods consist of a diversity of products that, while differing in a variety of characteristics, are so closely related in consumers' minds that they are considered as being one commodity.

It is possible to describe any particular property by the characteristics of its structure, environs and location. Let **z** be a vectors of descriptors of the physical characteristics of a property and its surroundings. The hedonic price function generally takes this form:

$$P = P(\mathbf{z}) \qquad (8.4)$$

In other words, the price of a property (P) is a function of **z**. The function is known as hedonic because it is determined by the different qualities of the differentiated good and the utility that these would bring to the purchaser. In empirical work, prices are regressed on characteristics **z**, and the regression coefficients give the implicit prices of each characteristic. A complication is that these values are not likely to be the same for all price ranges of houses. For this reason, the hedonic pricing model is often estimated in semi-log form with the natural log of price used as the dependent variable. The resulting coefficient estimates allow one to calculate the percentage change in price for a one-unit change in the given variable.

Empirical Studies: the Market Value of Brownfields Using Appraisal Methods

Chan (2000) reports that researchers working on contaminated property issues use various appraisal methods such as the direct comparison method (Patchin, 1994), the capitalization method (Patchin, 1988; Mundy, 1992; Neustein, 1992; Dixon, 1996), the impaired value (Wilson, 1994), the hypothetical development method (Simm, 1992; Liang, 1992), and the discounted cash flow method (Fisher et al., 1992; Gronow, 1998, 1999).

Neustein (1992) applies the income approach method for a contaminated industrial property in the Los Angeles area. He uses the reduction in occupancy rate as a substitute for the reduction in net income and he finds a 20.7 percent decrease in value.

Patchin (1988) proposes the capitalization method because it takes account of increased risks of ownership, difficulties in financing, etc. This method depends on three major factors: equity yield rate, mortgage terms available and anticipated future appreciation or depreciation. Using the sales comparison approach, Patchin (1994) computes the difference between unimpaired sale price and impaired sale price, which he attributes to stigma. He finds that properties that are in high demand and are hard to find in the market generally experience less stigma than those with many substitutes.

Wilson (1992) notes that the mere presence of environmental risk does not automatically imply devaluation. To devalue a property the environmental risk must: i) result in a cost to remediate the problem; ii) result in an increased operating cost; and/or iii) result in a perception in the marketplace that the property is less desirable than a property without that environmental risk present. He disagrees that the impaired value can be established through the sales comparison approach, claiming that each environmental impairment to value is as unique as a fingerprint and is generally not obvious or amenable to adjustments. Wilson concludes that the appraiser must rely on complex technical assessments performed by other experts to have the complete information of the site history.

In concluding, we note that all of these traditional methods encounter difficulties due to the lack of market data, and because every environmental problem has unique characteristics, making any further comparison with other properties difficult.

Empirical Studies: Valuing Brownfields Using the Hedonic Pricing Method

The hedonic pricing method has been applied in numerous studies to determine the influence of environmental contamination on the value of properties located in the proximity of these sites (see, for example, Roddewig, 1996, 1999, and Hirshfeld et al., 1992). Several studies (Ketkar 1992; Kiel, 1995; Kiel and McClain 1995; Kohlhase 1991; Smith and Desvousges 1986; and Thayer et al., 1992) have found that proximity to a hazardous site reduces housing prices by an amount that depends on distance from the site.

McCluskey and Rausser (1999) estimate the existence and duration of contamination stigma through a hedonic price model using sale prices of homes in Texas between 1979 and 1995 for a total of over 200 000 observations. This study uses repeat sales for the same property to examine post-cleanup property values, and temporary v. permanent price effects. Bond (2000) analyses sale transactions after remediation and then surveys residents to find out their perceptions of the sites contamination history. The stigma implies a decrease of 36 percent in sale price, but this may be offset by other positive characteristics of the site (cycle tracks, proximity to a river and playgrounds for children). Bible et al. (2001) use a sample of 1005 housing units sold between 1990 and 1998 in Northwest Louisiana, an area with many brownfields, establishing that proximity of a house to contaminated sites reduces the value of the property, even if the area has been remediated, which suggests the existence of stigma.

Kiel and Zabel (2001) estimate the appreciation in housing values associated with cleaning up a Superfund site in Woburn, Massachusetts, and use it to approximate the total benefits from cleanup. This study suggests that the benefits of cleanup are likely to outweigh the costs of cleanup, but should not generalized to all Superfund sites.

Jackson (2001) points out that the residential property value literature is concerned with situations in which the impacted properties are not the source of the contamination, but are affected by contamination generated from other sources and properties. There have been few attempts to model the price of commercial and industrial properties in a hedonic framework and even fewer studies that have looked at the effect of environmental contamination on industrial and commercial property values. The application of this technique to commercial and industrial properties is limited by the difficulty of assembling a sufficiently large number of transactions on relatively homogeneous properties.

Guntermann (1995) explores the impact that open and closed sanitary landfills have on surrounding industrial land values using 153 transactions of industrially zoned land in Phoenix, Arizona over 1984 to 1994. The results of this research indicate that an open solid waste landfill adversely affects the value of surrounding industrial land. There is no evidence that closed solid waste landfills adversely affect land values.

Munneke (1996) posits that if a parcels value in a redeveloped state increases relative to its value in its current use, then the probability of redevelopment increases. Support for this relationship is found using single-family dwellings in Vancouver, and land for commercial and industrial uses in Chicago. McGrath (2000) uses a similar model for 195 industrial properties sold in Chicago from August 1983 to November 1993. He models the land demolition costs as a function of environmental contamination variables. The results of this study support the conclusion that industrial land investors are discounting their bid to account for contamination risk, and within the city of Chicago, contamination risk appears to have been fully capitalized into industrial land values. Contamination risk reduces the value of land, which in the short term reduces the value differential available to an investor and increases the scale of financial capital required for redevelopment. But evidence suggests that investors could expect to recoup the expenditures required to remove contamination liability through the increase in land value after remediation. Another implication of this study is that on average, in his sample, a hypothetical cleanup of the parcel improves the probability of redevelopment.

Jackson (2002) examines the effects of environmental contamination on the sale prices of industrial properties using sales in Southern California from 1995 to 1999 and matched case-control approach. Industrial properties with unremediated contamination transact at prices approximately 30 percent less than unimpaired properties, but are undistinguishable after cleanup from comparable uncontaminated properties. This price reduction and rebound provides investment opportunities for venture capital and opportunity funds with investment objectives consistent with these levels of risk. Furthermore, this study provides strong statistical evidence of the temporary nature of market adjustments and the stigma effect for contaminated industrial real estate. In none of the models analysed was there any indication that the price effects of environmental contamination persist subsequent to remediation and cleanup.

Howland (2002) investigates if the cost of cleanup are so high relative to land values that government has to provide subsidies, and to what extent contamination deters central city revitalization. The study attempts to answer these questions by tracking all sales, the selling price, length of time on the market and presence of contamination in one industrial area southwest of Baltimore. She examines 740 parcels stated for industrial use, and the final number of parcels that went on the market over ten years is 161. She finds that contaminated properties do sell without government intervention, and that sellers and buyers have adjusted to contamination by lowering prices. In her sample the strongest barriers to redevelopment are: i) cleanup costs that raise expenditures beyond what a residential market can bear in a weak housing market; ii) outdated road configurations that make truck access difficult; iii) antiquated infrastructure and inadequate telecommunications linkages, iv) a mixture of incompatible and adjacent residential and industrial land uses, and v) obsolete uses which are expensive to demolish.

Schoenbaum (2002) investigates the effects of real environmental contamination on land value and economic development in a heavily industrialized area of Baltimore, Maryland, that has both brownfields and rapid recent economic development. She collects a time series dataset of all-non residential parcels continuously existing between 1963–1999. Land use is assumed to be a function of the characteristics of each specific property and its surroundings. She concludes that environmental contamination alone cannot account for the existence of vacant or underused industrial properties in central cities. Other unknown factors affect the industrial property transactions.

Ihlanfeldt and Taylor (2004) investigate the potential effects of hazardous waste sites on commercial and industrial property values in Fulton County, Georgia, which are more likely to be located near hazardous waste sites (HWS) as compared to residential properties, and to incur spillover-induced changes in value large enough that private cost-sharing and tax increment financing emerge as possible funding mechanisms for cleanup.

Empirical Studies: Alternative Brownfields Valuation Methods

Mclean and Mundy (1998) use three complementary approaches to estimate the value of a contaminated property: contingent valuation, conjoint analysis, and the perceived diminution approach among owners and prospective purchasers of property. The perceived diminution approach, in this application, measures an owner's own estimate of value diminution in his home due to the contamination using the owner's perceived value of a similar uncontaminated home as a basis.

They find that the use of the three approaches gives a range of damage estimates from $31 500 to $41 200 per residence in the affected area. They conclude that the contingent valuation estimate is the most defensible of the three because it is presented to property owners as compensation for the existence of the contamination, the probable loss in property value, and the loss of enjoyment and use of the property.

8.4   DISCUSSION: WHAT METHODS CAN BE USED TO VALUE THE PORTO MARGHERA SITE?

The Porto Marghera industrial site, which is situated very close to the Lagoon of Venice, covers about 2000 hectares, most of which are heavily polluted. A large part of Marghera is still an active industrial site: about 70 percent of the Italian chemical output is produced here, both for the Italian and the international market. Porto Marghera was placed on the National Priority List in 1998 (National Contaminated Sites Remediation Plan, Law 426/1998). Figure 8.1 shows a map of the Porto Marghera site.

At the time of this writing, only five properties had been sold at the Porto Marghera site during the last ten years. This means that the hedonic price method cannot be applied to estimate the effect of contamination in the industrial properties. Even appraisal techniques cannot be applied for lack of sufficient comparable properties.

Based on this, we decided that our best option for finding out how

Figure 8.1   The national interest site of Porto Marghera

developers can be enticed to clean-up and redevelop contaminated properties was to survey them and ask them to engage in choice experiments based on hypothetical projects and hypothetical government incentives, rather than attempting to predict the attractiveness (or unattractiveness) of contaminated sites by looking at their prices. The conjoint choice survey and the results of that study are reported in a separate chapter within this volume.

In sum, this chapter has looked at the factors that may influence the value of abandoned and contaminated industrial sites, including the uncertainty about the outcome of the cleanup, liability, stigma effects, delays in securing funding or project approval, etc. Despite these problems, municipalities and researchers feel that brownfield redevelopment is an important component of urban regeneration and sustainable urban growth.

Policy recommendations rely crucially on understanding how contamination and cleanup are captured into property prices, and this chapter provides a survey of possible approaches to doing exactly that. Appraisal methods are often of limited usefulness when used to assess the value of sites subject to contamination because of a lack of market data on real estate sales. Alternative approaches include the contingent valuation method and the hedonic price method. The latter has been widely used especially to determine the influence of environmental contamination on the contaminated properties values and on those located in their proximity.

Despite the large number of studies in the economic literature relating to the valuation of real estate property, relatively few of them have been able to infer the economic value of benefits deriving from the redevelopment of industrial and commercial properties. Further research is necessary to estimate all the economic benefits that may be derived from contaminated sites' redevelopment that can contribute to the regeneration of urban areas.

NOTES

1. Transaction cost is the amount of time, money and effort needed to establish, monitor, and enforce a particular policy.
2. Patchin reports that when contaminated properties, in particular single-family residential properties, sell before a remediation is undertaken, the difference between the unimpaired value and the actual selling price may be substantially greater than the cost of cleanup. Analysis of this disparity indicates that in addition to the costs of cleanup, the property value is $10 000 or $20 000 lower.

REFERENCES

Appraisal Institute of Canada (1998), 'Environmental Impacts', *Appraisal Guidelines*, available at http://www.pwgsc.gc.ca/realproperty/text/pubs_valuation/toc-e.html (last access: November 2005).

Bartsch, C., (2001), 'Financing Brownfield Cleanup and Redevelopment', available at http://www.nemw.org/brownfin.htm (last access: November 2005).

Bible, D.S., C. Hsieh, G. Joiner and D.W. Volentine (2001), 'Environmental Effects on Residential Property Values Resulting from the Contamination Effects of a Creosote Plant Site', paper presented at the 'I Congresso Mondiale della International Real Estate Society in Alyeska Resort', July 2001.

Bond, S. (2000), 'Estimating Stigma of Ex-Contaminated Land: the Buyer Beware Principle Reigns', paper presented at the 6th Conference of Pacific Rim Real Estate Society, Sydney, 23–27 January 2000.

Bond, S. (2001), 'Conjoint Analysis: Assessing Buyer Preferences for Property Attributes to Assist with the Estimation of Land Contamination Stigma', Paper presented to at the Conference of Pacific Rim Real Estate Society, Adelaide, 21–24 January, 2001.

Chan, N. (2000), 'How Australian Valuers Value Contaminated Land', paper presented at the Conference of Pacific Rim Real Estate Society, Sidney, 23–27 January 2000.

Chan, N. (2001), 'Stigma and its Assessment Methods', paper presented at the Conference of Pacific Rim Real Estate Society, Adelaide, 21–24 January 2001.

Dale, L., J.C. Murdoch, M.A. Thayer and P.A. Waddell (1997), 'Do Property Values Rebound from Environmental Stigmas? Evidence from Dallas', Law and Economics Consulting Group, Emeryville.

Dixon, T.J. (1996), 'Contaminated Land: a changing landscape', *Estate Gazette*, **9608**, 136–8.

Elliot-Jones, M. (1999), 'Markets for Contaminated Properties', Paper n. 19, Bala Research Inc.

Fisher, J.D., G.H. Lentz and K.S.M. Tse (1992), 'Valuation of Commercial Properties Contaminated With Asbestos', *Journal of Real Estate Research*, **7**, 331–50.

Gronow, S. (1998), 'Contaminated Land: The Inevitability of an Explicit Appraisal Model', *Property Management*, **16**(1), 24–32.

Gronow, S. (1999), 'Contaminated Land: Quantifying the Inputs to an Explicit Appraisal Model', *Property Management*, **17**(2), 169–85.

Guntermann, K.L. (1995), 'Sanitary Landfills, Stigma and Industrial Land Values', *The Journal of Real Estate Research*, **10**(5), 531–42.

Hirshfeld, S., P.A. Veslind and E.I. Pas (1992), 'Assessing the True Cost of Landfills', *Water Management and Research*, **10**, 471–84.

Howland, M. (2002), 'What Makes for a Successful Brownfield Redevelopment? Three Baltimore Case Studies', available at http://www.smartgrowth.umd.edu/research/researchpapers-landuseandenvironment.htm (last access: November 2005)

Hurd, B.H. (2002), 'Valuing Superfund Site Cleanup: Evidence of Recovering Stigmatized Property Values', *The Appraisal Journal*, **70**(4), 426–37.

Ihlanfeldt, K. R. and L.O. Taylor (2004), 'Externality Effects of Small-scale Hazardous Waste Sites: Evidence from Urban Commercial Property Markets', *Journal of Environmental Economics and Management*, **47**, 117–39.

International City/County Management Association (2001), *Brownfields Redevelopment: A Guidebook for Local Governments and Communities*, Second Edition, chapter 6.

Jackson, T.O. (2001), 'The Effect of Environmental Contamination on Real Estate: A Literature Review', *Journal of Real Estate Literature*, **9**(2), 93–116.

Jackson, T.O. (2002), 'Environmental Contamination and Industrial Real Estate Prices', *Journal of Real Estate Research*, **23**(1/2), 179–99.

Jackson, T.O. (2003), 'Appraisal Standards and Contaminated Property Valuation',

The Appraisal Journal, **71**(2), 127–33.

Keating, D.M (1994), 'Appraising Continuing Care Retirement Centers: The Income Approach', *The Appraisal Journal*, **62**(4), 546–52.

Ketkar, K. (1992), 'Hazardous Waste Sites and Property Values in the State of New Jersey', *Applied Economics*, **24**, 647–59.

Kiel, K.A. (1995), 'Measuring the Impact of the Discovery and Cleaning of Identified Hazardous Waste Sites on House Values', *Land Economics*, **71**, 428–35.

Kiel, K.A. and K.T. McClain (1995), 'House Price Recovery and Stigma after a Failed Siting', *Applied Economics*, **28**, 1351–8.

Kiel, K. and J. Zabel (2001), 'Estimating the Economic Benefits of Cleaning Up Superfund Sites: The case of Woburn, Massachusetts', *Journal of Real Estate Finance and Economics*, **22**(2/3), 163–84.

Kinnard, W.N. and E.W. Worzala (1999), 'How North American Appraisers Value Contaminated Property and Associated Stigma', *The Appraisal Journal*, **67**(3) 269–78.

Kohlhase, J.E. (1991), 'The Impact of Toxic Waste Sites on Housing Values', *Journal of Urban Economics*, **30**, 1–26.

Leon, H. (2003), 'Squeezing Green out of Brownfield Development', *National Real Estate Investor*, **45** (6), 48–51.

Liang, N. (1992), 'Putting a Price on the Problem – Valuation Issues', Conference paper, Drivers Jonas, London.

McCluskey, J.J. and G.C. Rausser (1999), *Stigmatized Asset Value: Is it Temporary or Permanent?*, College of Natural Resources, University of California, Berkeley.

McGrath, D.T. (2000), 'Urban Industrial Land Redevelopment and Contamination Risk', *Journal of Urban Economics*, **47**, 414–42.

McLean, D.G. and B. Mundy (1998), 'The Addition of Contingent Valuation and Conjoint Analysis to the Required Body of Knowledge for the Estimation of Environmental Damages to Real Property', *Journal of Real Estate Practice and Education*, **1**(1), 1–19.

Mundy, B. (1992), 'Stigma and Value', *The Appraisal Journal*, **60**(1), 7–13.

Munneke, H.J. (1996), 'Redevelopment Decisions for Commercial and Industrial Properties', *Journal of Urban Economics*, **39**, 229–53.

Neustein, R.A. (1992), 'Estimating Value Diminution by the Income Approach', *The Appraisal Journal*, **60**(2), 283–7.

OECD (2000), 'Urban Brownfields', OECD Territorial Development Service.

Patchin, P.J. (1988), 'Valuation of Contaminated Properties', *The Appraisal Journal*, **10**, 7–16.

Patchin, P.J. (1991), 'Contaminated Property: Stigma Revisited', *The Appraisal Journal*, **56** (1), 167–72.

Patchin, P.J. (1994), 'Contaminated Properties and the Sales Comparison Approach', *The Appraisal Journal*, **62**(3), 402–9.

Ramsett, D.E. (1998), 'The Cost Approach: An Alternative View', *The Appraisal Journal*, **20**, 172–80.

Roddewig, R.J. (1996), 'Stigma, Environmental Risk and Property Value: 10 Critical Inquiries', *Appraisal Journal*, **67**, 98–102.

Roddewig, R.J. (1999), 'Classifying the Level of Risk and Stigma Affecting Contaminated Properties', *Appraisal Journal*, **31**, 98–102.

Schoenbaum, M. (2002), 'Environmental Contamination, Brownfields Policy, and Economic Redevelopment in an Industrial Area of Baltimore, Maryland', *Land Economics*, **78**(1), 60–71.

Simm, G. (1992), 'Problems for the Valuation Surveyor', paper presented at Seminar on Environmental Assessment, Sheffield City Polytechnic, 5 March 1992.

Smith, V.K. and W.H. Desvousges (1986), The Value of Avoiding a LULU: Hazardous Waste Disposal Sites', *The Review of Economics and Statistics*, **68**, 293–9.

Strachota, R.J. (1998), *Stigma Damage: Recent Trends Affecting the Value of Contaminated Properties*, Shenehon Company, available at http://www.shenehon.com/ Library/valuation_viewpoint/stigma.htm (last access: November 2005).

Thayer, M., H. Albers and M. Rahmatian (1992), 'The Benefits of Reducing Exposure to Waste Disposal Sites: A Hedonic Housing Value Approach', *The Journal of Real Estate Research*, **7**(3), 265–82.

Urban Institute, Northeast-Midwest Institute, University of Louisville, University of Northern Kentucky (1997), *The Effect of Environmental Hazards and Regulation on Urban Redevelopment*, UI Project N. 06542-003-00.

US Environmental Protection Agency (2001), *The Brownfields Economic Redevelopment Initiative Proposal Guidelines for Brownfields Cleanup*, EPA 500-F-01-348.

Weber, B.R. (1997), 'The Valuation of Contaminated Land', *Journal of Real Estate Research*, **14**(3), 379–98.

Wilson, A.R. (1992), 'Environmentally Impaired Valuation: A Team Approach To a Balance Sheet Presentation, Technical Report: Measuring the Effects of Hazardous Materials Contamination on Real Estate Values: Techniques and Applications', *Appraisal Institute*, 23–42.

Wilson, A.R. (1994), The Environmental Opinion: Basis for an Impaired Value Opinion', *The Appraisal Journal*, **62**(3), 410–23.

Wolfe, C.R. (2000), 'Turning Brownfields Green is a Team Effort', available at http://www.djc.com/special/environment2000/wolfe.html (last access: November 2005).

9. Developer Preferences for Brownfield Policies

Anna Alberini, Alberto Longo, Stefania Tonin, Francesco Trombetta and Margherita Turvani

9.1 INTRODUCTION

This study examines different market-based mechanisms and other incentives intended to promote the environmental remediation and reuse of 'brownfields'. Brownfields are 'abandoned, idled or underused industrial and commercial properties where real or perceived contamination complicates expansion or redevelopment' (Simons, 1998). They were created through two concurrent factors: the downsizing and plant closings that started in the 1970s as the economy of the US and of Western European countries moved away from manufacturing, and the passage of legislation that holds responsible parties liable for the cost of cleanup at contaminated sites.

It is often argued that such legislation – in the US, the Comprehensive Environmental Response, Compensation and Liability Act (CERCLA, 1980) – has created disincentives to the redevelopment and reuse of potentially contaminated sites, as liability for the cost of cleanup has been construed to extend to lenders and property owners (Fogleman, 1992). In response, the latter have shied away from potentially contaminated properties.

Brownfield cleanup and reuse, however, are attractive to communities and policymakers for three reasons. First, they reduce the adverse effects of the site's soil and water pollution on human health and ecological systems. Second, they help stop the conversion of agricultural land and rural sites to urban uses and other development patterns that generate environmental problems, congestion and sprawl. Third, they promote economic growth in inner cities and are, therefore, potentially important components of sustainable growth.

Accordingly, federal, state and local initiatives have been recently established to encourage brownfield cleanup and regeneration. In the US, for example, in an effort to mitigate the disincentives created by CERCLA, the States have passed programs offering developers (a) reductions in regulatory burdens, (b) relief from liability for future cleanups and environmental damage once certain mitigation standards are met, and/or (c) financial support for regeneration of brownfields.[1] Similar initiatives are under consideration in several European countries, and voluntary cleanup agreements have been signed and are being implemented at several locales.

We examine the value of interventions and policies targeting brownfields from the point of view of the key economic agents involved – private real estate developers. In this chapter we ask three related questions: first, what economic incentives can be offered to developers to encourage cleanup and reuse of brownfields, and how effective are they? Although economic inducements have been offered for decades to economic agents, little empirical evidence exists documenting the impact of (a), (b) and (c) on brownfield cleanup and investments. Second, what kind of site characteristics and available infrastructure make a parcel attractive for cleanup and reuse, and to what kind of developers? If sites/developers can be identified that are more likely candidates for development, this may allow more effective targeting of policies based on economic incentives and liability or regulatory relief. Third, are developers truly influenced by contamination stigma, whereby a parcel's *potential* or *past* contamination makes it less desirable?

To answer these questions, we survey real estate developers using conjoint choice questions. Our survey questionnaire presents respondents with sets of redevelopment projects, where each project is defined by site attributes (location, contamination, access to transportation nodes) and a mix of government policies. Our policy mix attributes consist of (a) liability relief, (b) direct financial incentives, (c) and regulatory relief, in the form of fast-track approvals of plans and flexible cleanup standards. The survey was administered in person to a sample of developers and real estate professionals intercepted at random at the Marché International des Professionnels de l'Immobilier (MIPIM) in Cannes, France, in March 2002.

Conditional logit models of the responses to the choice questions indicate that developers find sites with contamination problems less attractive than others, and that they do value liability relief. This confirms our expectation that contaminated sites are less desirable because of the associated cleanup costs, but refutes earlier claims (Urban Institute et al., 1997) that liability does not matter. Liability relief is worth about 21 percent of the value of the median development project (€7 million, or approximately 7 million dollars).

Our developers are not deterred by prior contamination, once it has been cleaned up, suggesting that 'contamination stigma' is probably not very important, and appreciate fast-track review of development and remediation plans, direct financial incentives, and flexible cleanup standards.

The fact that liability relief is highly valued by developers provides support for recent trends in US environmental policy, where the States have increasingly resorted to liability relief to promote environmental remediation of contaminated sites. The attractiveness of subsidies, instead, varies across types of developers, and is influenced by prior experience of – and hence efficiency in taking advantage of – these incentives. For example, developers with prior experience with contaminated sites are more responsive to subsidies than other developers, whereas the other economic incentives work better for developers without such prior experience.

The remainder of the chapter is organized as follows: Section 9.2 provides some background information about brownfields. Section 9.3 describes the survey instrument, the conjoint choice questions and the administration of the survey. Section 9.4 discusses how economic incentives can influence the profitability of brownfield redevelopment projects, and presents the econometric model of the responses, as well as variables and hypotheses. Section 9.5 presents the results, and section 9.6 provides concluding remarks.[2]

9.2   BACKGROUND

A. How Did Brownfields Originate?

The problem of brownfields is the result of two concurrent factors: the numerous plant closings and downsizing that started in the 1970s as the US and Western Europe experienced a structural change of their economies away from manufacturing, and the passage of environmental legislation holding specified parties liable for the cost of cleanup at contaminated sites.

In the US, the Comprehensive Environmental Response, Compensation and Liability Act (1980, re-authorized and amended in 1986) holds parties that are responsible for the creation of contaminated sites liable for the cost of cleaning up those sites. Since responsible parties are sought among the owners and operators of the sites, liability has in some cases been construed to apply to those persons who acquire contaminated land, and to lenders that foreclose on contaminated properties.

Many observers believe that the fear of liability keeps investors away from brownfield properties. Fear of liability can have both direct and indirect effects on brownfield development. Developers might shy away from properties believed to be contaminated for fear of future liability, and because immediate cleanup costs may prove too high for the development project to be viable. These may be interpreted as the direct effects of liability. Regarding the indirect effects, developers may fear that lenders deny financing for brownfield projects to avoid possible involvement in liability over contamination, and/or undervalue the property as a collateral for the loan. In addition, it is often speculated that 'contamination stigma' may raise the uncertainty about demand for or reduce the revenue from the sale of contaminated sites.[3]

The most widely cited source of information about the number of brownfield sites in the US is a study by the General Accounting Office (1995), which estimates that there are 130 000 to 450 000 contaminated commercial and industrial sites in the US.[4] In Europe estimates of the size of the problem vary dramatically across countries, depending on the definition of brownfield (Grimski and Ferber, 1998).[5]

B. Policies for Contaminated Sites

In the US, where federal legislation addressing contaminated sites was passed over 20 years ago (CERCLA, 1980), state programs were recently established to encourage cleanup and redevelopment of potentially contaminated sites by offering liability relief, regulatory relief, simplified cleanup standards, and direct financial incentives to developers and landowners. Liability relief usually comes in the form of letters of no further action, certificates of cleanup completion, or covenants not to sue. The latter is generally regarded as the strongest form of liability relief, since it is essentially a contract by which the granting agency (usually the state department of environmental protection) commits not to sue the property owner, as long as the cleanup of the parcel (or any residual contamination) meets certain requirements.[6]

In Europe, some countries have crafted their own Superfund-like legislation, which includes, in certain cases, an innocent landowner disclaim (for example the Netherlands), and/or provisions for the municipality to take over remediation. Recent European Union directives emphasize the Union's support for the 'polluter pays' principle, and, in addition, some European countries rely on voluntary cleanup initiatives that resemble voluntary cleanup programs and brownfield initiatives in the US.[7]

C. Effects of Liability and Contamination on Parcel Prices and Development

Despite the claims about effects of liability on acquisition and development of brownfields, little empirical work has been done to assess the existence and magnitude of these effects, and the impacts, if any, of government incentives to developers for cleanup and redevelopment of brownfields, usually provided through voluntary cleanup and brownfield programs. To our knowledge, no study has attempted to relate the establishment of such programs to land prices or has sought to evaluate the impact of the various policy instruments to the number of parcels cleaned up and redeveloped and/or their location.[8] Urban Institute et al. (1997) rely on interviews, mostly of a qualitative nature, of developers to investigate a number of claims about the deterrent effect of contamination and liability, and possible policies for brownfields redevelopment.

Lacking evidence about the response of developers to brownfield contamination and policies, we turn to stated preference approaches[9] to answer the following questions. First, what economic incentives can be offered to developers to encourage cleanup and reuse of brownfields, and how effective are they? Second, what kind of site characteristics and available infrastructure make a parcel attractive for cleanup and reuse, and to what kind of developers? Third, are developers truly influenced by contamination stigma, whereby a parcel's possible or actual contamination results in its lower desirability?

9.3   STRUCTURE OF THE QUESTIONNAIRE AND SURVEY ADMINISTRATION

A. Conjoint Choice Questions

In our survey, we ask a sample of real estate developers to tell us which they prefer between two hypothetical alternative redevelopment projects, A and B, where each project is described by site attributes (for example location and contamination) and a policy mix.[10]

The policy mix includes (a) liability reduction in the form of a certificate of assurance that the developer is not going to be held responsible for future cleanups; (b) regulatory relief in the form of a faster notice of approvals and/or flexible cleanup standards; and (c) direct financial incentives to the developer.

These policies may affect different components of the costs and revenues associated with redeveloping the site. Liability relief, for example, reduces or eliminates the risk of future liability for cleanup costs, as long as the developer meets certain requirements. It may, in addition, help raise the revenue from the sale or rental of the site by avoiding the stigma due to existing or suspected contamination. For this attribute, we consider two possible levels: (a) certificate of assurance not available, and (b) certificate of assurance available upon completion of remediation.

Faster response times by the agency to the developer's application should reduce the costs of the project.[11] We use two levels of this attribute, setting response times within 6 months, and 24 months, respectively, of the date of the application.

Direct financial incentives can take the form of low-cost loans, tax credits, and cash rebates. In our survey, however, we do not specify what form they can take, and simply tell our respondents that they are for 10 percent, 20 percent and 30 percent of the value of the project.[12]

We reason that different policy mixes can have different appeal to developers, depending on the attributes of the site where the (re-)development project is undertaken. Accordingly, we include three more attributes to describe the project: The presence of contamination at the site, the availability of transportation networks near the site, and the presence of a city within 20 km of the site to capture access to markets and suppliers.

Regarding contamination, each alternative is characterized by one of three possibilities: (a) no contamination, (b) contamination, or (c) the site was previously contaminated but remediation has taken place. The latter level of the attribute allows us to check for developers' fears of contamination stigma even after the parcel is cleaned up. Finally, all sites are assumed to have regular access to highways, with some alternatives also served by rail, an airport, and a harbor.

In sum, each alternative is described by seven attributes: (i) presence/absence of contamination; (ii) cleanup standards; (iii) availability of transportation network within 20 km from the site; (iv) presence/absence of a certificate issued by a government agency that relieves the developer from liability for further cleanup; (v) time for approval of development/cleanup plans by the appropriate government agency; (vi) presence/absence of a city within 20 km; and (vii) government financial incentives, expressed as percentage of the value of the project.

B. Structure of the Questionnaire

The interview begins with a series of screening questions intended to determine whether the respondent is a developer. The questionnaire is comprised of four sections. The first section gathers more specific information on the business of the respondent's company, such as the typical project the company is involved in and its revenue, and whether the company has ever purchased, leased or developed sites located in industrial areas, or contaminated sites.

Section 2 provides information on cleanup responsibilities, highlights the advantages and disadvantages of developing contaminated sites, and describes the incentives available in some countries to encourage re-development of previously used sites. The respondent is then asked whether he is familiar with the cleanup legislation of the countries where his/her company does its business, and whether the company has ever benefited from financial assistance from the government for redeveloping used sites.

Section 3 is comprised of four conjoint choice exercises. Each exercise describes two hypothetical development projects (Site A and Site B). Each site is described by the above mentioned seven attributes. In each choice exercise, Site A differs from Site B in the level of two or more attributes. For each pair, the respondent is first asked which project he/she finds more attractive between A and B, and then is asked to choose between A, B and the option of not participating in either project. Box 9.1 displays an example of a conjoint choice question. Clearly, answering the conjoint choice questions requires trading off the attributes of the alternatives under consideration.

Finally, section 4 gathers further information about the respondent's

---

Box 9.1

Example of choice question

SECTION D

Site choice
Now, we would like to ask you to choose between two hypothetical areas to develop. For each question, you will be described two hypothetical sites and will be asked to choose which one you believe is the more attractive of these two sites, based on the characteristics of the site.

In answering the following questions, please imagine that you are considering development projects of value/size similar to those of your company's typical project. The development project will be in the country or countries where your company generally does its business. Please be assured that your answers will be kept strictly confidential.

CHOICE 1

Attributes	Site A	Site B
Site contamination	Present	Present
Transportation network available within 20 km	Highway	Highway and railroad
Certificate of no further action	Yes	No
Oversight by government agency	Response to developer's application within 6 months	Response to developer's application within 6 months
Cleanup standards	Flexible	Flexible
City within 20 km	Present	Present
Government financial incentives as % of the value of the project	20%	10%

Which project do you find more attractive between A and B?
A ☐   B ☐

If you were to choose between A, B, and the option of not participating in either of the two projects, which would you choose?
A ☐   B ☐   Neither ☐

characteristics, such as age and education, his or her position within the company, and role in the final investment decision about real estate development projects. The respondent is then asked to report the number of employees of the company and the level of sales in 2001.

C. Administration of the Survey Instrument

A preliminary draft of the survey questionnaire was tested on developers, real estate professionals, and city planning officials in the Venice, Italy, area in February 2002 to assess respondent comprehension of the questions and to solicit comments and suggestions. In general, the questionnaire was very well received. Subjects were comfortable with the conjoint questions, and suggested including questions about the type of projects generally undertaken by developers, and about the value of the projects. These suggestions were incorporated in a revised version of the questionnaire.

The survey was administered in person by five professionally trained interviewers at the Marché International des Professionnels de l'Immobilier (MIPIM),[13] Europe's largest international commercial property conference, in Cannes, France, on March 12–15, 2002.[14] Our sample is comprised of 293 developers randomly intercepted at the conference venue. The survey instrument was available in Italian (29 percent of the respondents), English (57 percent) and French (15 percent).

9.4   THE MODEL AND THE DATA

A. What are the Determinants of Brownfield Redevelopment?

The decision to invest or not to invest in a real estate development project should depend on the revenues and costs of the project. Formally, the profit π associated with a project is:

$$\pi = R - C - L + F \qquad (9.1)$$

where R is revenue, C is cost, L is expected liability costs, and F represents transfers to the developer.

The revenue of a real estate development project should depend on the characteristics of the land to be developed. The presence of contamination can influence the price received by the developer for the completed project, as can other location characteristics, such as proximity to transportation nodes and to a city.

Contamination should also influence the *costs* associated with the development project, raising them because of environmental assessment fees, remediation costs, legal expenses, and any other punitive and civil penalties linked to known or anticipated contamination. All of these expenses are incurred in addition to normal development costs, and are, presumably, relatively well known.

In addition, developers may fear liability, the risk that in the future additional costs may be incurred as a result of the discovery of previously unknown or unanticipated contamination, with the associated litigation and other uncertain events, including possible changes in remediation standards. The costs due to liability are generally thought to be highly uncertain.

Government policies can offset some of these components of the costs of development projects. They can, for example, offer letters of no further action, certificates of completion, or covenants not to sue that reduce or eliminate future liability risks. They can also reduce uncertainty about future changes in cleanup standards, and immediate cleanup costs, by offering a streamlined review of development project plans. Finally, they can offer direct financial incentives to the developers in the form of loans, grants, rebates and/or tax credits.

Equation (9.1) can, therefore, be amended to reflect its arguments' dependence on all of these factors:

$$\pi = R(\mathbf{C}, \mathbf{X}) - C(\mathbf{C}, \mathbf{X}, \mathbf{Z}) - L(\mathbf{C}, \mathbf{Z}) + F \qquad (9.2)$$

where $\mathbf{C}$ is a vector of variables denoting the presence and severity of contamination, and $\mathbf{X}$ is a vector of location and site characteristics. $C(\cdot)$ represents development costs, which include: (a) construction costs, a function of $\mathbf{X}$; (b) cleanup costs, a function of $\mathbf{C}$; and (c) policy instruments, $\mathbf{Z}$. L, the expected liability costs, should be influenced by the presence and type of contamination at the site, $\mathbf{C}$, and by policies offering relief from liability, $\mathbf{Z}$.

In our questionnaire, R is set to be equal to the size of the firm's typical project. When asked to choose between two projects, A and B, a developer should choose the one with the higher profits. When the choice set also includes the option of not undertaking either investment, a developer would be expected to choose the 'do nothing' option if the profits of projects A and B are negative or unacceptably low.

B. The Econometric Model

To motivate the statistical analysis of the responses, we assume that respondents select the alternative with the highest profit. We further assume that profits are a linear function of site attributes, $\mathbf{S}$, including its possible contamination,[15] and the policy mix:

$$V_{ij} = \alpha_0 + \mathbf{S}_{ij}\alpha_1 + \mathbf{Z}_{ij}\alpha_2 + \varepsilon_{ij} \qquad (9.3)$$

where $\mathbf{Z}$ is a vector of indicators and/or continuous variables capturing the extent of liability relief, regulatory relief and financial incentives, respectively, i denotes the individual and j the alternative. If the error terms ε are independent and identically distributed and follow the type I extreme value distribution, the probability that alternative k is selected out of K alternatives is:

$$\Pr(\text{resp. } i \text{ choses } k) = \exp(\mathbf{w}_{ik}\alpha) \Big/ \sum_{j=1}^{K} \exp(\mathbf{w}_{ij}\alpha) \qquad (9.4)$$

where $\mathbf{w}$ is the vector of project attributes and α is the vector of coefficients in (3).[16] Equation (9.4) is the contribution to the likelihood in a conditional logit model.

Once model (9.4) is estimated, the rate of tradeoff between any two attributes is the ratio of their respective α coefficients. The marginal value of each attribute is computed as the negative of the coefficient on that attribute, divided by the coefficient on the 'price' variable (here, the subsidy). To allow for heterogeneity among the respondents, the vector $\mathbf{w}$ in equation (9.4) can be augmented to include interactions between respondent or firm characteristics, and the attributes of the alternatives.

To further allow for heterogeneity – and to relax the assumption of independence of irrelevant alternatives (IIA) implicitly imposed by the conditional logit model[17] – we also estimate random-coefficient logit models. In a random-coefficient model, the vector of coefficients β breaks down into two components: its expectation, $\overline{\beta}$, and a vector of error terms, $\mathbf{u}_i$, that vary over respondents. The probability of choosing alternative k, given the realization of the individual-specific error $\mathbf{u}_i$, is:

$$\Pr(k \mid u_i) = \frac{\exp(\mathbf{w}_{ik}\beta)}{\sum_{j=1}^{K} \exp(\mathbf{w}_{ij}\beta)} = \frac{\exp(\mathbf{w}_{ik}\overline{\beta} + \mathbf{w}_{ik}\mathbf{u}_i)}{\sum_{j=1}^{K} \exp(\mathbf{w}_{ij}\overline{\beta} + \mathbf{w}_{ij}\mathbf{u}_i)} \qquad (9.5)$$

The individual-specific error term $\mathbf{u}$ creates correlation between the indirect utilities associated with the different alternatives, ruling out IIA.

To compute the (unconditional) probability of choosing project k one must, therefore, integrate equation (9.5) with respect to the joint density of the vector of error terms $\mathbf{u}$:

$$\Pr(k) = \int \dots \int \frac{\exp(\mathbf{w}_{ik}\overline{\beta} + \mathbf{w}_{ik}\mathbf{u}_i)}{\displaystyle\sum_{j=1}^{K} \exp(\mathbf{w}_{ij}\overline{\beta} + \mathbf{w}_{ij}\mathbf{u}_i)} f(\mathbf{u}_i)d\mathbf{u}_i \qquad (9.6)$$

where f is the joint density of the terms $\mathbf{u}$. Clearly, estimation of the likelihood function based on (9.6) requires that assumptions be made about which coefficients are random, and about the joint distribution of the individual-specific errors $\mathbf{u}_i$.

C. The Choice of Regressors

In our basic specification of the conditional logit model, the probability of choosing a project depends only on the attributes of the alternatives. In subsequent runs, we add interactions intended to test specific hypothesis about the attractiveness of the attributes to certain types of developers, and then experiment with further allowing for random coefficients.

We expect the coefficient of the contamination dummy (CONTAM_P) to be negative, reflecting the extra development costs associated with cleanup. Urban Institute et al. (1997) conclude that it is not the fear of liability that keeps investors away from contaminated sites, but the high costs of cleanup. We therefore formulate our Hypothesis I, that fear of liability does not matter but cleanup costs do. A negative coefficient on CONTAM_P and an insignificant coefficient on CERTIFIC, the dummy capturing whether or not a certificate of completion is offered, would provide empirical support for this hypothesis.

The coefficient of CONTAM_C (a dummy indicator denoting that contamination was present, but has been removed) should capture contamination stigma that persists even after the site has been remediated. We do not have any prior expectations on this coefficient. While many observers believe contamination stigma to exist, some recent empirical studies (for example Urban Institute et al., 1997) refute this notion. Others (Howland, 2000) argue that the market adjusts to contamination stigma by lowering the price of contaminated parcels, so that market activity is not deterred. We therefore wish to test the null hypothesis (Hypothesis II) that there is no contamination stigma, that is, that the coefficient on CONTAM_C is zero.

All else the same, one would expect sites at locales served by more means of transportation and sites located in the proximity of a city to be more attractive. Regarding the policy instruments, *ceteris paribus* we would expect direct financial incentives (INCENT), shorter response times (OVERS) by the agency to developer application, and the issuance of a certificate of completion (CERTIFIC) to increase the attractiveness of a project. Flexible standards should make a project more attractive, unless developers consider negotiation with the authorities lengthy and costly. The net effect is, therefore, an empirical issue.

D. Specific Hypotheses and Interaction Terms

As mentioned above, it is likely that some attributes may be more (less) attractive to certain types of developers than to others. Testing hypotheses about different impacts of attributes on different developers requires the use of interaction terms.

We create interactions between several project attributes and a dummy variable denoting whether the developer has prior experience with contaminated sites. Various project attributes may hold a different appeal to developers with contaminated site experience for several reasons. For example, developers with contaminated site experience may have different perceptions of cleanup costs, in which case the coefficient of CONTAM_P interacted with the dummy for experience with contaminated sites may partially or even fully offset that of CONTAM_P. In addition, their views of negotiable cleanup standards and of the value of a letter of completion may reflect their experience with the government agency in charge. In sum, our hypothesis III is that policy instruments and contamination appeal to or deter developers with contaminated site experience in a different way.

We also create interactions between selected project attributes and a dummy variable denoting whether the firm is a 'large' firm, in that its revenues are greater than the average. Several effects could be captured into the coefficients of these interactions. Some observers believe that large firms have traditionally been the target of EPA enforcement effort over Superfund because of their ability to pay for cleanup. This might make them more reluctant to take up contaminated sites, and perhaps more accepting of liability relief. On the other hand, large firms presumably rely more on their own financing than on borrowing from banks, which might insulate them from the indirect effects of liability through the lenders. Our Hypothesis IV is that larger firms have different preferences from smaller firms.

Developers who deal primarily with industrial and commercial sites may react to contamination to a different extent than developers who engage mostly in residential projects. This is our Hypothesis V, which could be due to the perception, discussed in Urban Institute et al. (1997), that financing costs are higher – and hence the effects of liability through the lenders more pronounced – at industrial sites, and to the expectation of higher cash flows at more densely developed sites, like residential projects and office buildings.

We also wonder whether liability and liability relief schemes impact developers differently if they transfer the property to others (Hypothesis VI).

We create an interaction term between CERTIFIC and SELL1 (a dummy that takes on a value of one if the developer sells its completed projects to other parties), and examine the sign and significance of the coefficient on this interaction. Finally, Urban Institute et al. (1997) emphasize the importance of familiarity with cleanup legislation. To test for this effect we include an interaction between attributes of the project and respondent familiarity with cleanup legislation and programs (Hypothesis VII).

9.5   RESULTS

A. Characteristics of the Respondents

Because our sample consists of developers intercepted at random at a professional conference, we cannot claim that it is representative of the universe of developers. Our first order of business is, therefore, to examine the characteristics of our respondents. Descriptive statistics for respondent characteristics and firm characteristics are reported in Table 9.1.

About 65 percent of the respondents stated that they bought and developed areas in order to sell the final projects, 38 percent to keep them for their business, and 27 percent to lease them to someone else. The most common type of projects in the last three years was commercial development projects (74 percent), followed by office complexes (68 percent) and residential projects (53 percent).

Roughly 58 percent of the companies in our sample do business in Southern Europe, 30 percent in Northern Europe, 62 percent in Western Europe, 36 percent in Eastern Europe, 17 percent in North America, almost 9 percent in Asia, and 8 percent in the rest of the world.[18] As one would expect of MIPIM attendees, the respondents' companies are considerably large: the average number of employees is 3733 people, and average level of sales is about €15 895 million. The typical project had a minimum size of about 231 868 m², and a building of at least 29 160 m². Median revenue was €7 million.

Approximately two-thirds of the respondents had previous experience with industrial sites, and 60 percent of them bought abandoned industrial areas, while 69 percent worked with industrial areas that are still used at the time of the acquisition. In our sample, 47 percent of the respondents stated having previous experience with contaminated sites. In addition, 77 percent of the respondents were familiar with the polluted site cleanup legislation in the countries where their company does business. Moreover, 39 percent of our interviewees reported to have benefited from government incentives to re-use abandoned areas.

Table 9.1 Descriptive statistics

	Sample average
Type of projects	
Industrial (*q3ind*)	48.97
Residential (*q3res*)	53.42
Commercial (*q3com*)	73.97
Offices (*q3off*)	68.15
Other (*q3oth*)	25.09
Sell (*sell1*)	64.85
Keep (*keep1*)	38.23
Lease (*lease1*)	26.96
Geography	
South Europe (*south_eu*)	57.88
North Europe (*north_eu*)	30.14
West Europe (*west_eu*)	61.64
East Europe (*east_eu*)	35.62
North America (*north_am*)	16.84
Asia (*asia*)	8.90
Rest of the World (*rest_of*)	8.25
Company characteristics	
Employees (*q11*)	3 733
Level of sales (*q11*)	€15 895 000
Typical project	
Minimum land area of project (*q1amin*)	231 868 m^2
Minimum building of project (*q1bmin*)	29 160 m^2
Minimum revenue of project (*q2min*)	€666 324 069
Experience	
Experience with industrial area (*q5*)	66.21
Experience with contaminated site (*q6*)	46.76
Abandoned area (*q5aban*)	59.90
Still used area (*q5used*)	67.71
Familiarity with legislation (*familiar*)	76.98
Has ever received govt financial incentives (*benefit*)	39.31
Characteristics of the respondent	
Visitor (*q9*)	51.45
Exhibitor (*q9*)	48.55
Male (*q15*)	82.00
Age (*q17*)	44
Makes decision (*q13*)	78.97
Gathers information for (*q14*)	93.75
College degree (*university*)	88.19
MBA (*mba*)	2.78
Master's degree, phd and post graduate (*masters_degree_or_phd*)	7.64

The majority of the respondents were males (82 percent), and the average age was 42. The respondents were highly educated: the majority (88 percent) had a college degree, and about 10 percent had a master's degree in business administration or had completed postgraduate work. Almost all of the respondents (94 percent) indicated that they are responsible for gathering information to support the decision to undertake a real estate development project, and roughly 79 percent actually participates in making the final decision.

Because an important policy question is what it takes to draw developers who have never worked with brownfields before to engage in brownfield projects, we compared the characteristics of brownfield-experienced and inexperienced developers. Developers with brownfield experience tend to engage in projects at larger sites and with larger buildings, and their revenue per project is greater. However, t tests indicate that the differences between the two groups are not statistically significant.[19] The primary activity of both experienced and inexperienced developers is developing commercial projects, followed by building offices, housing complexes and industrial projects.

B. Testing for Comprehension of the Choice Task

In conjoint choice experiments, and whenever survey participants are queried about hypothetical, and relatively complex, commodities, it is important to test for respondent comprehension of these commodities and of the choice tasks.

In informal debriefing conversations at the end of the interview, many respondents offered spontaneous comments that suggested that they understood the choice task and were comfortable with it. Some respondents even volunteered attributes of projects that they felt were more important to them than others.

In addition, we checked our responses for possibly abnormal response patterns. We used three criteria. First, we checked whether a disproportionate number of respondents selected the 'neither project' option when allowed to do so. This might indicate that respondents were unwilling to accept the proposed project alternatives, A and B, as reasonable. Our respondents chose the 'neither project' option in about 20 percent of the choice tasks that offered such an alternative, a frequency that seems reasonable.

Second, following Viscusi et al. (1991), we examined whether there were respondents who always chose alternative A or B, or always chose the 'neither project' option. It should be noted that always selecting answer A (or B) does not necessarily indicate that the respondent failed to trade off the attributes of the alternatives.[20] Even if that were the case, this behavior would be limited to a very small fraction of the sample: only 11 respondents (3.7 percent of the sample) always preferred alternative A, 11 respondents always preferred alternative B, and 16 people always preferred the 'neither A nor B' option (about 5 percent of the sample).

Finally, we checked for 'preference reversals'. A preference reversal occurs if a respondent selects A (B) in the initial choice between A and B, but prefers B (A) in the follow-up choice questions, where he is asked to choose between A, B and the 'neither' alternative. Once again, the random utility model framework (equations (9.3) and (9.4)) accommodates occurrences of this kind. In any case, only 8 respondents exhibited this type of behavior.

Based on these three criteria, we conclude that almost all of our respondents answered the choice questions in a reasonable fashion. For good measure, however, we run our logit models first on the full sample, and then after excluding respondents who engaged in any of the behaviors described in the second and third criterion above.

C. The Conditional Logit Model: Effects of the Attributes

The purpose of our conditional logit models is two-fold. First, we wish to determine what attributes actually matter to developers, a task we accomplish by performing statistical tests of significance of the associated coefficients. Second, we wish to estimate the marginal prices of the attributes and policy mechanisms.

Table 9.2 reports the results of conditional logit models based on attributes only, without interactions, for various subsets of the sample. The first column displays the results for the full sample, showing that contamination of the site, as expected, deters investments, and results in a lower probability that a project is selected. Interestingly, the coefficient on CONTAM_C is positive but insignificant, and is not statistically distinguishable from the coefficient of CONTAM_A, which indicates the absence of contamination. Regarding Hypothesis II, we therefore conclude that the stated preferences of developers do not provide support for the existence of contamination stigma, a result that is in line with claims by Urban Institute et al. (1997) and Howland (2000).

Regarding proximity to transportation, the negative sign of HIGHWAY should be interpreted to mean that a project is less preferred if only access to highway is available. By contrast, access to railroad, an airport and a port increases the attractiveness of a project, although the effect of railroad is not statistically significant. The presence of a city nearby is also deemed attractive, as shown by the positive and significant coefficient of this dummy indicator.

We were expecting the size of subsidies to the developers to be positively associated with the likelihood of selecting a project, and indeed this

Table 9.2   Basic model. Conditional logit model

	(1) Complete sample 2303 obs. Log L = −1631.026	(2) Cleaned sample* 2239 obs. Log L = −1574.78
Site Characteristics		
CONTAM_P (contamination present)	−0.8903 (−1.969)	−0.9994 (−2.124)
CONTAM_C (contamination was cleaned up)	0.3882 (0.855)	0.2848 (0.603)
CONTAM_A (contamination is absent)	0.3557 (0.788)	0.2524 (0.538)
HIGHWAY	−2.3170 (−1.733)	−2.2667 (−1.685)
PORT	0.3952 (4.533)	0.4095 (4.627)
RAILROAD	1.7802 (1.425)	1.8187 (1.453)
AIRPORT	0.3153 (3.731)	0.3117 (3.638)
CITYPRES (near a city)	1.0278 (14.039)	1.0562 (14.124)
Policies		
INCENT (subsidy)	0.0272 (6.295)	0.0274 (6.258)
CERTIFIC (certification of completion with liability relief)	0.5531 (7.689)	0.5740 (7.835)
OVERS (response times by agency)	−0.0413 (−10.477)	−0.0423 (−10.560)
FLEXSTDS (flexible cleanup standards)	0.2969 (4.297)	0.2895 (4.119)

Notes: T statistics in parentheses.
  *8 respondents exhibiting preference reversals (that is choose A between A and B, choose B between A, B and neither project) are excluded.

expectation is borne out in the data. The coefficient on INCENT is positive and strongly significant.

The negative coefficient of OVERS implies that longer response times by the agency to the developer's application tend to discourage investment in a project. The coefficient on CERTIFIC is positive and strongly significant. Taken together with the negative coefficient of CONTAM_P, this result implies that developers pay attention to both immediate cleanup costs and future liability, and thus dispels Hypothesis I. Finally, the availability of flexible cleanup standards is deemed attractive, suggesting that on the whole developers do not associate them with lengthy and costly processes.

Column (2) of Table 9.2 refers to a sample that excludes the 8 respondents who exhibited preference reversals. The results are very similar and virtually all coefficients are within 10 to 25 percent of their counterparts in column (1).[21]

D. The Conditional Logit Model: Interaction Terms

Tables 9.3–9.6 report the results of conditional logit models that include interactions between attributes and characteristics of respondents. The sample used to estimate these models excludes the eight cases of possible preference reversals.

Table 9.3   Conditional logit models with interactions between attributes and experience with contaminated sites

	Coefficient	T statistic
Site characteristics		
CONTAM_P	−1.2102	−2.532
CONTAM_C	0.2171	0.462
CONTAM_A	0.1968	0.424
HIGHWAY	−2.4220	−1.802
PORT	0.2164	4.658
RAILROAD	2.0647	1.650
AIRPORT	0.3186	3.697
CITYPRES	1.0657	14.159
Policies		
INCENT	0.0119	2.177
CERTIFIC	0.5836	5.771
OVERS	−0.0471	−8.765
FLEXSTDS	0.3513	3.543
Interaction terms		
INCENT × Experienced with contaminated sites	0.0335	4.600
CONTAM_P × Experienced with contaminated sites	0.2654	1.642
CERTIFIC × Experienced with contaminated sites	0.0145	0.099
OVERS × Experienced with contaminated sites	0.0085	1.151
FLEXSTDS × Experienced with contaminated sites	−0.1444	−1.053
Log likelihood function	−1552.36	

Notes: Cleaned sample only, respondents who exhibited preference reversals excluded. $N = 2239$.

Table 9.3 displays the results of the interactions between site or policy attributes and a dummy variable indicating whether the respondent's company has prior experience with contaminated sites. A likelihood ratio statistic of 44.84, which falls in the 1 percent upper tail of the chi square with 5 degrees of freedom, suggests that the interaction terms do significantly improve the fit of the model, and provides support for Hypothesis III, even though only one of the coefficients on the interaction terms is individually statistically significant at the 1 percent level (another is statistically significant at the 10 percent level).

Specifically, developers with contaminated site experience appear to be more sensitive to government subsidies: the coefficient on subsidies for these developers is $(0.0119 + 0.0335) = 0.0454$, whereas that for all other developers is 0.0119. This implies that – all else the same – increasing the

Table 9.4   Conditional logit models with interactions between attributes and large firms

	Coefficient	T statistic
Attributes		
CONTAM_P	−1.0200	−2.143
CONTAM_C	0.2652	0.563
CONTAM_A	0.2350	0.502
HIGHWAY	−2.0942	−1.562
PORT	0.4086	4.595
RAILROAD	1.6652	1.335
AIRPORT	0.3136	3.650
CITYPRES	1.0565	14.101
Policies		
INCENT	0.0347	6.752
CERTIFIC	0.6076	6.678
OVERS	−0.0472	−9.637
FLEXSTDS	0.2802	3.242
Interaction terms		
INCENT × Large firm	−0.0205	−2.767
CONTAM_P × Large firm	0.0142	0.087
CERTIFIC × Large firm	−0.1033	−0.697
OVERS × Large firm	0.0144	1.881
FLEXSTDS × Large firm	0.0278	0.193
Log likelihood function	−1569.67	

Notes: Cleaned sample only, respondents who exhibited preference reversals excluded. $N = 2239$.

incentive by the same amount raises the probability of selecting a site more for developers with experience than for developers without prior contaminated site experience. Developers with contaminated site experience also appear to be somewhat less deterred by the presence of contamination (the coefficient on this attribute is $[-1.2104 + 0.2654] = -0.945$, roughly three-quarters that for all other developers), but respond to other policies in a manner similar to that of all other developers.

Table 9.4 displays the results of the model with interactions between attributes and a dummy equal to one if the respondent's company has more than the average annual sales in the sample. The likelihood ratio test of the null hypothesis that the coefficients of all interactions are equal to zero is 10.22, failing to reject the null hypothesis at the conventional levels and providing little evidence for Hypothesis IV.

However, two coefficients – that on the interaction with the size of the financial incentives, and that on the interaction with response times by the agency in charge – are individually statistically significant at the 1 percent and 10 percent level, respectively. They imply that larger firms are less responsive to subsidies, and less deterred by slower response times by the agency. For large firms, the relevant coefficient is $(0.0347 - 0.0205) = 0.0142$, whereas for smaller firms it is 0.0347. Larger firms, however, do not value the existence of contamination and liability relief differently from smaller firms, despite their potentially larger exposure to liability. We also experimented with changing the definition of large firm, finding that, when we classified as 'large' a firm with revenues greater than the median, the results were qualitatively similar, but the differences between 'larger' and 'smaller' firms were no longer statistically significant.

Table 9.5 reveals that, in contrast to opinions voiced by some observers, primary involvement with residential or industrial projects is not likely to change the deterrent effect of contamination. We do not, therefore, find any support for hypothesis V. Table 9.6 also shows that developers who generally sell the properties they develop particularly appreciate the opportunity to receive a certificate of completion relieving them of liability, but are not different from other developers in terms of their reaction to the presence of contamination at the site. This provides some support for hypothesis VI.

Finally, regarding hypothesis VII, Table 9.6 implies that those respondents who are more familiar with contaminated site legislation are slightly less deterred by the presence of contamination and by slower response times by the agency, but distrust flexible cleanup standards. The magnitude of the coefficients on the interaction terms, however, implies that in practice the difference between those respondents who are and are not familiar with the applicable cleanup legislation is very small.

Other interaction terms between attributes of the alternative and

Table 9.5   Conditional logit models with interactions between attributes and other activities of the firm

	(A)	(B)	(C)
CONTAM_P	−1.0753	−1.0279	−1.0257
	(−2.250)	(−2.176)	(−2.174)
CONTAM_C	0.3049	0.2770	0.2868
	(0.648)	(0.589)	(0.608)
CONTAM_A	0.2735	0.2446	0.2532
	(0.584)	(0.521)	(0.537)
HIGHWAY	−2.4911	−2.2459	−2.2908
	(−1.855)	(−1.666)	(−1.704)
PORT	0.3998	0.4087	0.4064
	(4.502)	(4.619)	(4.589)
RAILROAD	2.0109	1.8065	1.8407
	(1.611)	(1.441)	(1.472)
AIRPORT	0.3162	0.3133	0.3111
	(3.681)	(3.656)	(3.629)
CITYPRES	1.0610	1.0564	1.0558
	(14.142)	(14.130)	(14.116)
INCENT	0.0276	0.0274	0.0275
	(6.280)	(6.256)	(6.282)
CERTIFIC	0.3260	0.5738	0.5752
	(2.899)	(7.835)	(7.851)
OVERS	−0.0423	−0.0425	−0.0424
	(−10.513)	(−10.572)	(−10.565)
FLEXSTDS	0.2884	0.2893	0.2907
	(4.090)	(4.116)	(4.134)
CONTAM_P × SELL1	0.1551	.	.
	(0.955)		
CERTIFIC × SELL1	0.4054	.	.
	(2.912)		
CONTAM_P × Primary activity is residential projects	.	0.1226	.
		(0.608)	
CONTAM_P × Primary activity is industrial projects	.	.	0.1761
			(0.841)
Log likelihood function	−1569.38	−1574.59	−1574.43

Notes: Cleaned sample, respondents who exhibited preference reversals excluded. $N = 2239$.
T statistics in parentheses.

Table 9.6   Conditional logit models with interactions between attributes and familiarity with legislation regarding contaminated sites

	Coefficient	T statistic
Attributes		
CONTAM_P	−1.1925	−2.459
CONTAM_C	0.2706	0.576
CONTAM_A	0.2408	0.515
HIGHWAY	−2.3566	−1.723
PORT	0.4205	4.723
RAILROAD	1.9185	1.504
AIRPORT	0.3047	3.539
CITYPRES	1.0611	14.172
Policies		
INCENT	0.0275	6.276
CERTIFIC	0.7784	6.131
OVERS	−0.0511	−8.115
FLEXSTDS	0.4706	4.136
Interaction Terms		
CONTAM_P × Familiarity	0.2571	1.519
CERTIFIC × Familiarity	−0.3014	−1.999
OVERS × Familiarity	0.0134	1.834
FLEXSTDS × Familiarity	−0.2791	−2.018
Log likelihood function	−1569.32	

Notes: Cleaned sample, respondents who exhibited preference reversals excluded. N = 2239.
T statistics in parentheses.

characteristics of the respondents and/or the respondent's firm were attempted and included in additional runs of the conditional logit model. For example, in runs not reported we examined whether respondents who have previously received incentives from the government have different preferences for contaminated sites and government financial assistance. We found that these developers are indeed more responsive to financial incentives, as the coefficient on financial incentives that applies to them is roughly one-half that for all other developers. They do not, however, have a different perception of the contamination problem.

It would have been interesting to examine if preferences vary with the country where the company or the respondent is based, reflecting his or her company's experience with local agencies and policies. Unfortunately, once the data were divided into subsamples for different countries or continents, the sample sizes were too small to obtain meaningful results. We attempted interactions between country or region dummies and policies, but did not identify significant differences across groups, a result we attribute to the relatively small number of observations per group.

E. Random Coefficient Models

To further account for heterogeneity of preferences across individual respondents, we allowed certain coefficients to be random in the models with interactions between type of developer and attributes of the project. In this section, we discuss the results of random-coefficient models with interactions between five attributes (contamination, plus the four policies) and prior experience with contaminated sites. We began with allowing the coefficients of all five interaction terms to be random, assuming that each such coefficient is normally distributed and independent of the others,[22] but found that only one of these coefficients, that on INCENT × experience with contamination, should be concluded to be random.

When the model is re-run imposing that the latter coefficient be random and normally distributed, and all others be non-stochastic, its expected value is estimated to be 0.0422 (s.e. 0.0092), and its standard deviation to be 0.0474. The corresponding coefficient for the remainder of developers is 0.0104. This implies that for roughly 74 percent of the developers with contaminated site experience the coefficient on the financial incentive is greater than that for developers without contaminated site experience, and that for 50 percent of the developers with contaminated site experience this coefficient is greater than 0.0422. All other coefficients are very similar to those of the conditional logit model of Table 9.3, and the predictions for the probabilities of choosing between alternatives and the estimated marginal prices of the attributes are virtually identical to those of the conditional logit model of Table 9.3.[23] In the next two sections, therefore, we report and discuss predicted probabilities and marginal prices based on the conditional logit.

F. Magnitude of the Effects

To illustrate the magnitude of the effects of the policies, we consider two sites, A and B, and compute the probability of choosing between them under various assumptions. We first assume that A is a contaminated site located close to all transportation modes and near a city, and that individual policies or combinations of them are offered at this site. By contrast, B is a pristine site with no applicable brownfield policies, but of comparable location characteristics.

The probability of choosing A, the contaminated site accompanied by the policy mix, is shown in Table 9.7 for various policy mixes for the entire

Table 9.7 Probability of selecting the contaminated site vis-à-vis a pristine site
Site A = contaminated site with policy incentives. Site B = pristine site with no policy incentives.

Probability of selecting A over B (Percent)

Policy incentive offered at site A	(1) All	(2) Developers with contaminated site experience	(3) Developers with no contaminated site experience	(4) Large firms	(5) Small firms
10% financial assistance	27.33	33.43	21.62	25.00	28.74
20% financial assistance	33.10	44.19	23.70	27.75	36.33
Liability relief alone	33.67	36.74	30.50	32.37	34.35
20% financial assistance + liability relief	46.76	59.01	35.77	38.87	51.16
Flexible cleanup standards	27.64	28.19	25.81	28.23	27.39
20% financial assistance + flexible cleanup standards	39.79	49.33	30.62	34.32	34.32
20% financial assistance + liability relief +flexible cleanup standards	53.98	63.91	44.17	46.39	46.39

sample and for various types of developers.[24] Column (1) shows the probability of selecting site A for all developers in our sample. With financial assistance for 10 percent of the project revenue, a developer chooses A, the contaminated site, with probability 27.33 percent. This probability increases to 33.10 percent when the subsidy is doubled.[25] Liability relief alone implies a probability of selecting A of 33.67 percent, which jumps to 46.76 percent when financial aid worth 20 percent of the project revenue is added. On further adding flexible cleanup standards, the likelihood of choosing the contaminated site project further increases to about 54 percent. It should also be noted that flexible cleanup standards alone imply a probability of selecting A of about 27 percent, and are thus roughly equivalent to offering financial assistance for 10 percent the value of the project.[26]

As shown in columns (2) and (3) of Table 9.7, there is a substantial difference in the propensity to engage in projects at contaminated sites between those developers who already have experience with this kind of sites, and those who do not. Specifically, when attention is restricted to financial assistance, developers with previous activity at contaminated sites have a higher probability of selecting the contaminated site at the lowest possible level of financial assistance (33.43 percent versus 21.62 percent), and are more responsive to an increase in financial assistance. Doubling the size of the subsidies to 20 percent raises the probability of opting for the contaminated site to 44.19 percent for developers with contaminated experience, but has little effect on developers with no contaminated site experience, for whom the probability of project A is now only 23.70 percent.[27]

On further incorporating liability relief, the probability of choosing A is 59 percent for developers with contaminated site experience, and 30.50 percent for developers without contaminated site experience. This suggests that liability experience is more important than subsidies for developers with no previous contamination experience, at least within the normal subsidy range.[28]

It is interesting that the likelihood of selecting A is similar – in that it differs by only 3 percentage points – for the two types of developers when the only policy instrument is flexible cleanup standards.[29] Finally, on combining 20 percent financial assistance, liability relief and flexible cleanup standards, the model predicts that the two types of developers will have probabilities of selecting A equal to 64 percent and 44 percent, respectively.[30]

Comparison between larger and smaller firms suggests that they are similar in terms of their preferences for liability relief and flexible cleanup standards. They do differ, however, in terms of their responsiveness to financial incentives. Larger firms have a lower probability of selecting A at all levels of the subsidy. When offered a policy package that includes a 20 percent subsidy, flexible cleanup standards and liability relief, for larger firms the likelihood of selecting project A is about 46 percent, whereas for smaller firms this probability is 58 percent.[31]

It is also possible to compute the probability of choosing one of two contaminated site alternatives, A and B, where A offers a subsidy, and B offers other incentives of a non-financial nature. For example, consider a contaminated site A with 10 percent financial incentive. If B offers only liability relief, the probability of choosing A is 46.40 percent for a developer with contaminated site experience, and 38 percent for a developer with no experience. While it takes a financial incentive equal to 14 percent of the value of the project for a developer with experience for him to be indifferent between the two projects, the financial incentive must be raised to 50 percent before an inexperienced developer is indifferent between the two projects.

When B is a contaminated site where the cleanup standards are flexible, about 56 percent of the developers with prior brownfield activity would choose A, the contaminated site with 10 percent financial assistance, and a similar percentage of inexperienced developers would prefer B. These examples once again illustrate how developers with contaminated site experience are more easily drawn to direct subsidies, while developers who have not dealt with contaminated sites before respond more to liability relief or other non-financial incentives.

G. Marginal Prices

Table 9.8 displays the marginal prices of the attributes for the sample as a whole and for specific groups of developers, based on the median value of a project (€7 million, or approximately $7 million).[32] The table shows that the presence of contamination is worth €2.5 million, in the sense that, all else the same, developers would require financial assistance for €2.5 million for a €7 million project involving a contaminated site where remediation has not been undertaken yet.[33] An alternative interpretation is that developers would be willing to sacrifice up to €2.5 million to obtain a pristine site. This accounts for almost 37 percent of the revenue of the project. There is, however, much variability in the value of avoiding contamination between different types of developers. Developers with contaminated site experience, for instance, would require only €1.46 million, smaller developers €2 million, and larger developers €5 million.

The certification of completion, which exempts the developer from future liability over contamination at the site, is worth about €1.5 million, implying that developers would sacrifice this amount to secure a letter of completion by the appropriate government agency.[34] This is approximately 21 percent of the revenue from the project. This time, it appears that developers with no

Table 9.8   Marginal prices in million of euros, based on the median project value (€7 million)

	Complete sample	Experience with contaminated sites	No experience with contaminated sites	Larger firms	Smaller firms
CONTAM_P	€2.549 (1.267)*	€1.455 (0.702)*	€7.119 (4.310)	€5.029 (3.306)	€2.081 (1.015)*
CERTIFIC	€1.464 (0.302)*	€0.921 (0.209)*	€3.433 (1.743)*	€2.521 (1.384)	€1.240 (0.271)*
OVERS	€0.108 (0.019)*	€0.059 (0.010)*	€0.277 (0.127)*	€0.164 (0.076)*	€0.096 (0.016)*
FLEXSTDS	€0.738 (0.222)*	€0.318 (0.164)	€2.066 (1.172)	€1.540 (1.029)	€0.572 (0.204)*

Notes: Standard errors in parentheses.
　　　　* Indicates that the marginal price is significant at the 5 percent level.

experience at contaminated sites are willing to pay more to obtain one such a letter (€3.4 million v. €0.9 million of developers with experience).

Our model also implies that each month of delay in the approval of cleanup plans is worth €108 000. It is interesting that developers who have previously engaged in projects at contaminated sites and smaller developers attach lower values to a delay of one month in the agency's response time (€59 000 and €96 000, respectively).

Finally, the marginal price of flexible standards is €738 000, implying that respondents would pay this amount to have the opportunity to negotiate the cleanup standards with the government agency. This figure represents roughly 10 percent of the value of the project here considered (€7 million).

9.6   CONCLUSIONS

We have illustrated the use of conjoint choice experiments to investigate real estate developers' preferences for public policies that encourage remediation and re-use of brownfields. Our survey instrument was administered in person to a sample of respondents intercepted at random at the MIPIM annual conference in Cannes, France, on March 12–15, 2002.

In our conjoint choice experiments, developers are asked to indicate which they prefer among projects characterized by site attributes and policies such as liability relief, flexible cleanup standards, fast-track oversight of plans, and subsidies.

The questionnaire worked well, in the sense that respondents did not report problems with the conjoint choice questions, and exhibited well-behaved response patterns. Conditional and random-coefficient logit models of the responses to the choice questions indicate that developers find sites with contamination problems less attractive than others, and that they do value liability relief. This confirms our expectation that contaminated sites are less desirable because of the associated cleanup costs, but refutes earlier claims (Urban Institute et al., 1997) that liability does not matter. This finding is comforting, in the sense that it provides support for state legislation and programs established in recent years in the US, which encourage voluntary cleanup in exchange for liability relief.

Our respondents are not deterred by prior contamination, once it has been cleaned up, suggesting that 'contamination stigma' is not very important, and appreciate fast-track review of development and remediation plans, direct financial incentives, and flexible cleanup standards.

Developers with prior experience with contaminated sites are more responsive to financial assistance than the others. The likelihood of selecting the contaminated site vis-à-vis a pristine site increases by roughly 11 percent points for every additional 10 percent subsidies for developers with contaminated site experience, but by only 2 percent points for developers without contaminated site experience. Those developers who are not experienced with contaminated sites are relatively insensitive to subsidies and more responsive to liability relief. Perhaps this reflects different expectations with respect to the cost of remediation, or subjective perceptions about the difficulties of and the transaction costs necessary to secure the subsidies.

Similar considerations hold for larger firms. Developers who sell their development projects, instead of using them themselves or renting them, value liability relief even more highly.

In regression not reported, we also find that developers who have previously availed themselves of government subsidies are more accepting of subsidies. This suggests that they have become efficient at securing those subsidies, and that they perhaps associate lower effort and transaction costs than developers that have not received government financial assistance before.

The fact that developers vary in their response to subsidies and liability relief also suggests that at locales where tax credits or cash rebates are offered to the developers for cleaning up and redeveloping contaminated land, one would expect these policies to attract primarily developers who have previous experience with contaminated land, rather than developers who have not worked with this type of sites before. At locales where virtually all prospective developers have not engaged in brownfield projects before, subsidies would, therefore, seem a relatively inefficient way of soliciting cleanup and redevelopment.

We calculate that for a project worth €7 million in revenue (the median revenue) developers need to be compensated €2.5 million for them to accept a contaminated site (in the absence of other policies), and are willing to give up €1.5 million to secure a certificate of completion that would exempt them from future liability. Each month's work of delay in obtaining approval of cleanup plans is valued as €108 000, while flexible cleanup standards are valued as €738 000.

In sum, our survey data suggest that developers generally are responsive to policies that encourage redevelopment and reuse of brownfields through market mechanisms, such as transfers and liability relief, and through regulatory relief. These policies can be used to influence land use. The impact of these policies, however, varies with the type of developer. This information, especially if confirmed by studies based on other techniques or on administering our survey instruments to samples of developers from different universes, should be useful in designing (and assessing the impacts of) brownfield policies.

NOTES

1. By late 2000, 47 states had instituted voluntary cleanup programs to promote reuse and cleanup of contaminated sites (Bartsch and Dorfman, 2000; Meyer and VanLandingham, 2000).
2. We wish to thank Peter B. Meyer and Kris Wernstedt for their help with and suggestions about the research, as well as the seminar participants at Queen's University, Belfast, and Fondazione Eni Enrico Mattei for their questions and comments.
3. Contamination stigma is defined as 'a market imposed penalty that can affect a property that is known or suspected to be contaminated, a property that was once contaminated but is now considered clean, or a never contaminated property located in proximity to a contaminated property' (Dybvig, 1992). Chan (2001) discusses other definitions of stigma, and refers to it as 'the detrimental impact on property value due to the presence of a risk perception driven market resistance'.
4. For comparison, the US Conference of Mayors (1996) estimates that there are 43 000 acres of browfields in 16 000 sites among the 39 cities surveyed, including about 20 larger cities with population over 100 000. One problem with this figure, however, is that the definition of brownfield varies across cities. Simons (1998) reports that as of 1994 brownfields in 31 US cities add to a total of 115 000 acres. Other estimates of the number of brownfields can be formed by examining the list of contaminated sites compiled by the US Environmental Protection Agency (EPA) and state agencies under various environmental programs. For example, the EPA maintains a registry of active contaminated sites (the CERCLA Information System, or CERCLIS), and has archived some 35 000 sites previously placed on CERCLIS and subsequently delisted because they were cleaned up or found not be contaminated in the first place. The EPA also maintains a registry documenting roughly 418 000 Leaking Underground Storage Tanks (LUSTs) (http://www.epa.gov/swerust1/cat/index.htm – last access: November 2005). On adding up several registries of contaminated sites, and correcting for sites that appear simultaneously on more than one registry, the total number of brownfields in the US is pegged at 384 000 (Simons, 1998).

5. With this caveat, Germany reportedly has 35 000 contaminated sites, mostly concentrated in former Eastern Germany (Meyer et al., 1995) for a total of 128 000 hectares (Grimski and Ferber, 1998). In reports to the European Union, the Netherlands claimed to have over 6 000 contaminated sites, Italy 5400, France 800 and Spain only 94 (Meyer et al., 1995). Other reports (Giangrasso and Tassoni, 2001) peg the number of sites suspected to be contaminated in Europe at the end of the 1980s at roughly 150 000, for a total of more than 100 million hectares, 20 million of which are in Western Europe.

6. Memoranda of understanding may be signed by the state and the US EPA through which the latter recognizes the state's authority in granting such documents and promises to refrain from prosecuting the property owner or developer for contamination, provided that certain conditions are met. See US General Accounting Office (1997).

7. These voluntary initiatives exist in addition to or in lieu of cleanup legislation. For instance, in France (Lévêque, 1996) much of the self-regulation of the chemical industry was launched in hopes of preventing the passage of an act similar to CERCLA, which was debated by the Parliament during the 1990s. In Italy, despite the existence of cleanup legislation (*Decreto* [Executive Order] *Ronchi*, approved in February 1997), at certain locales where no responsible parties can be found polluters have entered into voluntary agreements with the government (see Alberini et al., 2002).

8. McGrath (2000) estimates a switching regression model that relates the redevelopment of a parcel, and a parcel's sale price, to physical characteristics of the site and to its probability of being contaminated. This model assumes that the likelihood of redevelopment is affected by the odds of contamination both via the price of the parcel and through an independent effect. The effect of government policies, however, is not examined. Howland (2000) combines information on contamination and sale prices reported by owners of parcels in an industrial area of Baltimore with state records, finding that contamination reduces the sale price, but does not slow down transactions. This study, however, was completed before the passage of Maryland's Voluntary Cleanup program, and thus does not establish the effects of the latter – and of its economic incentives – on the prices and the rate of turnover of contaminated property.

9. Stated preference methods include conjoint choice, contingent valuation and contingent behavior. They are used to place a dollar value on environmental quality or natural resources, health endpoints, mortality risks reductions associated with public policies, and other public and private goods, and they rely on individuals stating what they would do under specified hypothetical circumstances (see Carson, 1991). Conjoint choice experiments ask individuals to choose between two or more hypothetical 'commodities' described by a vector of attributes. The levels of the attributes are varied across the alternatives, so that individuals trade off such attributes, and one of them is usually a dollar amount, so that the marginal prices of the attributes can be computed. See Louviere et al. (2000).

10. As explained in Section 9.3.B, each of these choice questions is followed by another where the respondent is asked to choose between A, B and not undertaking either project. We are not aware of previous research that has interviewed real estate developers about contaminated sites using this approach. Opaluch et al. (1993) use a variant of conjoint analysis to elicit residents' preferences for siting a landfill.

11. They may also eliminate some of the uncertainty typically associated with undertaking brownfield projects. Earlier research in this area (Urban Institute et al., 1997) suggests that reducing uncertainty may be an important component of effective brownfield programs.

12. These figures were based on a review of the legislation and programs in Italy and other European countries, and are similar to the levels of public subsidies in the US. Simons (1998) examines the role of public assistance and subsidies in a number of brownfield projects in the US. He finds that the average public subsidy is 20 percent. For comparison, remediation costs were typically 10 percent of a project's total value, but some projects using innovative remediation techniques kept the remediation costs to less than 5 percent of the project's value. Simons concludes that public subsidies are generally too high, and tend to support development costs other than the costs of remediation.

13. MIPIM is an annual conference. MIPIM 2002 was one of the busiest ever, with more than

15 000 visitors from 65 countries, and 4 830 end-users and investors, of which 988 were development companies and 1 008 real estate consultants.

14. We became interested in brownfield policies because there are many abandoned or underused contaminated sites in the industrial area of Marghera, near Venice, Italy. Ideally, we would have liked to survey local developers about their preferences for parcels at this locale, but were forced to abandon this plan for two reasons. First, we observed very little redevelopment activity at this locale. Second, we found it impossible to assemble a comprehensive list of developers at the local or national level from which a representative sample could be drawn. Moreover, we worried that, even if a representative sample could be obtained, only a very small fraction of developers would have previously dealt with contaminated sites, making it difficult for us to identify differences in preferences between those who do and do not have prior experience with such sites. Our MIPIM sample is, therefore, expected to be comprised of relatively large developers with international exposure. We also expect a greater proportion of developers that engage in projects at contaminated sites than in the universe of all developers.

15. **S** is, therefore, comprised of **X** and **C**, with **X** and **C** defined as in Section 9.4.A. We term 'project attributes' the entire set of attributes **S** and **Z**.

16. The intercept in equation (9.3) is not identified and is therefore normalized to zero.

17. Briefly, IIA, which follows from the assumption that the error term in (9.3) is i.i.d. type I extreme value, states that the ratio of the odds of choosing between any two alternatives does not depend on the attributes of any other alternative. IIA imposes a restrictive structure on substitution patterns. Specifically, a change in the attributes of one alternative changes the probabilities of the other alternatives proportionately to satisfy the conditional logit's requirement that the ratio of these probabilities remain the same (Train, 1999).

18. These percentages do not add to 100 because many firms do business in several parts of the world.

19. For developers with prior experience with contaminated sites, the average land area of a project is 298 000 m^2, whereas for developers that have not worked with contaminated areas before the average size of a project is 137 500 m^2. Buildings at the site are, on average, 37 000 and 23 000 m^2 respectively, and the median revenue for a typical project is 13.2 v. 5.7 million euro, respectively. These figures are not statistically different across developers with and without prior contaminated site experience.

20. If new error terms are drawn for every conjoint choice question, under certain conditions there is a positive probability that an individual chooses A (B) between A and B, but B (A) among A, B and the 'neither project' option.

21. Likelihood-ratio tests confirm that all site characteristics are significant (the likelihood-ratio statistic is 543.8, which under the null hypothesis is distributed as a chi square distribution with 8 degrees of freedom) and all policy instruments are significant (the likelihood-ratio statistic is 244.8, which falls in 1 percent upper tail of the chi square distribution with 4 degrees of freedom).

22. Train (1999) explains that skewed distributions defined on the positive semi-axis, such as the lognormal, are well suited for situations where individuals may attach a different value to the attributes, but all individual valuations share the same sign (for example all individuals perceive the attribute as attractive), whereas a symmetric density like the normal allows some individuals to attach a positive value, and others to attach a negative value, on the attribute in question.

23. The random coefficient logit probabilities are calculated as:

$$\int \ldots \int \frac{\exp(\mathbf{w}_A \boldsymbol{\beta})}{\exp(\mathbf{w}_A \boldsymbol{\beta}) + \exp(\mathbf{w}_B \boldsymbol{\beta})} g(\boldsymbol{\beta}) d\boldsymbol{\beta}$$

where g is a joint normal density with degenerate components for those coefficients that are not random. In practice, this is reduced to a single integral with respect to the (univariate) distribution of the coefficient on the interaction between INCENT and the dummy for developers with prior contamination experience. Our random-coefficient logit does not include individual-specific random effects, and thus treats all choice responses made by the same individual as independent of one another.

24. The probabilities shown in this table are based on the conditional logit models of tables 9.2, column (2), 9.3, and 9.4.
25. The elasticity with respect to the financial incentive is 0.1991. The formula for the elasticity is $\Pr(A) \times [1 - \Pr(A)] \times \beta_F \times F$, where β_F is the coefficient on the financial incentive attribute and F is the financial incentive. Our calculation refers to $F = 10$ percent.
26. The marginal effects of liability relief and flexible standards, defined as $\partial \Pr(A)/\partial w_{AJ}$ (1 denoting the attribute being considered) and computed as $\Pr(A) \times [1 - \Pr(A)] \times \beta_1$, are 0.1271 and 0.0579, respectively.
27. The elasticities of the probability of opting for A with respect to financial assistance are dramatically different across the two types of developers. The elasticity is 0.3022 for developers with prior experience with contaminated sites, and 0.0932 for developers without such prior experience.
28. The marginal effect of liability relief is the same for both types of respondents, and is equal to about 0.13.
29. The marginal effects of flexible standards are 0.04 for developers with prior contaminated site experience, and 0.06 for developers without such experience.
30. All of these results are confirmed when our preferred specification of the random coefficient logit model is used. Specifically, for developers with prior experience at contaminated sites the probability of preferring A is 34.07 percent with a 10 percent subsidy, 46.68 percent for a 20 percent subsidy, 59.50 percent with 20 percent subsidy and liability relief, 35.98 percent with liability relief alone, 26.92 percent with flexible cleanup alone, 50.91 percent when the flexible cleanup standards are paired with a 20 percent subsidy, and 63.94 percent when liability relief is further added. The corresponding probabilities for a developer without contamination experience are 21.13 percent, 22.94 percent, 34.64 percent, 30.05 percent, 25.48 percent, 29.67 percent, and 42.89 percent. Random-coefficient logit produces estimates of the marginal effects – computed using the formula $\int \beta_1 \times L(A)[1 - L(A)]g(\beta)d\beta$, where $L(A) = \exp(w_A\beta)/[\exp(w_A\beta) + \exp(w_B\beta)]$ that are virtually identical to those of the standard logit. Random-coefficient logit, however, results in elasticities with respect to the financial incentive – computed using the formula $\int \beta_F \times F \times L(A)[1 - L(A)][\Pr(A)]^{-1}g(\beta)d\beta$ that are farther apart across the two groups of developers. Specifically, the elasticity with respect to F is 0.3736 for developers with prior contaminated site experience, and 0.0791 for developers that have no such prior experience.
31. Similar calculations (not reported in Table 9.7) show that developers who generally sell the properties they develop particularly appreciate the opportunity to receive a certificate of completion relieving them of liability. A developer who sells his project to other parties has a predicted probability of 38.7 percent of choosing the contaminated site, A, in the presence of liability relief alone. This probability grows to 52.2 percent when a 20 percent financial incentive is also offered. For developers who do not sell their projects to others, the corresponding probabilities are 26.4 percent and 38.4 percent, respectively. Finally, familiarity with the relevant legislation appears to reduce the appeal of flexible cleanup standards, but this effect is weak: given the choice between a contaminated site, A, where negotiable cleanup standards are offered, and a completely pristine site, the probability of selecting the former is about 27.2 percent for those respondents who are familiar with the cleanup legislation, and 27.63 percent for those who said that they were not acquainted with such legislation.
32. At the time of the study, the Euro was equivalent to about 1 US dollar.
33. To interpret the concept of implicit marginal price of each attribute in this context, consider the indirect utility function in section 9.4.A, which is equal to profits. Profits are assumed to be

$$\pi = R - C(\text{Cont}, \mathbf{X}) - L(\text{Cont}) + F,$$

where C is development costs, L is liability costs, F is transfers to the developer and Cont is a dummy equal to one if the site is contaminated. Consider the expected profit associated with a pristine site:

$$\pi_0 = R - C(\text{Cont} = 0, \mathbf{X}) - L(\text{Cont} = 0).$$

In the absence of contamination, it is reasonable to assume that $L(\text{Cont} = 0) = 0$, reducing expected profit to $\pi_0 = R - C(\text{Cont} = 0, \mathbf{X})$. We wish to calculate the payment F that must be made to the developer for him or her to undertake a project at a site of identical characteristics, but where contamination exists. The expected profit with contamination and financial assistance is $\pi_1 = R - C(\text{Cont} = 1, \mathbf{X}) - L(\text{Cont} = 1) + F$. Because the respondent is asked to consider sites with equal revenue, R is identical across projects. Indifference between the two sites will be reached when the difference in profits is zero:

$$\Delta\pi = \pi_1 - \pi_0 = [C(\text{Cont} = 1, \mathbf{X}) - C(\text{Cont} = 0, \mathbf{X})] - L(\text{Cont} = 1) + F = 0.$$

This yields $F = [C(\text{Cont} = 1, \mathbf{X}) - C(\text{Cont} = 0, \mathbf{X})] + L(\text{Cont} = 1)$, implying that the direct payment required by the developer to undertake the project at the contaminated site must be equal to the full cost of contamination: that is the additional development costs – which are equal to the cost of cleaning up contamination – plus liability costs.

34. To interpret the marginal price of the certificate of completion, consider the profit in the presence and absence of certification (π_1 and π_0), assuming that certification fully removes liability at a contaminated site. Under this assumption, $\pi_1 = R - C(\text{Cont} = 1, \mathbf{X}) - L(\text{Cont} = 1, \text{Cert} = 1) = R - C(\text{Cont} = 1, \mathbf{X}) - 0$ and $\pi_0 = R - C(\text{Cont} = 1, \mathbf{X}) - L(\text{Cont} = 1, \text{Cert} = 0) + F$. On equating profit under the two alternative scenarios, we find that indifference is reached when $F = L(\text{Cont} = 1, \text{Cert} = 0)$. Because $L(\text{Cont} = 1, \text{Cert} = 0)$ is the liability cost, developers must be offered as much for them to give up certification, or are willing to pay as much to secure relief from liability. Our estimate suggests that on average developers expect the liability cost at a contaminated site worth €7 million in revenue to be €1.5 million.

REFERENCES

Alberini, A., A. Longo, S. Tonin, F. Trombetta and M. Turvani (2002), 'The Role of Liability, Regulation, and Economic Incentives in Brownfield Remediation and Redevelopment: Evidence from Surveys of Developers', AREC University of Maryland Discussion Paper 02–21, College Park, MD: November.

Bartsch, C. and B. Dorfman (2000), *Brownfields 'State of the States': An End-of-Session Review of Initiatives and Program Impacts in the 50 States*, Washington, DC: Northeast-Midwest Institute.

Carson, R.T. (1991), 'Constructed Markets', in J. Braden and C. Kolstad (eds), *Measuring the Demand for Environmental Commodities*, Amsterdam: North-Holland.

Chan, N. (2001), 'Stigma and its Assessments Methods', paper presented at the Pacific Rim Real Estate Conference, Adelaide, Australia.

Dybvig, L.O. (1992), 'Contaminated Real Estate Implications for Real Estate Appraisers', The Research and Development Fund, Appraisal Institute of Canada.

Fogelman, V.M. (1992), *Hazardous Waste Cleanup, Liability, and Litigation: A Comprehensive Guide to Superfund Law*, Westport, CT: Quorum.

Giangrasso, M. and E. Tassoni (2001), 'Il programma nazionale di bonifica e ripristino ambientale dei siti inquinati', *Ambiente e Sicurezza*, **10**, Milano: IlSole24Ore, April.

Grimski, D. and U. Ferber (2001), 'Urban Brownfields in Europe', *Land Contamination and Reclamation*, **9** (1), 143–8.

Howland, M. (2000), 'The Impact of Contamination on the Canton/Southeast Baltimore Land Market', *Journal of the American Planning Association*, **66** (4), 411–20.

Lèvêque, F. (1996), 'The Regulatory Game', in F. Lèvêque (ed.), *Environmental Policy in Europe. Industry, Competition and the Policy Process*, Cheltenham, UK and Brookfield, USA: Edward Elgar Publishing Ltd.

Louviere, J.J., D.A. Hensher and J.D. Swait (2000), *Stated Choice Methods. Analysis and Applications*, Cambridge: Cambridge University Press.

McGrath, D.T. (2000), 'Urban Industrial Land Redevelopment and Contamination Risk', *Journal of Urban Economics*, **47**, 414–42.

Meyer, P.B. and H.W. VanLandingham (2000), 'Reclamation and Economic Regeneration of Brownfields', *Reviews of Economic Development Literature and Practice*, 1, Washington, DC: U.S. Economic Development Administration.

Meyer, P.B., R.H. Williams and K.R. Yount (1995), *Contaminated Land. Reclamation, Redevelopment and Reuse in the United States and the European Union*, Aldershot, UK and Brookfield, USA: Edward Elgar Publishing Ltd.

Opaluch, J.J., S.K. Swallow, T. Weaver, C.W. Wessells and D. Wichelns (1993), 'Evaluating Impacts from Noxious Facilities: Including Public Preferences in Current Siting Mechanisms', *Journal of Environmental Economics and Management*, **24**(1), 41–59.

Simons, R.A. (1998), *Turning Brownfields into Greenbacks*, Washington, DC: Urban Land Institute.

Train, K.E. (1999), 'Mixed Logit Models for Recreation Demand', in J.A. Herriges and C.L. Kling (eds), *Valuing Recreation and the Environment. Revealed Preference Methods in Theory and Practice*, Cheltenham, UK: Edward Elgar Publishing.

Urban Institute, Northeast-Midwest Institute, University of Louisville and University of Northern Kentucky (1997), 'The Effects of Environmental Hazards and Regulation on Urban Redevelopment', report to the US Department of Urban Development, Washington, DC, August.

US Conference of Mayors (1996), 'Impact of Brownfields on US Cities: A 39-City Survey', Washington, DC.

US General Accounting Office (1995), 'Community Development: Reuse of Urban Industrial Sites', GAO/RCED 95-172, Washington, DC.

US General Accounting Office (1997), 'Superfund: State Voluntary Programs Provide Incentives to Encourage Cleanups', GAO/RCED-97-66, Washington, DC.

Viscusi, W.K., W.A. Magat and J. Huber (1991), 'Pricing Environmental Health Risks: Assessment of Risk–Risk and Risk–Dollar Tradeoffs for Chronic Bronchitis', *Journal of Environmental Economics and Management*, **21**, 32–51.

10. Governing Environmental Restoration: Institutions and Industrial Site Clean-ups

Francesco Trombetta and Margherita Turvani

10.1 INTRODUCTION

The Lagoon of Venice is a complex natural resource and ecological system that has been long subject to a variety of natural and anthropic stimuli. The contaminated sites of Marghera, the large chemical complex on the mainland side of the Lagoon, have contributed several such stimuli over the last decade, and in addition pose a potentially serious threat to public health. Cleaning up these sites, and redeveloping them when they are abandoned, is an important step towards reducing these negative externalities.

The contaminated sites of Marghera are an example of brownfields. Brownfields are defined by the US Environmental Protection Agency as

> abandoned, idled, or under-used industrial and commercial facilities where expansion or redevelopment is complicated by real or perceived environmental contamination.[1]

Brownfields are the result of two concurrent processes. The first is the transformation of the economy, with the downsizing and relocation of manufacturing and the increasingly larger role of the service sector. The second is institutional, and is the introduction of environmental legislation for the protection of public health and the environment that impose liability for the cost of cleanup at contaminated sites. For these reasons the brownfield problem is now common to all industrialized countries and is very serious in Eastern European countries, which face the consequences of the heavy impact of centrally planned economies on environmental contamination.

In this chapter we propose an explanation for such coevolution, providing a framework for the institutional setups that seek to address the brownfields problem. We discuss the possible approaches, their advantages and disadvantages, and examine what these approaches would entail for the Marghera sites.

The remainder of this chapter is organized as follows. In section 10.2, we describe briefly the nature of the Marghera brownfields, assess the seriousness of the brownfield problem, and discuss how economics traditionally classifies and addresses the problem of brownfields. Policy frameworks, including liability, voluntary cleanups and agreements, and co-regulation, are discussed in section 10.3. We discuss liability at length in section 10.4. In section 10.5, we present the agreements surrounding the Marghera sites. Section 10.6 concludes.

10.2   THE PROMISE AND LIMITATION OF THE ECONOMIC APPROACH TO THE BROWNFIELD PROBLEM

The Marghera Complex and Brownfields

The industrial area of Marghera lies on the mainland side of the Lagoon of Venice and hosts 70 percent of the oil-derived chemical production in Italy. It covers a total of 2000 hectares, most of which are nowadays considered heavily polluted.[2] Data collected in 2000 for the Italian National Priority List, which was established by Executive Order n. 468 by Ministry of the Environment dated 18 September 2001, define an even broader area that needs further investigation. According to the new criteria, 3825 hectares of land are classified as heavily polluted and are considered a contaminated area for NPL purposes – an area that is almost twice as large as the industrial zone of Marghera. In addition, 2311 hectares within the Lagoon of Venice are considered contaminated. These figures are impressive, although they should be interpreted with caution, as the pollution problem may have been overstated by local authorities in hopes of securing national funding for the cleanup.

In sum, soil, groundwater and surface water are contaminated at the Marghera industrial site, and contaminated sediments and leachates have migrated into the Lagoon. The Marghera site is a serious brownfield in terms of the severity of its contamination problem and the extent of the contaminated area, but is by no means the only example of a contaminated site in Italy: data from 1995 record more than 11 000 polluted sites in Italy, for a total of 260 000 hectares of soil and 70 000 of coastal areas corresponding to 280 km of coasts. The cost of cleanup interventions were estimated to be of the order of 30 000 billion lire (Gargiulo, 2001).

The remainder of the European Union is similarly affected. A survey conducted at the end of the 1980s found 150 000 presumably polluted sites for a total of 100 million hectares (Giangrasso and Tassoni, 2001). The cost of remediating the most heavily compromised areas for EU members has been estimated to be 1 percent of the internal gross product of the Union.

Contaminated sites are a serious problem in the US as well. At this time, over 1300 sites have been placed on the US National Priority List, a registry of contaminated sites to which priority in remedial action is given by law. However, the scale of the problem is much broader. DeLong (1995) holds a sharply critical view of US regulation on environmental liability, the so-called Superfund law, arguing that the number of sites that will eventually fall into the NPL might rise even to 6000 or 10 000 because of the breadth of the statutory definition of pollution at industrial sites. A 1993 survey estimated over 100 000 non-NPL sites, 40 000 of which needed attention. In 1995 the CERCLA Information System (CERCLIS) contained 39 692 sites, all of which required investigation to assess whether they posed a threat to human health and/or ecological systems. Site investigations found almost two-thirds of them to be within the allowed contamination limits. Site investigations, however, are costly and take considerable time and human resources on the part of the US Environmental Protection Agency.[3]

Traditional Economics and Brownfields

The large number and extension of brownfields is a substantial economic and territorial issue, and a serious environmental problem. Each brownfield site potentially creates four types of exernalities: (i) adverse effects of pollution on human health; (ii) adverse effects on other determinants of human welfare such as aesthetic values, urban congestion and degradation; (iii) damages to ecological systems; and (iv) perception of a subjective decrease in welfare of agents or of an increase in risk. These externalities may affect many parties, including residents, workers, tourists, and users of natural resources.

Externality is the core concept in environmental economics (Coase, 1960). Standard theory holds that externalities arise because of ill-defined property rights on natural resources that get impaired, damaged or depleted by pollution. Interpreted as market failures, externalities justify public agencies' intervention. If the origin of an externality is to be found in ill-defined property rights, the straightforward solution is the government redefining property rights via regulation or through the use of economic incentives.

Lèvêque (1996) argues that, even if the government could redesign property rights perfectly by means of law, bargaining between polluters and pollutees to compensate for welfare losses due to pollution is usually not possible: private negotiation works only when there are few polluters and pollutees which mutually know costs and preferences. In most cases, however, transaction costs are likely to be too high, property rights will remain ill-defined and a market will not emerge to deal with externalities.

Economic theory distinguishes two types of government intervention to correct environmental externalities (Lévêque, 1996): (i) economic instruments and incentives such as taxes, subsidies, tradeable permits, deposit refund systems, and liability; and (ii) command and control, or the regulatory approach, such as emission standards, concentration limits, and mandatory certification.

In theory, to produce the socially optimal regulation, the regulator must (a) possess and process all the relevant information at no cost and (b) act as benevolent maximizer of collective welfare (Pigou, 1946; Dixit, 1996). In practice no real regulator ever meets these requirements: perfect knowledge about pollution does not exist and uncertainty about eco-system and health effects inevitably hampers both private negotiation and public intervention.

But other problems arise from the procedural nature of regulation. In theory, as described by Baumol and Oates (1971), first the environmental goals are set in the political arena, and then the policy instruments are chosen to meet the stated goals. In practice, however, this stylized description overlooks the complexity and iterative character of real decision-making by government agencies.

An institutional perspective on regulation suggests framing both market and government failures within a holistic theoretical approach. Goals are not exogenous to feasible policy instruments. Regulation itself is an institution, a set of rules defining the game that agents are playing, both offering opportunities and imposing constraints. Regulation entails creating (i) new knowledge, (ii) some consensus around controversial environmental issues, (iii) new institutional structures and laws to address environmental issues, (iv) a monitoring system to evaluate the performance of the regulation itself and possible new externalities or undesired consequences, which in turn may create new stakeholders.

Traditional economics assumes that the regulator is benevolent and that it does not incur in regulating costs. Recent institutional theories emphasize that all forms of institutional governance fail, including markets and government agencies (Dixit, 1996; Williamson, 1995). Information asymmetries, monitoring and enforcement costs, uncertainty and *de facto* irreversibility of regulatory choices, all affect the evolution of regulation. Different interests converge in regulatory processes: the theory of capture (Tirole, 1994) explains how the regulator may collude either with the regulated industry or with environmentalist associations, producing a different kind of regulation accordingly. The choice of the policy instrument to deal with environmental problems is neither easy nor without consequences. Information problems are pervasive: real world regulators do not know firms' abatement costs and technologies for pollution reduction, and uncertainty on the effects on ecosystems hampers both decision-making of regulators and firms, private negotiations, and consensus building across public opinion.

As a result of this complex institutional evolution we observe nowadays hybrid forms of governance of environmental externalities such as co-regulation (when the public agency sets the goals and firms choose action plans to achieve them) or self-regulation (when firms, acting in a proactive manner, commit themselves to some environmental remediation practices) (Lévêque, 1996), which are neither pure market based nor pure government.

10.3 VOLUNTARY AND MANDATORY CLEANUP

From the perspective of the firm, it makes sense to regard cleanups as an investment that increases profits, but only when the firm operates on site and faces problem of relations with stakeholders such as workers, residents, the local community and institutions. In these cases, remedial actions are part of a broader investment strategy aimed at improving the safety of plants, reducing conflicts with local stakeholders, which in turns improves social and environmental sustainability, and developing customer-oriented marketing strategies.[4]

The rationale behind self-regulation is normally present also in more complex structures of co-regulation. The main Italian example is *Accordo di Programma per la Chimica a Marghera.*[5] We wish to emphasize that cleanups are *not* the main aim of this agreement, which is primarily driven by the need of restructuring the chemical industry, guaranteeing employment, and by specific features of the territory hosting the facilities. In Marghera an important goal is to deliver shipments of chemical feedstocks and intermediate goods to the plants located there: the removal of sediments obstructing channels is necessary to guarantee the normal operation of plants, but sediments are heavily polluted and therefore treatment must be planned and financed. *Accordo per la Chimica* provides funds jointly from the state and firms to deal with this problem.

Another recent trend is the reliance on voluntary cleanup, which has increasingly become economically feasible thanks to technological development and preferences both at the individual and societal level. Unless firms plan to stop production altogether, they must reduce opposition by environmentalists and residents, a goal that can be attained by undertaking voluntary cleanups.

A different argument, however, must be made for abandoned sites, where pollution is a sunk cost that can be transferred onto the community, and individual agents have no incentive to bear this cost. Why should anyone want to invest in an asset that is no longer productive, unless forced by law to compensate previous damages? A crucial feature for promoting voluntary cleanup is the possibility of a productive future utilization of the sites. On idle polluted sites the likelihood of a private firm financing remediation only out of economic reasons is virtually zero, unless the area has high location advantages so that its value in the cleaned-up, redeveloped state exceeds the cost of remediation. The cost–benefit balance of remedial action depends on two groups of factors:

1. site-specific factors such as proximity to important markets and networks, type of pollution, industrial history of the facilities and buildings on site;
2. external factors, such as laws, regulation, standards, innovation in remedial or mitigation techniques, advancement in risk-assessing and appraisal procedures, expectations about possible lawsuits, insurance for environmental costs and risks, etc.

Liability for the cost of remediation at contaminated sites is a widely adopted approach, but it too can create high costs or risks, to the point that potentially attractive sites are left idle, thus defeating one of the purposes of establishing the liability system. Many western countries have adopted a liability framework for handling contaminated sites, on the grounds that it is felt that the burden of environmental restoration should be placed on the responsible parties regardless of economic factors.

In the US, where the liability system was established in 1980, many – including residents, environmental organizations, and firms – question the effectiveness and fairness of holding responsible parties liable for the cost of cleanup, especially when they had disposed of the hazardous wastes in compliance with the laws and regulations of the time. Some observers argue that agencies do not try to reach effective results but pursue remediation *per se*, with an ethical bias regardless of actual results and a more efficient resources allocation. DeLong (1995) argues that reclaiming polluted land is not always valuable for the community, regardless of the costs and benefits of each specific intervention. Communities may prefer spending money on other sanitation or environmental issues, as long as risks at brownfields are below certain levels. Others argue that it is important to take into account uncertainty regarding future effects on human health and the ecological system, which makes remediation appropriate within a precautionary principle framework.

10.4   LIABILITY AND REGULATION

Different Approaches to Liability: the US and Italy

Liability forces firms to internalize the external damages of their production activities, and is thus regarded as an economic incentive to reduce pollution. It is the approach adopted to deal with hazardous waste sites in the US, Germany, the Netherlands and Italy.

The principle underlying liability is to define what is to be considered as polluted and to spell out criteria for identifying the parties that are held legally responsible for the pollution and must pay for remediation. Responsible parties can be obliged to clean up and sued if they fail to do so.

Liability can be either negligence-based or strict (in Italian *responsabilità soggettiva* or *oggettiva*). Under negligence-based liability the responsible parties must pay for the cost of remediation if their responsibility for pollution can be demonstrated, i.e., if they fail to meet a negligence standard. In the case of strict liability the owners or users of contaminated sites can be held responsible *per se* no matter how careful their behaviours were, and there is no burden of proof.

Liability can also be joint-and-several or in proportion to fault (in Italian: *responsabilità in solido* or *del singolo*). In the case of joint-and-several liability each of the parties responsible for the pollution can be held liable for and charged with the entire cost of the remedial actions. It is sometimes argued that a joint-and-several liability regime may encourage the government agency to pursue the 'deep pockets' (i.e., the firms who are solvent and can pay for the cleanup, even if their contribution to the contamination problem was modest; see Alberini and Austin, 1999, and Roddewig, 1996). Finally, liability can be retroactive in the sense that responsible parties are liable even when their disposal practices were in compliance with the applicable waste disposal laws.

National legal traditions differ very much and influence deeply the choice of the type of liability applied. In the US the *Comprehensive Environmental Response, Compensation and Liability Act* (CERCLA), commonly dubbed *Superfund*, was passed in 1980, amended as *Superfund Amendments and Reauthorization Act* (SARA) in 1986, and then reauthorized in 1991.

The common law tradition led to a strict, joint-and-several, and retroactive form of liability on a federal level. Contaminated sites that do not quality for federally funded or led cleanup fall on the shoulders of the individual states, which may or may not apply the same liability structure as the federal statute.[6]

DeLong (1995, p.16) claims that the Superfund liability regime actually slows down the cleanup process, because the most important item is the miasma of injustice that surrounds the program, generated by its core doctrines of polluter pays and liability that is strict, joint and several, and retroactive.

This view is supported by the fact that anyone who has come in contact with a Superfund contaminated site can be held liable:

> not only everyone who had any direct connection with the waste or the site but also whose connection is more removed – lenders, shareholders, corporate officers, parent and successor corporations, lessors and lessees, executors and trustees, and bankrupt estates. (DeLong, 1995, pp. 11–12)

An unintended consequence of this liability regime is that as a result 'hundreds and thousands of parcels of land are blighted for development while new industries are built on virgin ground' (p. 15). EPA staff members hold a completely different opinion, and point to the accomplishments of the program in reducing risks to public health, educating the public about contamination and health risks, and spurring research into new and cost-effective cleanup technologies.[7]

In Italy, contaminated sites were addressed only in 1997 – 15 years later than in other western countries – with the passage of Decreto Ronchi. Article 17 of D. Lgs. 22/1997 and its application, art. 9 of D. M. 471/1999, states that the party who is responsible for the pollution has to bear the cost of cleanup, even if pollutants are released into the environment by accident. Moreover, if no responsible party is found, or if the responsible parties do not comply with the remediation order, the municipality must start remedial action and sue the responsible parties for the money spent (or repossess the remediated areas in the case of orphan sites).

The US and Italy are thus very different in their application of the liability principle: here, legal tradition and history matters. The Italian legal tradition is strongly opposed to strict liability and retroactive laws, and environmental liability is not simply a matter of civil law but also entails penal responsibilities. Indeed, two principles governing the Constitution (*principio di riserva di legge* e *principio di tassatività*) state that only specified behaviours can be punished. In the case of remedial action for environmental pollution exceptions may arise in partial derogation of these principles:[8] as a result, the new owner of a contaminated site, even though he is not responsible for the pollution, may decide that it is better to start a cleanup action rather than bearing the risk of paying lawsuit fines if the national environmental protection agency or consultants of the court have the discretionary power to initiate and settle a lawsuit.

The opposition of lawyers and inconsistency of the new laws with hierarchically superior laws, such as the Constitution, may turn out to be major hindrances to judicial settlement for pollution, both by raising risk perceptions and stigma connected to known or suspected polluted areas, and by making law too strongly dependent on judicial interpretation and thus too uncertain in a system that is *not* based on common law. Uncertainty on liability standards may delay remediation at brownfields, thus defeating one of the purposes of the law. We conclude that both the US and the Italian laws may potentially create undesirable delays in the brownfield remediation process, but for completely different reasons.

Our inquiries at Comune di Venezia, Servizio Ambiente (Environmental Services Department of the City of Venice) suggest that many sites known to be polluted in Marghera are currently at a stalemate. Unilateral remediation orders by the municipality would inevitably lead to litigation with the responsible parties. This outcome is not a viable and desirable solution for either the authority or the private parties due to high costs and long time of litigation in Italy. Voluntary cleanups, on their part, are generally deemed to be too expensive, and only if the municipality negotiates with firms, offering something in exchange for cleanup, with no binding legal effect, would firms agree to voluntary cleanups.

In summary, the liability principle in practice may lead to very high costs of cleanup, both for private parties and for society, depending crucially on the effectiveness of the enforcement system. The legal tradition influences the likelihood of successfully governing the cleanup process. As a result, the Italian system appears to be much more prone to experiencing the adverse effects of firms' non-cooperative behaviours. This feature is confirmed by the predominance of voluntary agreements and by the contractual solution adopted in Marghera. Moreover, in Italy workers and end-users – two important categories of stakeholders in the cleanup and redevelopment process – are clearly at a disadvantage relative to industry, much more so than in the US.

From Command-and-Control to Cooperation

Although liability is an economic incentive to address pollution externalities, it is clear that it must rely on an enforcement system, and on an associated regulation to spell out the cleanup standards.

Shavell (1987) offers two criteria to describe enforcement in the case of pollution: (i) private v. public intervention, and (ii) ex-ante v. ex-post responsibility (liability and compensation for damages). These criteria are presented in Table 10.1.

According to this scheme, command-and-control approaches (regulation) are classified as ex ante modes of governance, as are economic incentives. Even ex ante approaches, however, must create ex post sanctions for non-

Table 10.1   Ex ante and ex post approaches to pollution

	Private initiative systems	Public initiative systems
Ex ante	Court injunctions	Command-and-control regulation Pollution taxes and economic incentives
Ex post	Tort liability	Fines for harm done

compliance. Indeed, every legal system allows for private action against damages by polluters.

In practice, environmental legislation in most countries resorts to a mix of all of the different instruments listed above. In Italy, civil action is always an option for damaged private parties according to art. 2043 Codice Civile. Moreover, law n. 349, enacted July 8, 1986, art.18, envisages civil payment to the State for collective damages to the environment, in addition to those suffered by private parties.[9]

What distinguishes a regulation system from another is the type and relative weight of the various instruments shown in Table 10.1. These differ across countries and over time, depending on: (i) the accumulation of knowledge; (ii) the legal tradition and approach towards regulation that favors/relies on the use of one or the other instrument; (iii) any redefinition of the system of values of the agents involved in the process generating externalities as they gather new knowledge, and (iv) any redefinition of stakeholders' positions and lobbying activities.

In countries with long judicial settlements and low probability of success in suing polluters, such as Italy, the parties who experience pollution damages tend to be less proactive than in others with more efficient legal systems and higher probability of successfully suing the polluters.

Recent developments in industrialized countries suggest that a common trend might be forming towards alternative forms of governance, where responsible parties, landowners and local collective agents cooperate, and/or remediation standards are locale-specific and depend on actual exposures to contaminants. Voluntary agreements (Amadei et al., 1998) and risk-based criteria driving the choice of remediation techniques in Italy (Decreto 471/99; see the recent debate on this executive order, *La Bonifica dei siti contaminati. Dall'esperienza in campo esempi di soluzioni alle problematiche*, Provincia di Milano, November 15, 2002) are examples of such trends. In this sense, Italy is experiencing a process similar to that of other countries, such as the US, the Netherlands and Germany, where the liability and remediation framework was established years ago.

Laws, incentives, deterrents and enforcement must be seen as parts of a unified system of governance of the remedial process. An institutional point of view looks at the variety of transactions involved in any process of cleanup at a brownfield as an emerging governance structure that must be analysed in its entirety (Williamson, 1995), taking into account the nature of transactions and the stakes involved along with a comparative approach to evaluate feasibility of specific processes of cleanup.

10.5   THE CASE OF MARGHERA

Regulatory action to curb pollution at industrial sites is frequently driven by locally sharpened public perception of environmental externalities and the subsequent shift in agent preferences. Pollution exposures may continue for several years, and health damages may affect workers or residents on a large scale before the remedial investigation begins. The demand for cleanup depends on various factors, including the accumulation of knowledge, agent preferences for health and income, and the legal tradition shaping regulation.

Legal action started at Marghera only in 1998, even though subpoenas (in Italian *avvisi di garanzia*) were issued to potentially responsible parties as far back as in 1994, after the inquiry, and immediately proved to be a costly and ineffective means of settlement of liability issues. Common knowledge about the risks connected with high pollution in Marghera had been building up among local stakeholders at least since the 1988 EniMont merger. It has even been argued that most of the deaths that occurred until the 1980s among workers at plants were presumably caused by exposures to toxic substances such as vinyl chloride.[10]

The building up and diffusion of awareness about health risks seems to have developed following a pattern similar to what happened in places such as Minamata, Japan, where pollution caused by organic mercury released from the Chisso Minamata Plant into Minamata Bay was first discovered in May 1956. The plant workers were exposed to hazardous substances on a daily basis, and knew the production processes very well, which helped them develop their own framework to interpret events. An important role was played by local individual healthcare practitioners, but neither the workers nor the physicians were able to raise concern by public health authority.

Despite the growing awareness of the environmental externalities created by the Marghera chemical complex, the local authorities were late in their actions. As late as the early 1990s the Venice Municipality acquired 43 hectares of land in the industrial park. Local residents that had previously worked at the Marghera chemical complex knew that the site was heavily polluted. The complex was not fenced, and had been used for a long time to dispose of waste from the production of aluminium.

No due diligence checks were conducted prior to the purchase and in 1995 the local authorities discovered that the site had to be cleaned up through very expensive procedures. Some observers have even claimed that the due diligence checks were omitted on purpose to benefit the potentially responsible parties. In practice the acquisition of the site started an on-going process of remediation funded with public monies.[11]

The workers' unions were even later participants in the process. They never made a strong case against pollution, mainly because their primary concern has historically been job protection. Environmental concerns became important only at a later stage, when the chemical plants underwent heavy restructuring, laying off a large number of workers.[12] Faced with the threat of further layoffs because of stricter environmental standards, the unions chose to focus on job protection. Only in 1998, when *Accordo per la Chimica a Marghera* was signed at the national level, the unions and the firms agreed on the need for a safer working environment, reconciling job creation and environmental care.

The trial that started in 1998 worked as a catalyst: On the one hand it broke away from the conservative approach of the Italian court system regarding environmental claims.[13, 14] On the other hand, it paved the way to new forms of cooperative regulation and self-regulation.

The Marghera lawsuit and trial worked as a sort of rehearsal of what may happen if litigation remains the only governance mechanism to deal with environmental externalities at brownfields. Since environmental regulation by law is frequently the product of rising public concern and growth of the relevant scientific knowledge, a gap may open between perceived externalities that threaten private and collective assets and the general system of rules which should cope with the problem.

Such a gap is rarely closed spontaneously by interactions among agents because transactions in brownfields are highly uncertain, very site-specific and generally very costly. This is confirmed by the fact that very little spontaneous redevelopment has occurred at the Marghera sites, despite their attractive location for business. All site sales during the last seven years were to publicly owned development corporations. Two major sales of abandoned/unutilized sites, for a total of 36 hectares, were carried out by Immobiliare Veneziana (IVE) and a third area (10 hectares) was purchased by Vega Science Park, a public consortium that rents space to high-tech firms.

Based on our interviews with private and government stakeholders, we believe that potential buyers in Marghera, even when they are attracted by the location, consider the environmental risk too high unless cooperation with public agents is offered to lessen the burden of the complex system of state-to-local rules and laws and the number of public agencies involved. In Marghera the market for polluted sites is very thin: there are no more than a dozen sellers and even fewer developers in the area. Potential end users for these sites feel confident enough to undertake remediation and redevelopment of brownfields only if they can find or buy areas that have already been cleaned up. Again Marghera shows evidence of this behaviour: 18 transportation firms bought a 10-hectare area (the so-called Azotati, previously used for the production of nitrogen fertilizers) from Immobiliare Veneziana, which offered it for sale after cleanup had been completed.

In this situation buyers develop specific competences and a competitive advantage in dealing with contaminated lands, as is demonstrated by their repeated transactions. The completion of a single transaction at a polluted site involves several steps, different forms of negotiation and complicated contracts. The design of such contracts involves multilateral negotiation among (i) sellers that might be held responsible for pollution, (ii) several levels of local authorities and (iii) potential buyers. For example, in Marghera cleanup was undertaken by the buyer, IVE, who tailored them to the needs of the end users, but paid for by the seller, who also petitioned for approval by the local authority. The whole process, which required approval by the City and certification of completion according to the standards established by Provincia di Venezia (Province of Venice), was expedited by the cooperative framework in which it took place.[15]

Accordo per la Chimica, the voluntary agreement governing remedial and safety-enhancing actions at the 800 hectares of active chemical facilities did so well as an instrument of co-regulation that a second step in that direction is now being taken: a round II/amendment has been signed by all of the public and private agents involved in the first round, and other firms operating in Marghera but outside of the chemical area are allowed to enter the process by signing up for the protocol.

In the end, the experience at Marghera may have had some input into the national statute, which now incorporates some form of cooperation in addressing contaminated sites. Art. 17 of the 1997 Decreto Ronchi is centered around a liability scheme, but the mandatory remedial action is covered in the subsequent 1999 law and reflects principles of economic feasibility similar to those of the 1998 *Accordo per la Chimica*.

10.6   CONCLUSIONS

The problems connected to industrial site divestment are the direct result of economic, productive and technological evolution, and are generated mainly by the changes in the industrial and manufacturing sectors. Both legislative and institutional factors contribute to trigger the processes of divestment and brownfields generation. On the one hand these factors have led to the definition of responsibilities for the damage caused, and on the other hand they carry with them very high management costs.

In the context of urban development policies, derelict areas are important for implementing urban renewal and re-qualification, especially in the framework of environmental safeguarding, human health and sustainable development. This objective is especially important now that the European Union wishes to develop a common strategy for soil protection and quality, as specified in the Sixth Environment Action Program. It is widely argued that urban and environmental re-qualification programmes have helped improve the economic, social and environmental conditions of these areas. Specifically, they have helped create new jobs, attract investment, improve existing infrastructure, reduce problems linked to sanitary risks, avoid future environmental contamination, reduce urban sprawl and pressure on greenfields and, finally, revitalize the socially degraded surrounding areas.

Many derelict sites, whether contaminated or not, lie in areas lacking the necessary economic resources to face the task of reclaiming them, and a central authority must step in to provide the institutional and economic tools necessary for managing the problem.

Indeed, it seems very unlikely that the private sector can react without the support of the public sector. Thin markets represent an important problem in the reclamation and redevelopment of contaminated industrial sites. Many sites remain unproductive not only because of high reclamation costs, but also because of the high level of uncertainty surrounding the reclamation processes themselves. Uncertainty may be about costs, techniques, end-use of the land, legislative pressure and so on. Experience suggests that it may be important to relax rigid standards (for example those that require recreating the 'original' conditions and background levels of the various contaminants), which do not address the problem of the actual costs and benefits connected to the intervention.

Another type of intervention is to encourage voluntary initiatives for the renewal of contaminated sites, by guaranteeing flexibility and limiting the financial responsibility for those involved. These are the conclusions we draw from our analysis of the institutional factors which may impede or foster redevelopment by influencing the overall costs of remediation. The case study of *Accordo per la Chimica* at Porto Marghera near Venice is an example of voluntary agreements; such agreements of course are not a panacea for solving the problems of industrial sites cleanups. They are demanding, requiring continuous effort in monitoring, negotiating and committing of the different stakeholders and agencies; yet they may be able to deal with the evolving character of externalities perception and of the economic dynamics.

NOTES

1. See http://www.epa.gov/swerosps/bf/glossary.htm#brow (last access: November 2005).
2. See http://www.ambiente.venezia.it/ (last access: November 2005) for details about the nature of the contaminants.
3. Estimates of these costs were provided at the Brownfields Conference held in Ferrara in October 2002. For sites de-listed immediately after document scrutiny, it takes about 1 person and 2–3 days' worth of work. For sites de-listed after perusal of papers, on-site inspection and soil or water samples, it takes about 1 person-month (Tom Voltaggio, US Environmental Protection Agency, personal communication).
4. An example is provided by the Responsible Care programme initiated by the chemical industry in the US and Canada (Hoffman, 1999). This programme is an example of what has been defined 'proactive' behaviour by firms: chemical producers adopted a form of self-regulation, by stating publicly their environmental improvements goals, monitoring performance, possibly involving third parties such as environmental associations in the monitoring system, and informing the public about the results attained.
5. *Accordo per la Chimica* was signed in Rome on 21 October 1998 and became effective on 12 February 1999. This is a major example of negotiated planning involving both agencies such as the Ministry of the Environment, the Ministry of Industry and private companies such as Enichem, European Vinyls Corporation, Elf Altochem, Agip Petroli, Esso Italiana, Api, Montefibre and Agip Gas, among others. The agreement spells out that much investment should be made in building safer plants. As of August 2000, 904 billion lire had already been invested out of the projected total of 1575 billion lire. One item was, for example, restoring channels around the area that tend to be obstructed by sediments. This will require digging 6 900 000 cubic metres of contaminated mud which must be treated or piled up and isolated by using capping devices to prevent migration of pollutants. All of this will be funded by public monies.
6. Alberini and Austin (1999) empirically study the determinants of adoption of one versus the other type of liability within a political economy framework.
7. See http://www.epa.gov/superfund/action/20years/preface.htm (last access: November 2005).
8. See Maurizio Bortolotto, JD, commenting on these topics on http://www.cahiers.org (last access: November 2005).
9. We note that this law is very difficult to apply, especially in a very conservative judicial environment such as the Italian one, as shown by the trial against alleged polluters of the chemical plants of Marghera. See http://www.petrolchimico.it (last access: November 2005).
10 Different parties count victims differently: according to the Prosecution, 157 out of 310 worker deaths were attributable to pollution in Marghera. However, since a direct link between pollutants and cancer is not easily established, the total number of victims of toxic substances exposures may shrink to 32 out of the 90 workers that washed trucks devoted to vinyl chloride transport, subsequently developed various forms of cancer and died. According to the lawyers of the operation managers at the chemical plants – the defendents – this figure may further diminish to 10 deaths during the 1960s (Battaglini and Mariotto, 2001).
11. As a result a pilot project on 10 out of 43 hectares was recently approved by the local authority in charge, the Provincia di Venezia (Province of Venice) in 1996: it envisaged the removal and treatment of surface waters, the separation and capping of toxic substances. The project was completed in 1998. The total cost was about 10 billion lire.
12. At the beginning of the 1980s, a total of 30 000 workers were employed at the Marghera industrial park, a figure that is over twice as large as today's 14 000.
13. The first-degree court announced the verdict on 2 November 2001: the defendants were not found guilty. This first-degree decision shows once again that the Italian legal system finds it difficult to deal with environmental issues.
14. The charge of environmental disaster by Prosecutor Felice Casson on behalf of the Italian Government against managers and owners of the plants was greeted by Italian public opinion, especially by local stakeholders, environmentalists, and communities facing similar problems nation-wide, as a pathbreaking legal action. No similar lawsuit had ever

been brought against alleged polluters. In Italy claims are routinely limited to health or other damages suffered by private parties: Only in a very few less important lawsuits was consideration ever given to collective environmental damages, and compensation required of the responsible parties.

15. It should be emphasized that the project was originated by an urban development corporation run by the City of Venice.

REFERENCES

Alberini, A. and D.H. Austin (1999), 'On and Off the Liability Bandwagon: Explaining State Adoptions of Strict Liability in Hazardous Waste Programs', *Journal of Regulatory Economics*, **15** (1), 41–64.

Amadei, P., E. Croci and G. Pesaro (1998), *Nuovi strumenti di politica ambientale. Gli accordi Volontari*, Milano: FrancoAngeli.

Baumol, W.J. and W.E. Oates (1971), 'The Use of Standards and Prices for Protection of the Environment', *Swedish Journal of Economics*, **73** (1), 42–54.

Battaglini, E. and A. Mariotto (2001), 'Porto Marghera: dai vincoli alle opportunità', *Formula,* **XVIII**, 1–2.

Coase, R. (1960), 'The Problem of Social Costs', *Journal of Law and Economics*, **3**, 1–44.

DeLong James, V. (1995), 'Privatizing Superfund: How to Clean up Hazardous Waste', *Cato Policy Analysis*, **247**.

Dixit, A.K. (1996), *The Making of Economic Policy: a Transaction-Cost Politics Perspective,* Cambridge, MA: MIT Press.

Gargiulo, C. (2001), (ed.), 'Processi di Trasformazione urbana e aree industriali dismesse: esperienze in atto in Italia', Venezia: Edizioni AUDIS.

Giangrasso, M. and E. Tassoni (2001), 'Il programma nazionale di bonifica e ripristino ambientale dei siti inquinati', *Ambiente e Sicurezza*, **10** (Aprile), Milano: IlSole24Ore.

Hoffman, A.J. (1999), 'Institutional Evolution and Change: Environmentalism and the U.S. Chemical Industry', *The Academy of Management Journal*, **42** (4), 351–71.

Lèvêque, F. (1996), 'The Regulatory Game', in F. Lèvêque, *Environmental Policy in Europe. Industry, Competition and the Policy Process*, Cheltenham, UK and Brookfield, USA: Edward Elgar.

Pigou, A.C. (1946), *The Economics of Welfare*, London: Macmillan.

Roddewig, R. (1996), 'Stigma, Environmental Risk and Property Value: 10 Critical Inquiries', *The Appraisal Journal*, **LXIV**, 375–87.

Shavell, S. (1987), *Economic Analysis of Accident Law*, Cambridge, MA: Harvard University Press.

Tirole, J. (1994), 'The Internal Organization of Government', *Oxford Economic Papers*, **46**, 1–29.

Williamson, O.E. (1995), *The Mechanisms of Governance*, Oxford: Oxford University Press.

Index

accelerated-life Weibull models 69–70, 71–2
access, Venice Lagoon islands 77, 92–4
accessibility maps 89
Accordo di Programma per la Chimica a Marghera 200, 207, 208, 209
Adamowicz, W.I. 20
aggregate demand function 27–8
Alberini, A. 3, 12, 191, 202, 210
Albers, H. 154
Amadei, P. 205
appraisal approach
  contaminated land 150–52, 153
  cost value 48–9
  dual approach 42–5
  hedonic value 50
  limitations of 50–51
  market value 46–8
  overview 40–42
  substitution value 49
  theory to practice 51–4
  transformation value 49–50
appraisal practice, relationships with economic theory 42
asymptotic distribution 11
Atkinson, G. 54
Austin, D.H. 202, 210
Australia, contaminated land 149
Azotati 208

Baltimore, valuation of contaminated land 155–6
Bartsch, C. 190
Bateman, I.J. 63
Battaglini, E. 192
Baumol, W.J. 199
Beal, D. 26, 29
Beggs, S. 15
Bell, F.W. 63
bequest value 6
Bevilacqua, P. 100

bias 19
Bible, D.S. 154
Bipolar City, Venice Lagoon 92
boating, Venice Lagoon 34–7
Boatto, V. 106
Bond, S. 149, 154
Bouyssou, D. 97
Brown, W.G. 26
brownfields
  creation of 196
  determinants of development 169–70
  economic approach to problems 197–200
  economic valuation 150–56
  empirical studies 153–6
  hedonic pricing method 152–3
  Marghera 207–8
  Marghera Complex 197–8
  overview 143
  and traditional economics 198–200
  valuation of contamination 144–9
  valuation of Porto Marghera site 157–8
  see also cleanup; developer preferences for brownfield policies; liability; stigma
Brunelli, G. 100
Bull, T. 28
Burano
  flood protection 94–5
  infrastructure 76–9
  residential properties valuation 91
  see also urban improvement

California, valuation of contaminated land 155
Cameron, T.A. 6, 8, 11
Caorle Lagoon 121
capitalization value 47, 48, 52, 153
Cardell, S. 15
Carson, R.T. 5, 9, 19, 20, 51, 191

213

case study, urban improvements 76–9
catch rates, recreational sport fishing
    116–32
census information 6
CERCLA (Comprehensive
    Environmental Response,
    Compensation and Liability Act)
    (1980), US 162, 164, 173, 202
    Information System (CERCLIS) 198
Chan, N. 144, 149, 150, 153, 190
Chattopadhyay, S. 75
Chicago, valuation of contaminated land
    155
Chioggia, Italy 100
Choe, K. 63
choke price 26–7, 32
Città Bipolare, Venice Lagoon 92
clam fishing practices, Venice Lagoon
    conjoint choice questionnaire 107–8
    identification of attributes/measured
        levels 105–7
    introduction of exotic clam species
        101–2
    management practices 100–101
    modeling fisherman behavior 102–5
    national resource problem 100–102
    overview 99–100
    survey design/questionnaire
        formulation 105–8
    survey evaluation results 108–12
Clawson, M. 23
cleanup, contaminated land 143, 145–6
    benefits 154
    costs 144, 146, 156
    demand for 206–8
    incentives for 162–4, 166–90
    uncertainties of 209
    voluntary/mandatory approaches
        200–201
Coase, R. 198
coastal environments, use of contingent
    valuation 63
coastal erosion, Venice Lagoon 61
Cochrane, H. 43
Coletto, L. 75
command-and-control regulation 204–6
commodities, selection of attributes 19
Common, M. 28
company size and brownfield
    development 173–90

compensating variation 4–5
compensation measures, contaminated
    land 152
competitive advantage, land reclamation
    208
complementary value *see* hedonic
    value
complex social value 41–2
Comprehensive Environmental
    Response, Compensation and
    Liability Act (CERCLA) *see*
    CERCLA
conditional logit (CLM) model 17–18,
    103, 104–5, 171, 172, 189
    effects of attributes 177–9
    interaction terms 179–84
conjoint choice methods 13–15
    analyses of responses 15–18
    claim fishing questionnaires 107–8
    compared to contingent valuation
        19–20
    design of study 18–19
    developer preferences 166–7
    Porto Marghera site 158
    testing for comprehension 176–7
    see also clam fishing practices,
        questionnaires; Venice Lagoon
conjoint choice questions 166–7
Constitution, Italy 203–4
consumer behavioural adjustment 24–8,
    42–5
contaminated sites
    abandonment of 200–201, 209
    costs of 146, 147–8
    effects of 165–6
    externalities value 148
    Marghera 196–200
    overview 144–6
    policies for 165
    prior experience of 173–90
    see also brownfields; liability; stigma
contingent ranking exercises 13–15
contingent valuation method 3–4
    compared to conjoint analysis 19–20
    recreational demand 34–7
    use on coastal environments 63
    see also S. Erasmo Island,
        environmental quality
convenience samples 7
Cooper, J.A. 3, 11, 12

cooperative approach to regulation 204–6
cooperative ownership, fishing vessels 108–13
corner solutions 31–2
cost types and user behaviour 28–31
cost value 47, 48–9, 52
cost–benefit analysis 40, 53, 201
Croci, E. 205
Cropper, M. 3
Curto, R. 75, 80

D'Apaos, C. 75, 79, 81, 96
Dale, L. 149
Dallas, Texas, contaminated land 149
Decreto Ronchi (1997), Italy 203, 208
Defrancesco, E. 34
DeLong, J.V. 198, 201, 202, 203
delta method 11
demand, sport fishing 116–32
Desvousges W.H. 5, 154
deterministic component of utility 16
developer preferences for brownfield policies
  choice of regressors 172–3
  conditional logit model 177–84
  conjoint choice questions 166–7
  determinants of development 169–70
  econometric model 170–72
  effects of liability and contamination 165–6
  effects of policies 184–7
  hypotheses/interaction terms 173–4
  marginal prices 187–8
  model/data 169–74
  origins of brownfields 164–5
  overview 162–4
  policies for contaminated sites 165
  questionnaire structure/survey administration 166–9
  random coefficient models 184
  respondent characteristics 174–6
  results 174–88
  testing for comprehension 176–7
development projects, contaminated land 147
development, effects of liability and contamination 165–6
Di Cocco, E. 55

Di Silvio, G. 101
dichotomous-choice payment questions 10
dichotomous-choice surveys 8–9, 11–12, 61, 65
digital maps 89
direct comparison method of valuation 153
discount rate choice 53–4
discounted cash flow method of valuation 153
Dixit, A.K. 199
Dixon, T.J. 153
'do nothing' alternative *see* status quo
Dorfman, B. 190
Dotinga, H.M. 102
double counting errors 51, 53
double-bounded approach 11–12
dual approach 42–5, 46
due diligence checks 206–7
Dybvig, L.O. 190

Eastern Europe, brownfields 196
ecological evaluation model 75–6
econometric models
  choice of regressors 121–2
  conjoint choice experiments 15–18
  developer preferences 170–72
  and welfare calculation 118–20
economic approach
  brownfield problem 197–200
  value of environment 40–41
economic characteristics, residential property 85
economic theory of consumer behaviour 24
economic theory, relationship with appraisal practice 42
economic valuation model 40–42, 75–6, 79–86
  implementation in GIS environment 87–91
  see also brownfields
ecosystem-friendly clam fishing *see* clam fishing practices
elicitation questions 7–9
Elliot-Jones, M. 149
empirical studies
  alternative brownfields valuation methods 156

valuing brownfields using appraisal
    methods 153
valuing brownfields using hedonic
    pricing method 154–6
EniMont 206
Environment Action Programs, EU 209
environment, definitions of 40–41
environmental damage
    from clam fishing 99–102, 106, 118
    from industrial pollution 115–16, 118
environmental economics 198–200
environmental policies, contaminated
    sites 165
environmental policies, developer
    preferences
    effects of liability and contamination
        165–6
    model/data 169–74
    origins of brownfields 164–5
    overview 162–4
    questionnaire structure/survey
        administration 166–9
    results 174–88
environmental pollution 49
environmental quality, S. Erasmo Island
    background/motivation 62–4
    discussion 72–34
    overview 61–2
    programme benefits 71–2
    questionnaire structure 64–5
    results 66–71
    sampling frame 65–6
environmental quality, Venice Lagoon
    125–6, 128–9
environmental restoration governance
    from command-and-control to
        cooperation 204–6
    liability approaches 202–4
    Marghera 206–8
    Marghera Complex/brownfields 197–8
    overview 196–7
    traditional economics/brownfields
        198–200
    voluntary/mandatory cleanup 200–201
environmental restoration/reproduction
    48–9
Environmental Services Department,
    City of Venice 204
equivalent variation 4–5
Europe, contaminated sites 191, 197–8

European Council, definition of
    environment 40
European Union (EU)
    definition of environment 40
    liability policies 165
    strategy for soil protection/quality 209
ex ante/ex post approaches to pollution
    204–5
Executive Order n. 468, Italy 197
existence value 6
exotic clam species, Venice Lagoon
    101–2, 115
externalities 48–9, 148, 198, 204, 206
extreme-value type 1 distribution 103

factor maps 89–90
Famularo, N. 41
Feather, P. 121
*Federazione Italiana Agenti Immobiliari
    Professionisti* 81
Ferber, U. 165
Fisher, A.C. 53
Fisher, J.D. 153
fisherman behavior
    estimation of utility parameters 103–5
    random utility model 102–3
fishing *see* clam fishing; recreational
    sport fishing
fixed costs 23, 28–31
flood protection, Venice Lagoon 94–5
Flores, N.E. 15
flow fixed costs 23, 28–34, 37–8
Fogleman, V.M. 162
follow-up questions 8–9, 11–12
Forte, C. 41
France, contaminated sites 191
Freeman A.M. 38, 73, 132
Fulton County, Georgia, contaminated
    land 156
Fusco Girard, L. 41

Galletto, L. 106
Gardiulo, C. 197
Garrod, G.D. 75
Geographical Information System (GIS)
    75–6, 87–91
Georgiou, S. 63
Gerlowski, D.A. 63
Germany, contaminated sites 191
Giangrasso, M. 198

Giorgiutti, E. 100
Giovanardi, O. 1–2, 115
Giupponi, C. 75
Gollier, C. 53
governance, environmental restoration
   see environmental restoration
   governance
Great Britain *see* UK
Green Book, European Commission 40
Greene, W.H. 120
Grimski, D. 165
Gronow, S. 153
Groom, D. 53
Gum, R.L. 26
Guntermann, K.L. 154

Halstead, J.M. 63
Hanemann, W.M. 5, 8, 20, 103
Hanley, N. 14, 15, 19, 29
Hausman, J.A. 3, 15
hazardous waste sites (HWS) 156
hedonic pricing method 51, 62
   contaminated land 149, 152–3, 154–6
hedonic value 47, 50, 52
Hensher, D.A. 14, 103
Hepburn, B. 53
Hirshfeld, S. 154
Hoehn, J.P, 8
Hotelling, H. 23
Howe, C. 40, 53
Howland, M. 155, 177, 191
Hsieh, C. 154
Huber, J. 176
Hudson, S.P. 5
Huppert, D.D. 8
hypothetical bias 19
hypothetical development method of
   valuation 153

Idrisi Kilimanharo software
   Cost Analysis module 89
   Micro Modeler 87–8
Ihlanfeldt, K.R. 156
Immobiliare Veneziana (IVE) 207, 208
impaired value method of valuation 153
improvement evaluation, urban
   improvement 91–5
in person interviews 6
incentive-compatible approaches 8
income method of valuation 151, 153

Independence of Irrelevant Alternatives
   (IIA) 18
indirect utility 15–18
Individual approach (ITCM) 25–6
   recreational demand 34–7
individual ownership, fishing vessels
   108–13
infrastructure
   construction 61–73
   Venice Lagoon islands 76–9
internal scope test 20
internal validity of WTP responses
   12–13
   environmental improvements 69–71
Interventi per la salvaguardia di Venezia
   (Law N.171) 62
investment decisions, brownfields
   169–76
Italian Federation of Professional Real
   Estate Agents 81
Italy
   approach to liability 202–4
   brownfields 197

Jackson, T.O. 148, 152, 154, 155
Joiner, G. 154
joint-and-several liability 202

Kanninen, B.J. 8, 12, 19
Keating, D.M. 151
Ketkar, K. 154
Kiel, K. 154
Kinnard, W.N. 149
Kohlhase, J.E. 154
Kontogianni, A. 63
Kooistra, W.H.C.F. 102
Koundoury, P. 53
Krutilla, J. 41, 53

land use, Venice Lagoon islands 77
landfill sites 154–5
Langford, I.H. 63
Lauria, D.T. 63
legal tradition, Italy 203–4
Lentz, G.H. 153
Leon, H. 144
Lesvos, Greece, wetland protection 63
Lèvêque, F. 191, 198, 199, 200
liability, contaminated land 146
   approaches to 202–4

costs 201
effects of 165–6
regimes 143
relief from 163–5, 166–76
risks 201
Liang, N. 153
litigation 206, 207
Local Council Noise Classification Plan,
     Venice 89
location characteristics, residential
     property 81, 83, 84
logistic distribution of WTP 10–11
Longo, A. 191–7
Loomis, J. 8
Los Angeles, valuation of contaminated
     land 153
Louisiana, valuation of contaminated
     land 154
Louviere, J.J. 14, 20, 103

MacFadden, D. 103
Magat, W.A. 13, 176
mail surveys 6, 118
Maine, beach protection programmes 63
management practices, clam fishing
     100–101, 107–8, 110
mandatory approach to cleanup 200–201
Manila clam *see Tapes philippinarum*
Marano Lagoon 121, 126
Marchant, Th. 97
Marché International des Professionnels
     de l'Immobilier (MIPIM) 163, 169,
     174, 188
Marella, G. 75, 79, 81, 96
Marghera 204, 206–8
Marghera Complex 196–8
     see also Porto Marghera
marginal prices 187–8
Mariotto, A. 192
Markandya, A. 53
market comparison approach to
     valuation 151
market demand, brownfields 145
market price 50–51
market value 46–8, 52, 153
Martin, K.M. 19
Martin, W.E. 26
Maximilian's Tower 64, 91
McClain, K.T. 154
McCluskey, J.J. 149, 154

McConnell, K.E. 63, 121
McGilvray, J. 6
McGrath, D.T. 155, 191
McLean, D.G. 151, 152, 156
mean willingness to pay 9–10, 12
median willingness to pay 12
Medici, G. 48, 50, 55
Melaku, C.D. 114
Merlo, M. 48
Mestre 92
Ministry of the Environment, Italy 197
Mitchell, R.C. 5, 51
Molesti, R. 40
mono-parametric procedures 83
Monte-Carlo technique 149
Mourato, S. 14, 15, 19, 54
multi-parametric procedures 83
multinomial probit model 18
multiple criteria evaluation model 80–81
Mundy, B. 151, 152, 153, 156
Munneke, H.J. 155
Murano
     flood protection 94–5
     infrastructure 76–9
     residential properties improvement 90,
          91
     subway connection 92–3
     see also urban improvement
Murdoch, J.C. 149

National Contaminated Sites
     Remediation Plan (Law 426/1998),
     Italy 157
National Oil and Hazardous Substances
     Pollution Contingency Plan, US
     150
National Priority List
     Italy 197
     US 198
natural resource problem, Venice Lagoon
     100–102
Nawas, F. 26
negligence-based liability 202
net realizable value *see* transformation
     value
Netherlands, contaminated sites 191
Neustein, R.A. 153
New Hampshire, beach protection
     programmes 63
New Jersey, beach nourishment 63

Nicholson, W. 43
Ninni, E. 100
non-use values 5–6, 41–2, 46, 61, 62–3,
  65, 68–9, 71–4
normally distributed willingness to pay
  10
Nunes, P.A.L.D. 102

Oates, W.E. 199
Opaluch, J.J. 191
open access fishing 100
open-ended questions 7, 9
option value 5–6
Orel, G. 101, 106
ownership regimes, fishing vessels
  108–13
Oxera, D. 54

Page, T. 53
pairwise comparison techniques 81, 82
parcel prices, effects of contamination
  and liability 165–6
Pas, E.I. 154
passive use *see* non-use
Pastres, R. 114
Patchin, P.J. 148, 153, 158
payment card approach 8
payment questions 9, 10
payment vehicle 7
Pearce, D. 53, 54
Pellizzato, M. 100, 106, 114
Peperzak, L. 102
perceived diminution approach to
  valuation 156
Perman, R. 6
Perny, P. 97
Pesaro, G. 205
Pessa, G. 101
Phoenix, Arizona, valuation of
  contaminated land 154–5
Pigou, A.K. 199
Pirlot, M. 97
Po River Delta 121
policies, magnitude of effects 184–7
Porto Marghera industrial site, Venice
  115, 143, 157–8
Pranovi, F. 102, 115
preference reversals 177, 179–81
price effect on recreational demand 24–8
primal approach 43

probit logic regression 10–11
production processes, inputs 49
production value 47
property characteristics, Venice Lagoon
  islands 77
property rights 198–9
protest behaviours 20
public transport, Venice Lagoon Islands
  78, 89, 92–4
Punta Sabbioni 77

quasi option value 6
questionnaires
  developer preferences 166–9
  ecosystem friendly clam fishing 105–8
  elicitation questions 7–9
  recreational demand 34–7
  recreational sport fishing 117–18,
    134–40
  respondent characteristics 122, 174–6
  respondent comprehension 176–7
  sampling frame 65–6
  statistical analysis of responses 9–12
  structure 7, 64–5, 117–18, 167–9

Ragland, S. 6
Rahmatian, M. 154
Ramsett, D.E. 151
Ramsey, F.P. 53
Randall, A. 8, 28
random coefficient logit model 18, 171,
  184, 189
random utility model (RUM) 16
  fisherman behavior 102–3
random-effects Tobit models 120, 125,
  126–9
Rausser, G.C. 149, 154
real estate market Venice Lagoon islands
  77–9
real estate values 49–50
recreational demand
  application 34–7
  flow fixed costs 31–4
  overview 23
  price effects 24–8
  Travel Cost Method 28–34
  user behaviour/types of cost 28–31
recreational sport fishing, Venice Lagoon
  angler surplus 129–30
  data 122–6

econometric model 118–22
fishing trips by scenario 122–5
overview 115–16
perceptions of environmental quality
    125–6
questionnaire structure/survey
    administration 117–18, 134–40
random-effects Tobit models 126–9
respondent characteristics/current
    behavior 122
results 126–31
Travel Cost Model (TCM) 116–17
referendum format 61
regressors, econometric model 121–2,
    172–3
regulation, approaches to 204–6
replacement cost approach to valuation
    151
residential demand, Venice Lagoon
    Islands 78
residential properties, market value
    75–6, 79–96
retroactive liability 202
revealed preference techniques 3, 19,
    144
Rhode Island, beach use 63
river pollution 49
robust lower-bound estimate of
    willingness to pay 12
Roddewig, R.J. 149, 154, 202
Rosato, P. 34, 75, 79, 81, 96
Rosen, S. 79
Rossetto, L. 106
Rossi, R. 114
Ruby, M.C. 5

S. Erasmo Island, environmental quality
    background/motivation 62–4
    data 66–8
    discussion 72–3
    flood protection 94–5
    infrastructure 75–9
    overview 61–2
    programme benefits 71–2
    questionnaire structure 64–5
    residential properties values 90, 91
    results 66–71
    sampling frame 65–6
    willingness to pay 68–71
    see also urban improvement

Saaty, T. 81, 82
sales comparison approach to valuation
    153
sample average 9
sample selection bias 6
sampling frame 65–6
sampling structure 65–6
SARA (Superfund Amendments and
    Reauthorization Act) (1980), US
    202–3
Scarpa, R. 75
Schlesinger, M. 72
Schoenbaum, M. 156
scientific approach to value of
    environment 40
scope effect 13
    sensitivity of willingness to pay 19–20
Scotland, rock-climbing 15
Scrobicularia plana 100
Sfriso,A. 102, 106
Shavell, S. 204
Shaw, W.D. 6, 121
Silberman, J. 63
Silvestri, S. 106
Simm, G. 153
Simonotti, M. 46
Simons, R.A. 162, 190, 191
Skourtos, M. 63
Smith, V.K. 154
social approach to value of environment
    41–2
social discount rate 53–4
socio-demographics 7
Solidoro, C. 101
Spain, contaminated sites 191
Spash, C.L. 29
stated preferences 144
    analysis of conjoint responses 15–18
    conjoint choice methods 13–15
    contingent valuation compared to
        conjoint analysis 19–20
    contingent valuation method 3–4
    design of conjoint analysis study
        18–19
    elicitation questions 7–9
    internal validity of responses 12–13
    questionnaire structure 7
    statistical analyses of responses 9–12
    survey methods 6–7
    use/non-use values 5–6

willingness to accept/willingness to pay 3–5
statistical analysis of questionnaire responses 9–12
status quo 14, 19
Stellin, G. 75, 79, 81, 96
stigma from contaminated sites 148–9, 153, 154, 155, 163, 164–5, 167, 172, 177
Stoeckl, N. 28
Strachota, R.J. 147, 148
Strand, I.E. 121
strict liability 202
Structured Query Language (SQL) 87
subsidies, brownfield development 166–76
substitution cost 51
substitution elasticity 5
substitution value 47, 48, 49, 52
subway construction, Venice Lagoon 92–4
Superfund Amendments and Reauthorization Act (SARA) *see* SARA
survey administration
  developer preferences 166–9
  recreational sport fishing 117–18
survey design, clam fishing 105–8
survey methods 6–7
survey valuation results, clam fishing 108–12
Swait, J.D. 14, 20, 103
Swallow, S.K. 191

Tapes decussates 100
Tapes philippinarum 99, 101, 118, 122, 125
Tassoni, E. 198
Taylor, L.O. 156
technological intensive fishing equipment 99, 100–102, 106
telephone surveys 6, 63–6
Tessera 77, 92, 93
Texas, contaminated land 154
Thayer, M.A. 149, 154
thematic maps 87, 89–90
theory of capture 199–200
theory of prospects 5
time-declining discount rate 53–4
Tirole, J. 38, 199

Tonin, S. 191
total economic value (TEV) 41–2, 46, 54
toxic substances 206
traditional appraisal theory 150–52
traditional economics and brownfields 198–200
traditional fishing systems 106
Train, K.E. 192
transformation value 47, 48, 49–50, 51, 52
Travel Cost Method (TCM) 23, 62
  and flow fixed costs 31–4
  and price effect 24–8
  recreational fishing trips 116–17, 121
travel generator function 28
Treporti 77
Trombetta, F. 191
Tse, K.S.M. 153
Tsoukiàs Vincke, Ph. 97
Tupper, H.C. 63
Turvani, M. 191
typology factors, residential property 82, 84

unimpaired valuation approach, contaminated land 150
University of Padua 65
UK, contaminated land 149
unobserved willingness to pay 10
urban improvement, Venice Lagoon islands
  case study 76–9
  construction of subway 92–4
  economic valuation model 79–86
  evaluation of improvement scenarios 91–5
  flood protection 94–5
  implementation of economic model in GIS environment 87–91
  overview 75–6
US
  brownfields 150, 154–6, 162, 165, 198
  development of brownfields 145–7, 149
  liability system 163–5, 189, 201, 202–4
US Environmental Protection Agency 143, 148, 173, 196, 198, 203
use values 5–6, 41–2, 65, 67, 68–9, 71–4
user behaviour, recreation demand 28–31

utility
    fishermen 103–5
    maximization 24–31, 42–5

vacation homes, Venice Lagoon islands
    78
value, definitions of 40–42
Van den Bergh, J.C.J.M. 102
Vancouver, valuation of contaminated
    land 155
Vaske, J.J. 63
Vega Science Park 207
Venice Lagoon
    boating use 34–7
    environmental quality 125–6
    flood protection 94–5
    subway under 92–4
    see also clam fishing practices;
        environmental restoration
        governance; recreation sport
        fishing; S. Erasmo island;
        urban improvement
Veslind, P.A. 154
Viscusi, W.K. 13, 176
Volentine, D.W. 154
voluntary approach to cleanup 163, 165,
    200–201, 204, 209
Vrieling, E.G. 102

Waddell, P.A. 149
Walsh, R.G. 23, 29
Ward, F.A. 26, 29
warm-up questions 7
Weaver, T. 191
Weber, B.R. 149
Weibull with parameters 9–10
    see also accelerated-life Weibull
        models
Weitzman, M. 53

welfare calculations 118–20, 129–31
welfare losses, compensation for 198–9
Wessells, C,W. 191
wetland reclamation projects 48
White Book European Commission 40
Whittington, D. 63
Wichelns, D. 191
Williams, N.A. 63
Williamson, O.E. 199, 206
willingness to accept (WTA) 3–5
    ecosystem friendly clam fishing
        practices 105, 109–13
willingness to pay (WTP) 3–5
    ecosystem friendly clam fishing
        practices 105, 109–13
    elicitation questions 7–9
    environmental improvements 61–2,
        64–73
    internal validity of responses 12–13,
        69–71
    statistical analysis of responses 9–12
Willis, K.G. 75
Wilson, A.R. 150, 153
Woburn, Massachusetts, contaminated
    land 154
Wolfe, C.R. 145
World Health Organisation, definition of
    environment 40
Worzala, E.W. 149
Wright, J.L. 19
Wright, R.E. 14, 15, 19

Yohe, G. 72
Yue, M. 6

Zabel, J. 154
Zentilin, A. 106
Zolezzi, G. 100
Zonal approach (ZTCM) 25–6